MOON

P9-CBE-580

BUDAPEST & BEYOND

JENNIFER D. WALKER

CONTENTS

Discover Budapest & Beyond ...5

My Favorite Experiences 6

Explore Budapest & Beyond 14

Before You Go 27

Budapest **31**

& Beyond

Gödöllő 134

Szentendre.......................142

Danube Bend......................155

Lake Balaton......................172

Eger 193

Hollókő.............................205

Sopron 216

Pécs.................................233

Essentials........................252

Index...............................268

1 souvenir shop in Szentendre

2 Esztergom city center

3 tourist train in Eger

4 Lion's Pharmacy in Sopron

5 food market in central Budapest

6 people resting in front of
St. Stephen's Basilica

DISCOVER
BUDAPEST & BEYOND

Once three distinct cities—Buda, Pest, and Óbuda—Budapest has a long history that expresses itself in the tapestry of the city's architecture, from the excavated remains of the Roman city of Aquincum to medieval ruins left behind from the monasteries of Margaret Island; from domed Ottoman baths and Habsburg grandeur to Communist brutalism. It's a complex and vibrant city where you can go to a thermal bath in the early morning, spelunking before lunch, do a spot of sightseeing in the afternoon, and party till dawn. You can crisscross the city from Buda, dominated by tree-clad hills interwoven with hiking trails, to cosmopolitan Pest, where large Parisian-style boulevards are interspersed with dilapidated ruin bars and a vibrant café culture. And don't forget Óbuda: the oldest part of the city is strewn with Roman ruins, factories, and shady beaches that lead you right down to the Danube River.

But Hungary is more than just Budapest. The country is small and compact, making it easy to branch out from the capital and see more of the country with a day or an overnight trip. Head south to recline on a beach at Lake Balaton, Central Europe's largest lake. Head north and take a boat down the beautiful Danube Bend. Or jet off to other cities in Hungary if you want to escape the tour crowds. Visit Eger for its Baroque architecture and wine cellars. Discover Sopron on the Austrian-Hungarian border for its beautiful medieval architecture. Go south to Pécs for its blend of Art Nouveau and Ottoman architecture. Or, you can stay closer to Budapest with a jaunt to the picturesque towns of Szentendre, rustic Hollókő, or regal Gödöllő.

MY FAVORITE
EXPERIENCES

1 Soaking in **Budapest's thermal baths.** From opulent multi-pool complexes to low-key local spots, relaxing in the healing waters is the perfect activity on the morning after a night out. (page 81).

^^^

2 Drinking a *pálinka* or Unicum in a ruin bar or *kert* in **Budapest's Jewish Quarter** (page 88).

3 Taking in views over the Danube from Budapest's **Fisherman's Bastion** (page 47).

4 Cycling along the Danube to **Szentendre** or **Vác,** stopping for a few *fröccs* (a white or rosé wine spritzer) at one of the riverside bars along the way (page 152).

>>>

5 Kicking back with the locals on a **Lake Balaton beach** (page 190).

>>>

6 Immersing yourself in Habsburg grandeur at **Gödöllő Royal Palace** (page 137).

7 Visiting the Danube Bend town of **Esztergom,** home to a grand basilica with sweeping views, then taking the slow boat back to Budapest at golden hour (around 4pm) (page 169).

>>>

8 Sampling local wine in the **Valley of Beautiful Women** (page 202) or at the hillside wineries near **Badacsony** (page 186).

<<<

9 Discovering rural life in the museums of the living folk village of **Hollókő** (page 210).

>>>

10 Learning about the history of Hungary's famous glazed porcelain in the **Zsolnay Cultural Quarter in Pécs** (page 244).

<<<

EXPLORE
BUDAPEST & BEYOND

Three or four days is enough to immerse yourself in Budapest's best sights, along with some of its more unusual ones. However, it's easy enough to hop on a bus or a train and get out to explore more of the country. Some destinations are nearby and take less than an hour to get to: **Szentendre, Gödöllő,** and the **Danube Bend** can all be reached in just over an hour (or less) by train or bus, and they make good day-trip destinations or can be combined into longer excursions. Other destinations (**Eger, Hollókő, Sopron, Lake Balaton,** and **Pécs**) are farther afield, requiring a journey of two or three hours, so you need to either travel early or stay overnight. The good news is that all are reachable by bus or rail, so you can access them, even if you don't have your own car.

sailing on the Danube Bend

the Castle Garden Bazaar entrance

BEST OF BUDAPEST & BEYOND

This itinerary covers the must-see highlights for any first-time visitor, with a mix of Habsburg palaces, museums, rooftop and ruin bars, and even a thermal bath. This will keep you busy from dawn till dusk on days 1 and 2, with day 3 (a short trip to nearby Gödöllő) being more relaxing. You will want to make sure your camera is fully charged for the next three days.

This itinerary is accessible with public transport. Since you'll be based in Budapest for three days, you won't need to worry about luggage storage as you can just keep everything at your hotel.

›DAY 1

- Start your trip in style with a coffee or a decadent breakfast at the **New York Café.** It's a little pricey, but it is one of the most beautiful cafés in the world, so it's the perfect way to kick off your trip.

- Grab the **number 5 bus** from Blaha Lujza tér metro station to go to Buda. Keep an eye out for the views while you ride, especially when crossing the river!

- Get off the bus at Szarvas tér and head toward the river. You'll see the **Castle Garden Bazaar** stretch out in front of you. Walk along and follow the colonnade leading up the hill until you reach the escalators.

- Take the escalators up to the top and you've reached the top of **Castle Hill.** Wander along, admire the views, and take many photos.

- Buy a ticket for the **Hungarian National Gallery** in the **Royal**

15

Hungarian Parliament building

Palace and spend a couple hours exploring the museum to learn more about Hungarian art. Make sure you climb up inside the dome of the Royal Palace (if the season permits).

- Stroll over the winding cobbled streets to Matthias Church and Fisherman's Bastion. This will give you the best views in the city.

- If you're hungry, there are plenty of options here; if you're feeling spendy, Pierrot won't disappoint.

>DAY 2

Try to make yourself get up early and go to the Széchenyi Baths before the crowds arrive. Expect to spend a good couple of hours here—the complex is massive and the architecture is stunning inside and out.

- Once you've had a good soak, explore the surroundings at City Park. Wander the grounds of Vajdahunyad Castle and pay a visit to the Anonymous statue.

- At the Vienna Gate, grab the 16 bus to Deák Ferenc tér metro station. Head south and pass the Great Synagogue and walk down Wesselényi utca till you reach Kazinczy utca and turn right.

- Grab some street food at Karavan, and then head into Szimpla Kert, Budapest's most famous ruin bar, for a few drinks to wrap up the night.

- If you're in the mood to party, bar-hop over to nearby Instant and Fogas Ház, Anker't, or Doboz.

Fisherman's Bastion in Budapest

- Head to **Bagolyvár** for a filling lunch.

- Now, it's on to some major sightseeing. First, walk over to **Heroes' Square** and snap a few pictures.

- Take metro 1, also known as the Millennium Underground, to Opera. Keep walking down Andrássy Avenue until you reach Bajcsy-Zsilinszky út. Cross over and head to **St. Stephen's Basilica.** Try to get up to the viewing platform at the top of the dome.

- Walk a few blocks northwest toward the river until you get to the **Hungarian Parliament** building. Take it easy and just admire the exterior.

- Head down to the Danube Banks in front of the Parliament to the **Shoes on the Danube** memorial.

- End the evening at a rooftop bar, such as the bar (or ice rink in the winter) at the **Hotel President** with views over the Royal Postal Savings Bank, the High Note Bar at the **Aria Hotel** for a vista overlooking St. Stephen's Basilica, or return to Andrássy Avenue to **360 Bar.**

>DAY 3: DAY TRIP TO GÖDÖLLŐ

Get out of the city and escape to the nearby town of Gödöllő for a spot of Habsburg grandeur and opulence. Before you leave, call the **Royal Palace of Gödöllő** to find out if you can visit **Horthy's Bunker** or the **Baroque Theater.** During peak seasons, large tour groups get priority, and the palace can only tell you that day whether you can visit these extras or not. Once you get the times for the tours, you can plan your day and slot in a visit to Horthy's Bunker and the Baroque Theater when a spot is available.

The Baroque Theater is the oldest theater in the country, and is still used for performances.

- Take metro line 2 to Örs Vezér tere and take the suburban railway

(HÉV) to **Gödöllő** and get off at Gödöllő, Szabadság tér 50 minutes later.

- If you're hungry, grab a bite to eat at **Solier Café,** a five-minute walk from the train station.

- Head over to the Royal Palace of Gödöllő. Pay a visit to the castle interior and the elegantly furbished rooms. Once you're done with the museum and tours (or you have some waiting time), make sure you explore the lush park grounds surrounding the palace.

- Once you're done for the day, grab the suburban railway back to Budapest.

WHERE TO GO FROM BUDAPEST

If You Want...	Destination	Why Go?	Distance/Travel Time from Budapest	How Long to Stay
Habsburg palaces	Gödöllő (page 134)	Tour an opulent palace within easy striking distance of Budapest.	25-50 minutes by train	half to full day
Local artwork	Szentendre (page 142)	Explore Hungarian village life in an open-air museum, then shop for handicrafts in this local artists' colony.	40 minutes by train; 1.5 hours by boat	half to full day
Scenery	Danube Bend (page 155)	Visit historic small towns, a medieval citadel, and a looming basilica with international views on the banks of the Danube. Travel back to Budapest by boat if you can.	25 minutes-1 hour by train; 1.5 hours by bus; or 40 minutes-1.5 hours by boat, depending on your destination	two days
	Lake Balaton (page 172)	Hike into the hills or swim and kick back on a lakeside beach at this favorite Hungarian vacation spot.	1.5-3 hours by train, depending on your destination	two days
Wine tasting	Eger (page 193)	Explore a fortress-like castle, then duck into wine cellars housed in natural caves in the Valley of Beautiful Women.	2 hours by train or bus	two days
	Badacsony (Lake Balaton) (page 185)	Trek up a volcanic hill to reach vineyards and wineries with a view of Lake Balaton.	3 hours by train	overnight

SZENTENDRE AND THE DANUBE BEND

Follow the Danube upstream from the Hungarian capital through an undulating landscape that twists and turns with the river. The Danube Bend is one of the most beautiful parts of the country, its forest-covered hills punctuated by village churches, ruined medieval citadels, and one of Europe's largest basilicas. It has the added advantage of being very close to Budapest and easily accessible by public transport.

Although you can get up to Szentendre on the local suburban train, taking a boat is the best and most fun way to reach the town. Pack light,

If You Want...	Destination	Why Go?	Distance/Travel Time from Budapest	How Long to Stay
Beaches	Siófok (Lake Balaton) (page 188)	Join the locals at golden lakeside beaches and energetic pubs.	1.5 hours by train	overnight
Hungarian village life	Hollókő (page 205)	Explore quirky museums and get an authentic taste of Hungarian life in this traditional village, which is also home to an impressive 13th century castle.	2 hours by bus	one day
	Sopron (page 216)	Wander the historic Old Town of this city perched on the border of Austria, and don't miss tasting some of the local wine.	2.5 hours by train	overnight
Architecture	Pécs (page 233)	Soak in Art Nouveau details, visit a spectacular Ottoman mosque, and tour the factory where gorgeous Zsolnay tiles and ceramics were once produced.	3 hours by train	two days

because you won't have anywhere to store luggage while you explore Szentendre on day 1 and Esztergom on day 3. Book your ticket in advance (even if it's just the day before) to guarantee a seat for the 10:40am hydrofoil bound for Esztergom on day 3.

>DAY 1: BUDAPEST TO SZENTENDRE TO VISEGRÁD

- Head up to **Szentendre** in the morning. You can take the suburban railway (HÉV line 5, takes 40 minutes from Batthyány tér) or the boat (1.5 hours).

- Explore the picturesque downtown and do some shopping in this former art colony. Pay a visit to the **Blagoveštenska**

Blagoveštenska Orthodox Church

Church to see a little of the town's Serbian heritage.

- Grab lunch in **Mjam** before heading over to the **Art Mill.** Walk back through the town to the bus station next to the suburban railway stop.

- Get on the bus going to **Visegrád** (45 minutes).

- Check into your hotel, then grab a cab to the **Visegrád Citadel** for the amazing views. If you're feeling athletic, hike down the southern side of the citadel to the Solomon Tower.

- Get dinner at the **Renaissance Restaurant** before retiring for the night.

>DAY 2: VISEGRÁD TO VÁC

- In the morning, visit the **Renaissance Palace.**

- Take the hourly ferry over to Nagymaros (15 minutes) and get the train down to **Vác** (15 minutes). Check into your hotel and freshen up before you head out to explore the town.

Getting ready to take off beyond Budapest? Here are some tips to help you plan your excursion.

CAR RENTALS

All the destinations in this book are accessible via bus or train; however, renting a car will give you the flexibility to link them together as you like. In Budapest, you can rent cars from international rental companies such as **Hertz** (tel. 06/1-296-0999 for local reservations, tel. 06/1-235-6008 for international reservations, www.hertz.hu), **Europcar** (tel. 06/1-421-8333, www.europcar.hu), and **Avis** (tel. 06/30-934-4050, www.avis.hu). You'll find all these rental companies at the airport or in the Inner City.

You can rent a car easily in downtown Budapest, too: **Hertz** on Apaczai Csere Janos utca in the V District is one option. Car rental costs around HUF 10,000-25,000 per day.

LUGGAGE STORAGE

Packing light for a mini-excursion beyond city limits? You can find various luggage storage facilities in Budapest. Try **Budapest Luggage Storage** (www.budapestluggagestorage.com, €10 per 24 hours per bag) that has a seven luggage storage facilities all over the city center, from close to the Basilica to the Jewish Quarter, or check out **BagBnB** (www.bagbnb.com/luggage-storage/budapest) for more options.

- Pay a visit to **Vác Cathedral** and the **Memento Mori Exhibition.**

- Take a leisurely hike along the river to the **Hekk Terrace** if you want a long scenic walk before lunch.

- Spend the afternoon in Vác at your own pace. Grab a cake or a coffee and watch life go by, or watch the sun set from the riverside.

EXPLORE

the state border between Slovakia and Hungary on the Mária Valéria bridge across the Danube River

>DAY 3: VÁC TO ESZTERGOM TO BUDAPEST

- Make sure you hop on the 10:40 hydrofoil bound for **Esztergom** (50 minutes). Book your ticket in advance, even if it's only the day before, from the Mahart Passnave website to guarantee a seat. Sit back and enjoy the Danube Bend views from the boat.

- You'll get to Esztergom around lunchtime. The town is small, but if you want to see amazing views of Esztergom and sneak another country in, cross the **Mária Valéria bridge** over to Štúrovo, Slovakia, for wonderful vistas of the basilica and the city. Cross back over and head up toward the basilica. Stop for lunch at **Padlizsán** on the way.

- When you arrive at **Esztergom Basilica,** make sure you go up to the dome for amazing views over the city.

- Get the local bus or a taxi to the train station and take the train back to Budapest (1 hour).

Esztergom Basilica

LAKE BALATON

Get out of the city and relax on Lake Balaton for a few days with beautiful views, boat rides, and plenty of good food and wine. Balaton is not so much about sightseeing but rather taking in the little pleasures—a walk along the water, a day at the beach, or trying the excellent local wines.

All three of these towns are accessible by rail or bus, making this itinerary possible without a car. Drop your luggage off when you get into town and go exploring right away.

>DAY 1: BUDAPEST TO BALATONFÜRED

- From Budapest, catch an early train (2-2.5 hours) to **Balatonfüred.** Trains depart Budapest's Budapest-Déli train station hourly (every half hour in peak seasons). No reservations are necessary; just get a ticket and go. However, in the summer it's best to buy a ticket in advance so you are guaranteed a seat.

- The train will drop you off just a 15-minute walk from the center of the town. Settle into your hotel, take a stroll along the river on the **Tagore Prominade,** and grab lunch at **DOCK Bistro.** Take it easy for the rest of the afternoon, and just enjoy the views over the lake.

- If you're in an adventurous mood and don't want to simply relax, you can grab a local bus from the train station to **Tihany** (15-20 minutes). Visit **Tihany Abbey** and get a cake at the **Rege Cukrázda.** Go for a walk down by the Inner Lake and pick up some lavender souvenirs before taking the bus back to Balatonfüred.

>DAY 2: DAY TRIP TO BADACSONY

- Take the train to **Badacsony,** which will take an hour or less.

- Hike up the hill to **Szőlőhegy Bistro** for lunch with an amazing view over the lake. You can try a few wines here, but don't be shy about exploring several other wineries in the area, like the nearby **Laposa winery.** This is not a day to run around and sightsee but to enjoy the wonderful views.

- Take the train back to **Balatonfüred,** then treat yourself to a meal at **Horváth House Wine Gallery.**

Lake Balaton

>DAY 3: BALATONFÜRED TO SIÓFOK

- After a good breakfast, take a ferry across the lake to **Siófok,** which will take around an hour.

- If you can, get settled into your hotel and head down to **Siófok Main Beach** to catch the sun.

- Fuel up at **Calvados** before climbing up the **Siófok Water Tower** and riding the **Siófok Ferris Wheel.**

- At night, head down to **Petőfi Promenade** for the nightlife. Try the **Renegade Pub** if you're looking for a lively vibe.

>DAY 4: SIÓFOK TO BUDAPEST

- Enjoy one last walk by the lake before grabbing your luggage and taking the train back to Budapest. The journey takes approximately an hour and a half, so you have plenty of time to relax in the morning.

Swans flock on the Lake Balaton in Siófok with the Ferris wheel in the background.

EGER, THE VALLEY OF BEAUTIFUL WOMEN, AND HOLLÓKŐ

Explore a different side of Hungary in the historic city of Eger, famous for its medieval castle, wine cellars, winding Baroque streets, and remnants from the Ottoman occupation. Then, head even deeper into the countryside to the living folk village of Hollókő in the Cserhát Hills to get a feel for rural life and culture, as well as shop for some unique folk art to take home.

It's very easy to get to Eger with public transport, but going from Eger to Hollókő is more of a challenge. Although Hollókő is only an hour and a half by car, it can take around four hours by local bus because you need to change twice and take a detour to get there. For this itinerary, I'd recommend renting a car in Budapest before setting out.

>DAY 1: BUDAPEST TO EGER

Before leaving for Eger, consider where you'll park your car. The **Hotel Park & Eger** has parking for HUF 600 per night, and the **Hotel Senator** also includes reserved parking for guests, so if you're booked at either of those you're sorted for parking. Otherwise, you can park in a number of parking lots in the downtown area, like at the base of Eger Castle on Dobó István utca, or at the underground parking garage on Katona tér. Parking in Eger costs between HUF 200 and 360 per hour.

- Drive two hours due northeast on the M3 (via Füzesabony) to Eger. Check in, settle into your hotel, and head into town.

- Grab a coffee on Dobó István tér before hiking up to **Eger Castle.** Expect to spend a good couple of hours exploring the museums within the castle walls. Grab lunch at **1552** before descending.

- Wander over to the **Eger Minaret.** If you want to climb up, make sure you're physically fit and not claustrophobic or suffering from

23

a fountain in front of Eger Castle

vertigo. The minaret is a tight climb with 100 steps going up, and while the view at the top is amazing, it will make you feel dizzy. Coming down is harder.

- You'll be exhausted after all that climbing, so find somewhere for an early dinner, such as **Depresso Kávéház és Étterem,** and return to relax at the hotel.

>DAY 2: EGER AND THE VALLEY OF BEAUTIFUL WOMEN

- Take in an organ concert at **Eger Basilica** in the morning.

- After the concert, walk down Klapka utca to the small trackless train. The train leaves at half-past every hour and costs HUF 1,000—keep your ticket, as you can use it on the journey back. In 15 minutes you will be in the **Valley of Beautiful Women,** which is in the suburbs.

- The valley is home to almost 200 wine cellars set in carved-out caves, with some being better than others. Expect to spend the afternoon here. Make sure you don't miss the **Hagymási Cellar,** which looks like a church. You can also grab some snacks in the

Eger Basilica

cellars from cheese plates, bread smothered in pork or duck fat, or freshly baked pastries filled with cheese and herbs.

›DAY 3: EGER TO HOLLÓKŐ TO BUDAPEST

- Leave Eger after breakfast and make your way to **Hollókő.** Take the road northwestward for 90 minutes on route 23.

- Once you get to Hollókő, park your car then grab lunch at the **Muskátli Vendéglő.** At the main parking lot, parking costs HUF 400 per hour or HUF 1,200 for a day.

- In the afternoon, explore the village—check out a few of the artisanal shops in the area and

- In the evening, take the train back and grab dinner at **Macok Bisztró.**

some of the many tiny museums dotted around the whitewashed houses, such as the **Village Museum** or the **Palóc Doll Museum.**

- Just past the Palóc Doll Museum, follow the signs leading up to **Hollókő Castle.** Hike up and around the castle.

- When you're ready, head back to the car and return to Budapest. Drive south on the M3 back to the city (90 minutes).

Kossuth Street in the UNESCO World Heritage village Hollókő

TRAVEL LIKE A LOCAL

Central Market Hall, Budapest

Like many cities in Europe, Budapest suffers from the challenges that come with over-tourism. You'll feel the pressure in the height of summer or a Saturday night in the VII District when bachelor and bachelorette parties crowd the bars. Step back to appreciate this amazing city from the ground up like a local. Although the big sights and top bars are famous for a reason, there is certain pleasure getting off the beaten path and learning more about the real Budapest outside the tourist hubs. A few tips:

- **Stay outside the V, VII, and I districts.** Go for less-touristy neighborhoods like the VIII, IX, or XIII districts in Pest, and residential parts of Buda outside the I District.

- **Take public transport.** Instead of the sightseeing buses and boat rides, you can see the best of Budapest from its excellent public transport network. The number 2 tram is one of the most beautiful ways to see the city, and you can also jump on one of the BKK (Budapest's Center of Transport) boats for HUF 750.

- **Have lunch in a market.** Markets are a great place to grab inexpensive food. The quality in their food courts may vary, and the food tends to be on the heavy and greasy side, but you'll hobnob with the locals and save money.

- **Go off the beaten track.** Explore the outer districts and enjoy the lesser-known gems in the city. Go up to Római Part in the summer for a few glasses of *fröccs* by the river, hike up the Buda Hills, or explore the bohemian VIII District.

- **Dress the part.** Locals don't really wear running shoes unless they are out for jog. The hip younger crowd sometimes wears high-end sport shoes that are clean and pristine, but sneakers are a big giveaway you're from out of town. Another big clue is baseball caps; you'll seldom see Hungarians sporting them.

- **Avoid carrying selfie sticks, big maps, and big backpacks.** Sometimes you can't avoid these, but they will clue locals in that you're a tourist. If you want to be discreet but still know where you're going, you can pre-download a map onto your phone with Google maps and save it on the offline setting.

- **Get out of Budapest.** Hungary is more than just the capital, and since Hungary is so small, you can see a lot of the country on a day trip. In the heat of the summer, travel to Lake Balaton (which is what the locals do to escape the heat of the urban jungle and the crowds of tourists). Take the train and watch the landscape roll by—this is especially fun if you get on one of the trains with a bar on board.

BEFORE YOU GO

WHEN TO GO

HIGH SEASON (JUNE-AUG. AND DEC.)

Summers in Hungary can be scorching (sometimes rising above 40°C/104°F) and often come punctuated with flash storms. But this is when you can sail along the Danube, sunbathe on a beach by Lake Balaton, or grab a picnic in a leafy park. Skip July and August if you want to avoid the crowds, especially when the Sziget Festival is in full swing. December, when the Christmas markets set up shop, is also a busy time in each city.

SHOULDER SEASON (APRIL-MAY AND SEPT.-NOV.)

If you're outdoorsy, spring and fall may be your best bet. You get to escape intense temperatures of the summer months and the dreary cold weather of the winter. In the spring, cherry and apricot blossoms burst into bloom, and in the fall, the trees paint the landscape with a palette of rusty colors. Culinary and wine festivals take over the public spaces of the towns and cities—like the wine festival in Buda Castle—so if you're a

Budapest's Fisherman's Bastion in winter

foodie it's a good time to visit, with fewer crowds than you'll experience in summer or December.

LOW SEASON (JAN.-MAR.)

Winters can dip down to sub-zero temperatures (as low as -15°C/5°F), yet Central Europe is at its most beautiful in the snow. When the temperatures plunge, you can escape the chill in a museum or a cozy café with its own curious cast of local characters. Going off-season can be easier on the wallet, as hotels often have rooms available at lower prices, but many outdoor attractions close down or operate with limited opening hours.

WHAT YOU NEED TO KNOW

- **Currency:** Hungarian Forint (HUF)

- **Conversion rate:** $1=HUF 299, €1=HUF 333, £1=HUF 367 at the time of writing.

- **Entry Requirements:** Citizens from the US, UK, EU, Canada, Australia, and New Zealand can enter Hungary visa-free as part of the Schengen Agreement. South Africans will have to apply for a Schengen Visa to enter the EU, with the application being made to the embassy or consulate of the first country entered.

- **Emergency number:** 112

- **Time Zone:** CET

- **Electrical system:** 230 V and 50 Hz

TRANSPORTATION

GETTING THERE

Budapest's **Liszt Ferenc International Airport** (BUD, Budapest 1185, tel. 06/296-9696, www.bud.hu) receives flights from across Europe including the UK, as well as flights from outside Europe including North America. There are no direct flights from Australia, New Zealand, or South Africa.

tram number 2 in Budapest

GETTING AROUND IN BUDAPEST

Budapest is easy to explore on foot, but the public transport run by the **BKK** (Budapest's public transport network) is also very efficient. There are four metro lines and several bus and tram lines, such as the 4/6 running along the entire stretch of the Grand Boulevard and the tram 2 that gives you front-row seats for the banks of the Danube.

OUTSIDE BUDAPEST

Getting to the main towns in Hungary is easy if you're going from Budapest. However, if you're looking to combine day trips, you may want to rent a car to cut down journey times. Cities like Eger, Pécs, Sopron, Esztergom, Vác, or towns on Lake Balaton are all accessible by train. Hollókő and

Visegrád are only accessible directly by bus, and Szentendre and Gödöllő are easiest to reach with the local suburban railway. You can also take the boat or hydrofoil to many towns on the Danube Bend, and there are even ferries going across Lake Balaton from the northern to the southern shore.

Cities outside Budapest are compact and easy to get around on foot, but if you are planning to spend the night and have luggage, it's best to grab a cab from the train station. Otherwise, you can walk around the cities pretty easily.

WHAT TO PACK

- **Swimsuit.** So you can enjoy the wonderful thermal baths. You may want to bring slippers, a towel, and a swimming cap, too.

- **An umbrella.** Even in the hot summer, Hungary is prone to sudden flash downpours.

- **Closed-toe shoes** if you're planning to go hiking or spelunking.

- **Something smart for the opera.** People tend to dress up for the opera, theater, and concerts in

BUDGETING

- **Beer:** HUF 400-900

- **Glass of wine:** HUF 400-1,500

- **Lunch or dinner:** HUF 2,500-6,000

- **Hotel:** HUF 10,000-200,000 per night

- **Car rental:** HUF 10,000-25,000 per day

- **Gasoline:** HUF 365-415 (per liter)

- **Parking:** HUF 265-440 per hour

- **Public transport ticket:** HUF 350-450

- **Museum entry:** HUF 800-2800

- **Thermal bath entry:** HUF 2,500-6,500

fountain on Deák Ferenc Square in Budapest

Budapest, so bring something smart-casual or smart for a night out at the opera.

- **Plug adapter.** Hungary uses the Continental European plug sockets, so if you're coming from the US or the UK you will need an adapter to use your electronics.

- **A refillable water bottle.** It can get very hot in the summer, so it's important to stay hydrated—but try to be eco-friendly. Also, having a refillable water bottle means you can fill it up at the thermal water fountains next to the Rudas, Széchenyi, and Lukács baths.

29

- **Memory cards.** Budapest is a very photogenic city, so it's easy to run out of camera space. Bring something to back up your pictures to!

- **Backpack or day pack.** Most rural places won't have luggage storage facilities, so if you're planning an excursion or two, bring something you can travel light with, and leave the rest of your luggage in storage or at a hotel in Budapest.

SIGHTSEEING PASSES

IN BUDAPEST

The **Budapest Card** (www.budapest-card.com, 24-hour card €22; 48-hour card €33; 72-hour card €44) includes public transport, free entrance to 17 museums (including the museums in Buda Castle, the Hungarian National Museum, and Memento Park), two walking tours, free entrance to the Lukács Baths, a free cave tour, and discounts. The Budapest Card is available at Budapestinfo Points, and you can also buy it online. If you're planning to pack a number of museums into your trip and use public transport often, it's worth investing in a card.

OUTSIDE BUDAPEST

Pécs has a sightseeing pass called the **Visit Pécs! Card,** which costs HUF 2,990 per day and can be extended at HUF 500 per day. It gives you free or discounted entry to more than 20 town attractions, including the museums in the Zsolnay Cultural Quarter, the Sopianae Early Christian Museum, the Mosque of Pasha Qasim, and the Csontváry Museum, to name a few.

DAILY REMINDERS

IN BUDAPEST

Most museums, including popular sights such as the Hungarian National Museum, close on **Monday.** All Jewish sites, such as synagogues, close on **Saturdays.** ("Sparties," on the other hand, only take place Saturday nights.) On **Sundays,** a weekly farmer's market is held in Szimpla Kert ruin bar.

Some churches close to visitors during Mass, and outdoor sites like the Budapest Zoo or Memento Park shift their opening hours based on the time the sun sets. Budapest's thermal baths are open daily.

BEYOND BUDAPEST

Like in Budapest, most of the popular sites are open every day, including Eger Castle and the Royal Palace of Gödöllő. However, many museums, such as those in the Zsolnay Quarter in Pécs, are closed on **Mondays.** Museums are open daily in Hollókő, even Mondays, but in winter the castle may close in snowy or icy weather.

KEY RESERVATIONS

Book your ticket for the **Hungarian Parliament** in Budapest before going on the day (ideally book the day before or even earlier in the week). Spots are limited and fill up quickly in high season. If you're traveling in high season (summertime or around Christmas), I recommend booking at least a few days in advance.

Zsolnay Fountain in Pécs

BUDAPEST

Divided by the Danube River,

Budapest is a city with two personalities. On the Buda side, hills curve up from the river, topped with palaces and citadels. Game-filled forests and ivy-covered villas stand above an underworld of caves. The Pest side spreads out on a plane built up with wide boulevards and grand monuments.

Budapest began as three separate towns: Buda, Pest, and Óbuda. Built on the Roman ruins of the city of Aquincum, modern Budapest is punctuated by medieval relics, Ottoman monuments, Habsburg grandeur, ceramic-clad Art Nouveau

Orientation
    and Planning 37
Itinerary Ideas 40
Sights 44
Thermal Baths 81
Bars and Nightlife......88
Performing Arts........94
Festivals and Events....96
Recreation
    and Activities 99
Shopping..............105
Food 110
Accommodations 123
Information
    and Services 129
Transportation.........131

HIGHLIGHTS

✪ **BUDA CASTLE:** This Habsburg palace houses the Hungarian National Gallery and Budapest History Museum. It stands on the ruins of castles that have been razed and rebuilt over time (page 44).

✪ **FISHERMAN'S BASTION:** This neo-Gothic lookout platform offers spectacular views over the Danube (page 47).

✪ **HUNGARIAN PARLIAMENT BUILDING:** Whether you view it from the Danube or take a tour, the country's political powerhouse dominates the cityscape with its towering spires and claret-hued rooftop (page 49).

✪ **ST. STEPHEN'S BASILICA:** Climb the dome for 360-degree views over Budapest. Then, stop to see the mummified hand of St. Stephen in a jewel-encrusted box (page 56).

✪ **DOHÁNY STREET SYNAGOGUE:** The second-largest synagogue in the world is the heart of the historic Jewish Quarter (page 58).

✪ **HUNGARIAN STATE OPERA:** A bastion of Hungary's excellent classical music scene, and one of the most important buildings on the UNESCO-protected Andrássy Avenue (page 60).

✪ **GELLÉRT HILL:** Take a hike up this hill beside the Danube for the best views over Budapest (page 70).

✪ **MEMENTO PARK:** This graveyard for Communist statues turned open-air museum is the best place to visit to glimpse Hungary's Communist past (page 72).

✪ **HUNGARIAN NATIONAL MUSEUM:** The largest museum in the country, with an eclectic collection of artifacts from Roman times to the 19th century (page 76).

✪ **SZÉCHENYI BATHS:** Budapest's most famous thermal bath with its canary-yellow pools is one of Central Europe's largest thermal bath complexes. It's also notorious for its "Sparties," raucous parties held on summer weekends (page 84).

✪ **RUIN BARS:** These watering holes have sprung up in condemned buildings in the city. Head to Szimpla Kert, the ruin bar that started the craze, for a beer in its labyrinth of graffiti-covered crumbling rooms (page 88).

buildings, and Communist brutalism. It's this architectural diversity, along with an attractive tax incentive, that draws Hollywood producers to Budapest to shoot on location.

But you don't need to go to the movies for compelling stories—Budapest's complex and diverse history is written on its bullet-scarred walls and within the memories of its residents.

Hungarians are renowned for their creativity and innovation, boasting 13 Nobel Prize winners and inventions like the Rubik's Cube and the ballpoint pen. This innovation spills out into the city's showrooms, eccentric bars, art galleries, and into the basement that birthed the world's first room escape game.

While rougher around the edges than Prague and Vienna, Budapest has made dilapidation part of its attraction. Flaking buildings now house vibrant ruin bars—unique watering holes that marry eccentric junk with art. These bars serve as alternative culture hubs. Today, revelers flock to former apartment blocks and factories for shots of *pálinka* or local craft beer and party until the early hours of the morning. Get to know Budapest by wandering the winding streets of the Castle District. Stop for views over the Danube, or ride a boat on the river. Explore the Jewish District's synagogues and the bars that spice up the quarter at night. Revel in the paprika-laden aromas of Hungarian cuisine and enjoy a spicy *Bikavér,* a red wine from Eger. Budapest is a city to be experienced, not just seen. Dare to venture beyond the ruin bars and discover where the locals go to enjoy life, celebrate, and give a toast to each other's health with *egészségedre* ("cheers" in Hungarian).

HISTORY

A tale of three cities, Budapest's history is long and complicated. It unified into the capital we know today when the towns of Buda, Pest, and Óbuda merged in 1873. History is on the walls of Budapest, in the scars left behind by shots fired during World War II and the 1956 uprising. There's also much to learn in the Roman ruins and Ottoman baths scattered around the city.

The region of the Carpathian Basin (the area between the Carpathian Mountains and the Alps) has been populated for hundreds of

thousands of years by Celtic tribes (who arrived around today's Budapest in the 3rd century BC). The Romans set up camp on the Danube in the 1st century BC. Eventually, the town of Aquincum grew into one of the largest Roman settlements—but it came crashing down when Attila and the Huns razed the city in the 5th century AD. (Despite the English name for the country, the Huns played only a short part in Hungary's history.) Following Attila's death, Germanic tribes occupied the region for a century. The Avars (Eurasian nomads) controlled the Carpathian Basin in the 6th century. Charlemagne later conquered the area around today's Budapest and incorporated it into the Frankish Empire.

The Magyars, a nomadic people, arrived in the Carpathian Basin around the 9th century, conquering and settling the land under the leadership of Árpád, a chief military commander. In 1000, King Stephen I founded the Hungarian State and embraced Christianity as the new country's religion. The cities of Buda and Pest were villages at the time; they only became a principal seat of the nation following the Mongol invasion in the 13th century. King Béla IV rebuilt the devastated country and founded a fortress in the Buda Hills, but Buda saw most of its development during the Renaissance under the rule of King Matthias, who transformed Hungary into one of the leading powers in Europe at the time.

In the 16th century, the Turks invaded Hungary and defeated the Hungarian army in the southern town of Mohács in 1526. Large parts of Hungary, including Buda (occupied in 1541), existed under Ottoman rule for 150 years.

Budapest

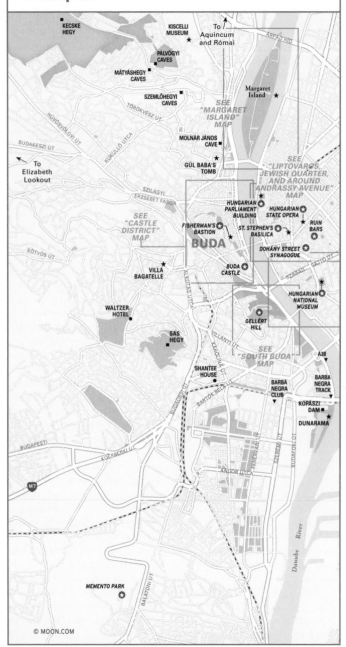

KECSKE HEGY

KISCELLI MUSEUM

To Aquincum and Római

ÁRPÁD HÍD

PÁLVÖLGYI CAVES

MÁTYÁSHEGY CAVES

SZEMLŐHEGYI CAVES

Margaret Island

HŰVÖSVÖLGYI ÚT

KUKULLÓ UTCA

TÖRÖKVÉSZ ÚT

SEE "MARGARET ISLAND" MAP

BUDAKESZI ÚT

MOLNÁR JÁNOS CAVE

To Elizabeth Lookout

GÜL BABA'S TOMB

SEE "LIPTOVÁROS, JEWISH QUARTER, AND AROUND ANDRÁSSY AVENUE" MAP

SZILÁGYI ERZSÉBET FASOR

HUNGARIAN PARLIAMENT BUILDING

HUNGARIAN STATE OPERA

SEE "CASTLE DISTRICT" MAP

FISHERMAN'S BASTION

ST. STEPHEN'S BASILICA

RUIN BARS

BUDA

EÖTVÖS ÚT

DOHÁNY STREET SYNAGOGUE

SZABAD SAJTÓ ÚT

VILLA BAGATELLE

BUDA CASTLE

HUNGARIAN NATIONAL MUSEUM

WALTZER HOTEL

ALKOTÁS UTCA

GELLÉRT HILL

SAS HEGY

VILLÁNYI ÚT

SEE "SOUTH BUDA" MAP

A38

KAROLINA ÚT

SHANTEE HOUSE

BARBA NEGRA TRACK

BARTÓK BÉLA ÚT

BARBA NEGRA CLUB

KOPÁSZI DAM

BUDAPESTI

BUDAFOKI ÚT

SZEREM

DUNARAMA

KŐÉRBERKI ÚT

M7

ANDOR UTCA

TETÉNYI ÚT

Danube River

MEMENTO PARK

BALATONI ÚT

© MOON.COM

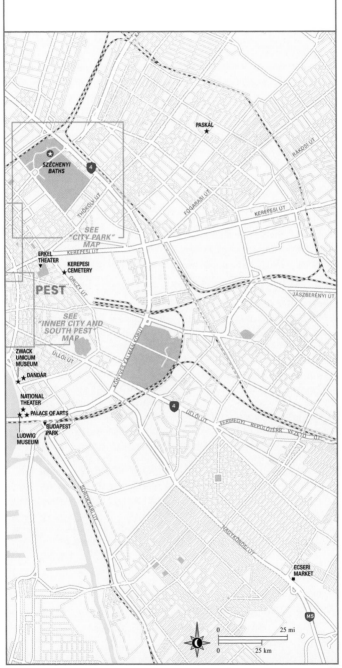

PASKÁL ★

★ SZÉCHENYI BATHS

4

THÖKÖLY ÚT

RÁKOSI ÚT

FOGARASI ÚT

KEREPESI ÚT

SEE "CITY PARK" MAP

KEREPESI ÚT

ERKEL THEATER ▲

★ KEREPESI CEMETERY

ORCZY ÚT

JÁSZBERÉNYI ÚT

PEST

SEE "INNER CITY AND SOUTH PEST" MAP

KÖNYVES KÁLMÁN KÖRÚT

ZWACK UNICUM MUSEUM ★

★ DANDÁR

ÜLLŐI ÚT

ÜLLŐI ÚT

ÜLLŐI ÚT

FERIHEGYI REPÜLŐTÉRRE VEZETŐ ÚT

4

NATIONAL THEATER ★

★★ PALACE OF ARTS

LUDWIG MUSEUM

BUDAPEST PARK

SOROKSÁRI ÚT

NAGYKŐRÖS ÚT

ECSERI MARKET ■

M5

0   25 mi

0   25 km

35

After the Ottomans came the Habsburgs, who liberated Buda and Pest in 1686, and Austria absorbed Hungary into the Habsburg Empire. Buda and Pest were rebuilt in the Baroque style, shaping the Castle District's current look. Pest also grew rapidly around the Inner City in today's V District.

A strengthening desire for Hungarian independence surfaced, but the failed Hungarian Revolution of 1848 against the Habsburgs shook the empire. Austria weakened after its defeat by Prussia in 1866. The Austro-Hungarian Compromise of 1867 sought to strengthen the empire. It allowed for two self-governing states to be created under a dual monarchy with two capitals, Vienna and Budapest. Emperor Franz Joseph I provided Hungary full autonomy. Following the compromise, Budapest flourished, with the streets of Pest rebuilt with Paris as its model, featuring wide boulevards and grand, eclectic buildings. By the end of the 1900s, Budapest had become one of Europe's most significant cultural centers.

Budapest suffered severe economic setbacks after World War I, the collapse of the Habsburg Empire, and the Treaty of Trianon (1920) that redrew the boundaries of the new, smaller Republic of Hungary. Trying to reclaim some of its territory, Hungary ended up on the side of Nazi Germany in World War II. However, when leftists attempted to negotiate peace, Germany stormed in and occupied the country in 1944. The Hungarian fascist Arrow Cross Party rose to power and rounded up Budapest's Jews—and immediately began deporting hundreds of thousands to Auschwitz. In 1945, Hungary was liberated by the Soviet Army, but not before the Germans blew up all the bridges upon retreating following the 50-day-long Siege of Budapest by the Red Army.

Communists had assumed full control of the country by 1949. Industry became nationalized, and estates were divided among the proletariat. The next revolution, however, was percolating—and it came to a head on October 23, 1956, when student demonstrators demanded the withdrawal of Soviet troops, and shots were fired. On November 4, Soviet tanks moved into Budapest and violently crushed the uprising. The fighting ended just one week later, on November 11. Some 25,000 people died within that short time. Over 20,000 were arrested in the aftermath, and 250,000 fled the country. Over time, Hungary's branch of Communism loosened into a limited market system, and by 1989, the Iron Curtain fell.

Once Communism fell in 1989, Hungary became a republic once again, and the first democratic elections were held in 1990. The last Soviet troops left in 1991. Hungary became a member of the EU in 2004 and entered the Schengen Area in 2007.

Orientation and Planning

ORIENTATION

The Danube River divides the city into Buda (western side) and Pest (eastern side). Budapest is also split up into 23 numbered municipal districts (*kerület*) that spiral out almost clockwise from the Castle District. White placards on street corners are labeled with the Roman numeral district number, the neighborhood name (*Erzsébetváros*), followed by the street name and the numbering of the houses on the block. If you're asking for directions, you can refer to the district number (for example, ask where "the seventh district" is if you're trying to get to VII District).

With street names, it's important to know your *utca* (street) from your *út* (boulevard or avenue), so you don't, for example, confuse Váci utca (a shopping artery in the Inner City) with Váci út (a long road leading to industrial suburbs). Other names are *tér* (square), *körút* (ring road or boulevard), *sor* (row), and *rakpart* (embankment). In some locations, you may notice street signs crossed out in red, which denote former place names that have been changed following the Communist regime; these have been replaced with the new name on the placard below.

CASTLE DISTRICT (I DISTRICT)

Budapest's I District (on the Buda side of the river) centers on Castle Hill, which rises sharply above the Danube, and is crowned by **Buda Castle.** The Castle District packs history into a dense space. Traces of the old medieval city can be seen in the excavated ruins near Buda Castle, but much of the original Buda lies in rubble or is hidden away. Much of the district is dominated by **cobbled, narrow streets, pastel-hued Baroque houses,** and romantic stone staircases that lead up the hill.

LIPÓTVÁROS

Where Váci utca ends (at Vörösmarty tér) is where the neighborhood of Lipótváros begins. This is where you'll find the most famous landmarks, like the **Hungarian Parliament** and **St. Stephen's Basilica.** Around the Parliament Building and Liberty Square, keep your eyes peeled for incredible specimens of **Art Nouveau architecture.**

JEWISH QUARTER (VII DISTRICT)

Though the neighborhood itself is older, the Jewish Quarter lies inside the former 1944 ghetto. **Memorials** on both Dohány and Király utca mark the location of the former wall. You can still find signs of Jewish life scattered about the streets of the inner VII District, from the grand **Dohány Street Synagogue** to kosher restaurants, bakeries, butchers, and Hebrew lettering on building doors. Most tourists flock to this part of the VII District after dark, when the Jewish Quarter energizes with its vibrant **nightlife,** including Budapest's most famous ruin pub, **Szimpla Kert.** This neighborhood is located east of the Inner City.

AROUND ANDRÁSSY AVENUE (VI DISTRICT)

Some consider Andrássy Avenue (Andrássy út), which stretches northeast from the Inner City, to be Budapest's answer to the Champs-Élysées. This elegant, wide boulevard, lined with eclectic palatial apartment blocks and slender trees, stretches about 3 kilometers (2 miles). The avenue itself falls under UNESCO World Heritage protection. The first half is dominated by luxury boutiques; it shifts to palatial villas enclosing embassies up in the vicinity of City Park.

CITY PARK AND AROUND (XIV DISTRICT)

City Park, northeast of the Jewish Quarter, is one of Pest's main green lungs, a place of recreation with thermal baths, picnic spots, and a popular ice-skating rink in the winter. City Park lies in the residential XIV District, but there's plenty to see and do in and around the park, from the Budapest Zoo to the sites at Vajdahunyad Castle. There are also plans to turn this area into a museum quarter by 2020.

MARGARET ISLAND AND AROUND (II AND XIII DISTRICTS)

When the sun comes out, locals head to Margaret Island (Margitsziget) in the Danube. It's accessible by Margaret Bridge and Árpád Bridge for picnics, strolls, and sunbathing. The island is mostly car-free (local bus service and taxis do operate). The island is over 2.5 kilometers (1.5 miles) long and 500 meters (550 yards) wide. You'll find medieval ruins, thermal baths, and abundant green parkland here. (This is also allegedly where German composer Richard Wagner almost drowned after falling from a boat.) Flanking the island on the mainland, the northern parts of Buda and Pest have a few points of interest, from Turkish remains to quirky museums.

SOUTH BUDA (XI DISTRICT)

The area stretching south of the Castle District spills into the XI District, and it's mostly off the tourist track. There's plenty to do, from hiking up Gellért Hill to sipping a coffee in a trendy café on lively Bartók Béla Avenue. Although you may need to use public transport to get to some of the area's sites, you can be sure to escape the crowds and see a bit more of less touristy Budapest. Head further down along the river to Kopaszi dam (Kopaszi gát) for a Danube beach area with riverside cafés and water sports.

INNER CITY AND SOUTH PEST (V, VIII, AND IX DISTRICTS)

The Inner City (V District), located right on the riverbank in Pest, exudes elegance, from its promenades dotted with riverside cafés to grand buildings with elaborate friezes, columns, and wrought iron façades. Pedestrianized Váci utca is the main road for shopping and dining.

Stretching south of the Jewish Quarter and the Inner City, the VIII and IX Districts lie slightly off the beaten track for most tourists. However, you can take a walk past the grand, palatial apartments of the Palace District or head down to the Danube banks around the formerly industrial IX District, where old factories have been converted into cultural centers or craft beer bars, and you'll find a different, more laid-back side of Budapest.

The Millennium Quarter along

Soroksári út, up by Rákóczi híd, is a new cultural hub for the city, with the Palace of Art, the Ludwig Gallery, and the National Theater.

ÓBUDA (III DISTRICT)

Óbuda (meaning Old Buda) was once a city in its own right, and it's outside the boundaries of historic Buda and Pest. Today, Roman ruins lie beneath Communist-era apartment blocks, and two-story Baroque townhouses back onto industrial complexes. It has a different character from the rest of Budapest. While far-flung from the center, it has plenty to offer, from dining around Kolosy tér to beaches and riverside bars at Római Part. Meanwhile, Óbuda Island hosts one of Europe's largest music festivals—Sziget—in August.

BUDA HILLS (II, III, AND XII DISTRICTS)

What distinguishes Buda from mostly flat Pest is its hills. Gellért Hill and Castle Hill are the most prominent in the city center; the hills out in the II, III, and XII districts feel like they belong somewhere in the countryside and not in a capital city. You'll find lookout points offering views over the city, hiking trails, and even networks of caves running below the city for miles on end. The Children's Railway, a small railway run by children as a relic left over from Communist times, is located here.

PLANNING YOUR TIME

You can easily see the main sights in Budapest in two days, with one day in Buda and another in Pest. But at least three days will give you time to fully appreciate the city's charm, unique nightlife, and culture.

DAILY REMINDERS

Most museums close on Monday, and all Jewish sites, such as synagogues, close on Saturday. Some churches close to visitors during Mass, and outdoor sites like the Budapest Zoo or Memento Park shift their opening hours based on the hour the sun sets.

Budapest's thermal baths are open daily.

Saturday

All Jewish sights, such as synagogues, are closed. "Sparties," on the other hand, only take place Saturday nights.

Sunday

A weekly farmer's market is held in Szimpla Kert ruin bar; Klauzál Square Market (an antiques market) is open.

These attractions are closed:
- National Széchényi Library
- Hungarian House of Art Nouveau (Bedő House)
- Cave Church
- Central Market Hall
- Zwack Unicum Museum

Monday

Most museums are closed, including:
- Hungarian National Gallery
- Budapest History Museum
- National Széchényi Library
- House of Terror
- Vajdahunyad Castle
- Miksa Róth Memorial House
- Budapest Pinball Museum
- Hungarian National Museum
- Holocaust Memorial Center
- Ludwig Museum
- Aquincum
- Kiscelli Museum

ADVANCE RESERVATIONS AND TIME-SAVING TIPS

You can buy tickets online for popular sites like the Hungarian National

Gallery or the Hungarian Parliament Building. Buying online will help you skip the queues, but at most of the sites, you can just buy tickets when you arrive without any issues. Some places (like the Parliament or the synagogues and Jewish museums) may want you to put your bags through a security check, so account for a little extra time for that as well.

If you want to go to a "Sparty" (a rowdy party in a thermal bath, www.spartybooking.com, €50, over 18 only), make sure you buy a ticket in advance from the website, as these sell out fast.

Itinerary Ideas

Budapest is compact and you can divide the main sites between the Buda and Pest sides. To get away from the crowds, explore the Buda Hills to see a different side of the city.

And you will want to save one of Budapest's iconic experiences—soaking in a thermal bath—for the last day. It'll be a relaxing end to your trip.

DAY 1

Spend Day 1 in Budapest's Castle District.

1 Start the day at one of Budapest's most spectacular bridges, the Chain Bridge, with amazing views over the river.

2 From the bridge and Clark Ádám Square take Hunyadi János út heading uphill north of the Chain Bridge and keep walking till you reach the stairs leading up to Fisherman's Bastion. Usually, this is one of Budapest's most crowded sites, but early in the morning there are only a few people here, and it's the perfect spot for snapping a few photos of the river.

3 There are plenty of breakfast options up in the Castle District. Baltazár, which is a five-minute walk down Országút, will keep you fueled up for the morning.

4 Return to Matthias Church next to Fisherman's Bastion for its incredible frescoes. If you make it on the hour, get a ticket and go up the church tower.

5 For something offbeat, head over to the Hospital in the Rock just five minutes away for a subterranean journey back in time to World War II, the 1956 revolution, and the Cold War.

6 Stop at Ruszwurm, the oldest café and confectionary in Budapest, which you will have passed on the way to the museum.

7 In the afternoon, you'll want to spend a couple of hours at the Hungarian National Gallery in the Royal Palace, just a 10-minute walk away.

8 Once you're done learning about the history of Hungarian art, take the elevator in the Castle Garden down to the Castle Garden Bazaar for the scenic route down the castle and get on the 41 or 19 tram to Gárdonyi tér.

9 Have dinner and drinks at Hadik, a former literary hangout in the early 1900s that's now a trendy bistro.

DAY 2

On your second day, explore around the Parliament and Inner City.

1 Kick-start your morning with breakfast in a classic café, like Central Café in the old part of the Inner City.

2 Walk five minutes toward the Danube and get on the number 2 tram. Get off at the Széchenyi István tér and turn around and take some pictures of the Royal Palace, the river, and Chain Bridge from the Pest side of the city.

3 Turn into Zrínyi street and pay a visit to St. Stephen's Basilica. Make sure you head up to the top inside to the dome, where amazing 360-degree views await.

4 It's a good time for a lunch break, and restaurants and cafés spill out onto the squares and streets surrounding the Basilica. Zeller Bisztró on Hercegprímás utca is a good option.

5 Once you've eaten, stroll over to Hold utca for the Royal Postal Savings Bank by Ödön Lechner two blocks away. If you want to see the rooftop from above, go into the Hotel President across the street to the rooftop café—it's worth it for the view.

6 Stroll over to Freedom Square and head over to the Hungarian Parliament. Get on one of the English-language tours of the Hungarian Parliament—it's easier to get on a tour if you buy a ticket online—to see inside this amazing building.

7 Get yourself on a Danube cruise. Take the tram number 2 to Vígadó and get on a boat organized by Legenda.

8 Once the boat docks, walk up to Vörösmarty tér and take the metro to Opera. Turn into Székely Mihály utca and then Kazinczy utca, passing the Art Nouveau Kazinczy Street Synagogue.

Itinerary Ideas

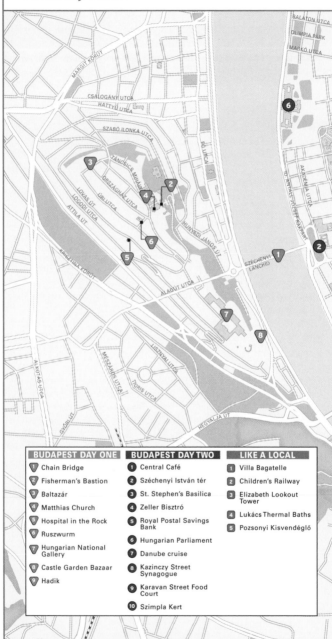

BUDAPEST DAY ONE

1. Chain Bridge
2. Fisherman's Bastion
3. Baltazár
4. Matthias Church
5. Hospital in the Rock
6. Ruszwurm
7. Hungarian National Gallery
8. Castle Garden Bazaar
9. Hadik

BUDAPEST DAY TWO

1. Central Café
2. Széchenyi István tér
3. St. Stephen's Basilica
4. Zeller Bisztró
5. Royal Postal Savings Bank
6. Hungarian Parliament
7. Danube cruise
8. Kazinczy Street Synagogue
9. Karavan Street Food Court
10. Szimpla Kert

LIKE A LOCAL

1. Villa Bagatelle
2. Children's Railway
3. Elizabeth Lookout Tower
4. Lukács Thermal Baths
5. Pozsonyi Kisvendéglő

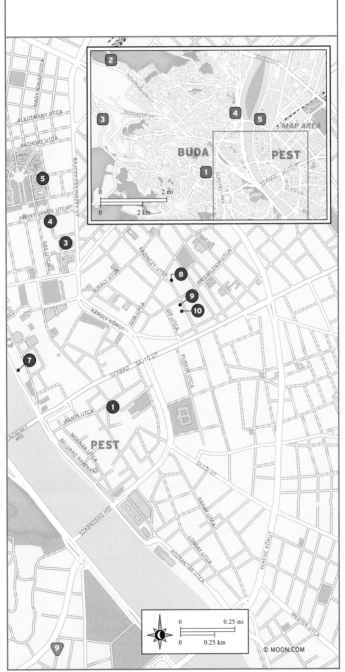

9 Grab a bite to eat at the Karavan Street Food Court at the end of Kazinczy utca.

10 End the night at Budapest's most famous ruin bar, Szimpla Kert, located just next door.

BUDAPEST LIKE A LOCAL

Today, head outside Budapest's center and into the Buda Hills.

1 Start with a decadent breakfast at the beautiful Villa Bagatelle at the base of the Buda Hills.

2 Walk down the hill five minutes and take the 61 tram to the end of the line at Hűvösvölgy. Take the carved wooden staircase leading up the hill pointing you in the direction of the Children's Railway and hop on this retro locomotive operated by children under 14 (drivers and engineers excepted) that will take you through the wilderness of the Buda Hills.

3 Get off the train at János Hegy and hike 20-30 minutes from the train station up to the Elizabeth Lookout Tower, following the signposts up to Budapest's highest point.

4 At the base of the tower, take the chairlift down to Zugliget, where you can connect with the 291 bus and get off at the Margit híd, Budai hídfő stop. Cross the road and head north through Elvis Presley Park to the Lukács Thermal Baths for a soak and swim.

5 After relaxing a little at the baths, take the number 9 bus to Jászai Mari tér and walk 10 minutes north to the Pozsonyi Kisvendéglő for a hearty Hungarian dinner.

Sights

CASTLE DISTRICT

The Castle District was razed and rebuilt, occupied by Turks for over a century, left in ruins following the Habsburg liberation in the 17th century, besieged again in the 1849 revolution, and then damaged during the Siege of Budapest in 1945. When exploring, think of the district as a patchwork of history, where you'll find stories within the details.

✪ BUDA CASTLE

Buda Castle is a symbol of the city, perched on top of the hill overlooking the Danube. Its neo-Baroque façade spreads out in columns under a copper-green dome, and it's worth the hike up for the views from the terrace.

Despite centuries of history, the palace you see today is fairly new in the Budapest cityscape. The original Gothic and Renaissance palace was

Castle District

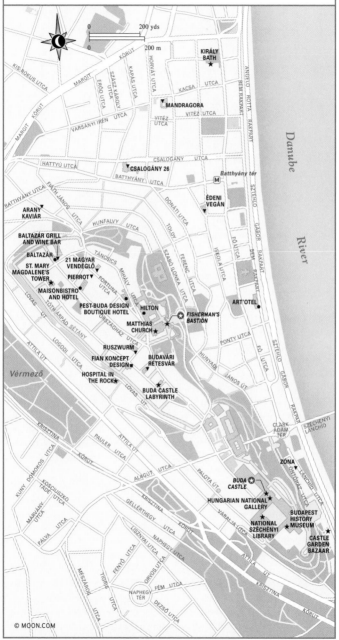

© MOON.COM

courtyards of Buda Castle

where you can see the layers of history in the stones lying around, and the reconstructed turrets and walls capture the historic essence of the building. The herb garden next to the Budapest History Museum is a hidden, quiet spot that can be a relief from the crowds packed onto the main terrace. If you take the steps down through the old tower and out the old gate toward Tabán, you'll even find a cluster of Ottoman tombstones under the tree.

funicular to the castle

destroyed during the liberation from the Turkish occupation in 1686, then rebuilt from scratch in a Baroque style. Much of today's façade, including its iconic dome, comes from a post-World War II reconstruction after much of the castle was damaged during the Siege of Budapest. However, you can still find traces of the old castle around the reconstructed turrets or in the foundations in the on-site Budapest History Museum.

Inside, the spartan walls offer a stark contrast to the Habsburg opulence you'd find in Vienna, as the interior was severely damaged in the war. Later, the interior was gutted and "modernized" under the Communist regime of the 1950s. Today, Buda Castle is an important cultural center, home to two museums and the National Széchenyi Library.

You can easily access the castle via the Habsburg steps next to the funicular, at the end of the flagpole-lined promenade, or take the back way via the elevator and escalators from the Castle Garden Bazaar, which leads out into the older part of the castle. This is my favorite part of the castle,

Hungarian National Gallery

Szent György tér 2, tel. 06/20-439-7331,
www.mng.hu, Tue-Sun 10am-6pm,
HUF 2,800 permanent exhibition,
audio guides HUF 800

The Hungarian National Gallery occupies the river-facing wings of Buda Castle, and it chronicles Hungarian art from the Middle Ages to the avant-garde in the period following 1945. Highlights include late-Gothic winged altarpieces, the realism of Mihály Munkácsy, and the explosive colors from Hungarian Expressionists.

Don't miss the dreamlike paintings by Tivadar Csontváry Kosztka on the staircase landing between the first and second floors. Climb up into the cupola and its terrace (open between April and October) for views across the city, or lie on beanbags and look up at hanging wire sculptures. You can easily spend two to three hours here, especially if you decide to see one of the temporary exhibitions.

Budapest History Museum

Szent György tér 2, tel. 06/1-487-8800, www.btm.hu, Tue-Sun 10am-6pm Mar-Oct, 10am-4pm Nov-Feb, HUF 2,000 entrance, HUF 1,200 audio guide

The Budapest History Museum sits in the south wing of Buda Castle and is split into three floors. In the basement, you'll find traces of Renaissance and medieval relics of Buda Castle, including parts of the older palace like the 14th-century tower chapel and vaulted palace rooms dating back to the 15th century. There is an exquisite collection of Gothic statues on the ground floor, and a unique Hungarian-Angevin tapestry dating to the Middle Ages. The first floor offers further insight into the history of the palace plus an interactive exhibition on the history of Budapest from the Romans to the Communist era. The top floor is dedicated to the Romans and prehistory. If you're passionate about history, you love Gothic sculpture, or you simply want to explore a part of the castle hidden away, the history museum is worth a couple hours of your time.

St. Mary Magdalene's Tower

Kapisztran tér 6, www.budatower.hu, daily 10am-6pm Mar-Dec, Sat-Sun 10am-6pm Jan-Feb, HUF 1,500

Take a stroll around the Castle District and you may notice a lone church tower hovering above the two-story houses at the corner between Kapisztrán tér and Országház utca. The original church was built in the 13th century as a Franciscan church for Hungarian-speaking worshippers. Under the Ottoman occupation, it was the only place of worship

for Christians in Buda, as the rest of the churches had been converted into mosques. Catholics were confined to the chancel and the Protestants to the nave, both of which were destroyed in World War II. Only the 15th-century bell tower and a reconstructed window survived the bombing. You can go up the tower if you want a view over Castle Hill; otherwise, it's enough to see the grounds from below.

National Széchényi Library

Szent György tér 4-6, tel. 06/1-224-3700, www.oszk.hu, Tue-Fri 9am-5pm, Sat 9am-2pm, HUF 400 for museum and exhibitions

At the back end of Buda Castle overlooking the Buda Hills, you'll find the National Széchényi Library, home to a collection of codices, manuscripts, and everything that has been published in Hungary. It's only open to members of the library for research purposes. So unless you're a traveling academic looking to delve into a historic manuscript, most of the library will be inaccessible. However, if you really want a peek inside, there are some temporary exhibitions to view, along with a permanent library museum.

TOP EXPERIENCE

✪ FISHERMAN'S BASTION

Halászbástya, Szentháromság tér, Mar-Apr 9am-7pm, May-Oct 9am-8pm, HUF 1,000

Glimmering white above the Danube, the romantic Fisherman's Bastion overlooks the Hungarian Parliament Building and the rooftops of Pest. Built as a spectacular viewing platform by Frigyes Schulek between 1890 and 1905, it's still one of Budapest's most beautiful structures. Its seven turrets represent the seven tribes that came to the Carpathian Basin back in the 9th century. With winding staircases and arched colonnades, it may look medieval, but it's a 19th century folly.

Why the odd-sounding name? In the Middle Ages, it was very close to a fish market. The Guild of Fisherman defended that portion of the castle wall.

In the summer, the colonnade below turns into a café. It certainly has one of the best views in the city, but let's say it's not necessarily a place locals would go to hang out.

Fisherman's Bastion, a scenic lookout point on Castle Hill

If you want to skip the crowds and the price tag that comes with getting to the top of the viewing platform, then head to the main staircase in the middle—you'll see medieval-style carvings in the arches. The view through those arches is one of the most beautiful over the bastion.

MATTHIAS CHURCH

Mátyás Templom, Szentháromság ter 2, tel. 06/1-488-7716, www.matyas-templom. hu, Mon-Fri 9am-5pm, Sat 9am-noon, Sun 1pm-5pm, HUF 1,800 church admission, HUF 1,800 tower visit

The Church of Our Lady of Buda Castle (more colloquially known as Matthias Church after the Renaissance monarch was married twice in this church) presents an eclectic architectural tapestry, beginning as early as the 1200s. The colorful interior, painted with frescoes of angels, saints, and floral and leaf motifs, can be traced back to the 19th century. Like the rest of the historic district, Matthias Church has seen significant damage (at one point, the Turks turned it into a mosque, stripped it bare, and painted its walls). For a different perspective, climb the intricately carved neo-Gothic stairway to the gallery for views across the church and to see exquisite stained-glass windows illuminating the nave from above.

HOSPITAL IN THE ROCK

Lovas út 4/C, tel. 06/70-701-0101, www. sziklakorhaz.eu, daily 7am-10pm, English language tours depart on the hour or every 30 minutes in peak season, HUF 4,000

Hospital in the Rock is a curiosity built into the caves under Castle Hill. After beginning life as a wine cellar, it was reinforced with concrete in the 1930s and was used as an underground military hospital during World War II (and again in the 1956 Uprising). Later, it was used as a prison for revolutionaries and then as a secret nuclear bunker during the Cold War. Declassified in 2002, it now houses one of Budapest's most fascinating museums. All the medical equipment on display is original, and the eerie waxwork figures give a lifelike depiction to the hospital. You can only visit the hospital with a guide, but tours run on the hour for English speakers. The tour ends in the decontamination chambers of the shelter (reinforced to withstand nuclear and chemical attack).

BUDA CASTLE LABYRINTH

Labirintus, Úri utca 9, tel. 06/1-212-0207, www.labirintus.eu, daily 10am-7pm, HUF 3,000 (cash only)

The entire Castle District sits on top of

hollow marl and limestone caves, and underneath each street is a tunnel of similar length. Initially, these natural subterranean pockets were used only as cellars, storage rooms, and wells. The Turks later connected many of these underground chambers for strategic reasons, digging more than a kilometer (almost a mile) of tunnels.

Today, you can visit a section of this labyrinth at Buda Castle. The labyrinth winds past a surreal waxwork exhibition with figures dressed in costumes once belonging to the Hungarian State Opera House. You'll then wander into smoky chambers illuminated with eerie blue light where Vlad the Impaler was allegedly imprisoned.

You'll also see marble and limestone relics from Buda's medieval past, along with Turkish tombstones. For an adrenaline-pumping experience, head to the ticket office at 6pm and pick up an oil lantern to guide you through the tunnels when the lights go out. (This is something I do not recommend doing alone—unless stumbling around a dark labyrinth alone sounds like an enjoyable experience).

CASTLE GARDEN BAZAAR

Várkert Bazár, Ybl Miklós tér 6,
tel. 06/1-225-0554, www.varkertbazar.hu,
tram 41, 19

Originally built in the 19th century as a pleasure park along the Danube, the Castle Garden Bazaar fell into decay over the decades—but it was renovated in 2014. Today, this neo-Renaissance stretch of sloping promenades featuring statues, fountains, and elegant pavilions has reopened as a cultural center with exhibition halls, film screening space, and restaurants and shops. Head up the walkway and you'll come to the neo-Renaissance

gardens. You'll find an escalator and an elevator (if needed) that can carry you up to Buda Castle without having to hike up or take the bus or the funicular railway.

LIPÓTVÁROS

✪ HUNGARIAN PARLIAMENT BUILDING

Kossúth tér 1-3, tel. 06/1-441-4904,
http://latogatokozpont.parlament.hu/en,
daily 8am-6pm Apr-Oct, daily 8am-4pm
Nov-Mar, tours daily 10am-4pm, HUF 6,700
non-EU citizens including guide, metro 2

Facing the Danube, in carved blocks of white Hungarian marble and topped with neo-Gothic spires on a wine-hued rooftop crowned with a dome, the Hungarian Parliament Building is a symbol of the city. An architectural wonder designed by Imre Steindl and completed in 1902, its 691 rooms exist in a labyrinth of gold-gilded corridors and grand staircases. It's still in use today, which is why you'll only see part of the building on the tour (and only with a guide).

You can head to the visitor center underground to join a 45-minute tour—but first, you'll want to guarantee your place by buying a ticket online (www.jegymester.hu) because openings will fill quickly. You'll have a time allocated for your English-language tour, and you'll need to go through a security checkpoint (similar to an airport check) before you're handed a headset.

The tour takes you up a golden staircase (there is an elevator as an alternative to the 100-plus stairs). The staircase leads to a corridor lined with stained-glass windows and accents of real gold. (More than 40 kilograms/88 pounds) of gold was used to create the gold leaf that covers the Parliament Building.)

Liptóváros, Jewish Quarter, and Around

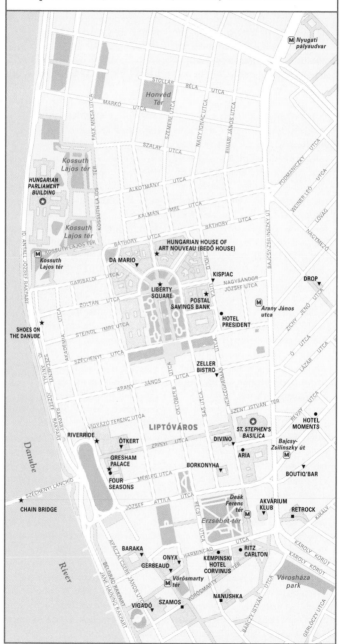

Ⓜ Nyugati pályaudvar

STOLLAR BÉLA UTCA

Honvéd Tér

MARKO UTCA

FALK MIKSA UTCA

SZEMERE UTCA

NAGY IGNAC UTCA

BIHARI JANOS UTCA

PODMANICZKY UTCA

SZALAY UTCA

Kossuth Lajos tér

WEINER LEÓ UTCA

LOVÁG

HUNGARIAN PARLIAMENT BUILDING ✪

ALKOTMANY UTCA

NAGYMEZO

KALMAN IMRE UTCA

BAJCSY-ZSILINSZKY UT

Kossuth Lajos tér

BATHORY UTCA

ID. ANTALL JÓZSEF RAKPART

KOSSUTH LAJOS TÉR

BATHORY UTCA

HUNGARIAN HOUSE OF ART NOUVEAU (BEDŐ HOUSE) ★

Ⓜ Kossuth Lajos tér

★ **DA MARIO** ▾

GARIBALDI UTCA

KISP!AC ▾

NAGYSANDOR JÓZSEF UTCA

DROP ▾

LIBERTY SQUARE ★

ZOLTAN UTCA

POSTAL SAVINGS BANK ★

Ⓜ Arany János utca

ZICHY JENŐ UTCA

Ó UTCA

STEINDL IMRE UTCA

AKADEMIA

HOTEL PRESIDENT ▾

LAZAR UTCA

★ **SHOES ON THE DANUBE**

SZÉCHENYI UTCA

ID. ANTALL JÓZSEF RAKPART

SZÉCHENYI RAKPART

ARANY JÁNOS UTCA

OKTÓBER 6 UTCA

SAS UTCA

HERCEGPRÍMÁS

ZELLER BISTRO ▾

SZENT ISTVÁN TÉR

REVAY UTCA

VIGYÁZO FERENC UTCA

LIPTÓVÁROS

ST. STEPHEN'S BASILICA ✪

HOTEL MOMENTS ▾

Danube

RIVERRIDE ▾

ÖTKERT ▾

ZRINYI UTCA

DIVINO ▾

Bajcsy-Zsilinszky út Ⓜ

GRESHAM PALACE ★

BORKONYHA ▾

ARIA ▾

BOUTIQ'BAR ▾

FOUR SEASONS ★

MERLEG UTCA

River

SZÉCHENYI LÁNCHID

JÓZSEF ATTILA UTCA

BECSI UTCA

Deák Ferenc tér

AKVÁRIUM KLUB ▾

Ⓜ

RETROCK ▪

★ **CHAIN BRIDGE**

Erzsébet-tér

KIRALY

BELGRAD RAKPART

JANE HAINING RAKPART

APACZAI CSERE JÁNOS UTCA

HARMINCAD UTCA

KAROLY KÖRÚT

BARAKA ▾

ONYX ▾

RITZ CARLTON ▾

KAROLY KÖRÚT

GERBEAUD ▾

KEMPINSKI HOTEL CORVINUS ●

Városháza park

Vörösmarty tér Ⓜ

VIGADÓ ▾

SZAMOS ▾

VÖRÖSMARTY UTCA

NANUSHKA ▾

BARCZY ISTVÁN UTCA

GERLOCZY UTCA

Andrassy Avenue

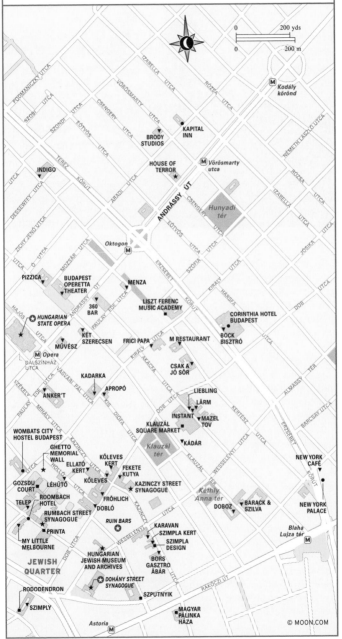

0   200 yds
0   200 m

M Kodály
körönd

IZABELLA UTCA
RÓZSA UTCA
PODMANICZKY UTCA
SZOBI UTCA
VÖRÖSMARTY UTCA
CSENGERY UTCA
SZONDI UTCA
EÖTVÖS UTCA

NÉMETH LÁSZLÓ UTCA

▼ KAPITAL
INN
▼ BRODY
STUDIOS

M Vörösmarty
utca

HOUSE OF
TERROR
★

RÓZSA UTCA
IZABELLA UTCA

JÓSIKA UTCA
UTCA

▼ INDIGO

ANDRÁSSY ÚT
CSENGERY UTCA

Hunyadi
tér

DESSEWFFY UTCA
TERÉZ KÖRÚT
ARADI UTCA
ZICHY JENŐ UTCA

EÖTVÖS UTCA

Oktogon M
ERZSÉBET KÖRÚT

SZOFIA UTCA

▼ PIZZICA

Ó UTCA
MOZSÁR UTCA

▼ BUDAPEST
OPERETTA
THEATER

▼ MENZA

KIRÁLY UTCA

UTCA

ANDRÁSSY ÚT
PAULAY EDE UTCA

LISZT FERENC
MUSIC ACADEMY ■

HARSFA UTCA

DOB UTCA

CORINTHIA HOTEL
BUDAPEST

★ HUNGARIAN
STATE OPERA

HAJÓS UTCA

▼ 360
BAR

▼ KÉT
SZERECSEN
▼ MŰVÉSZ

FRICI PAPA ▼

M RESTAURANT ▼

BÖCK
BISZTRÓ ▼

M Opera
DALSZÍNHÁZ
UTCA

HAJÓS UTCA
NAGYMEZŐ UTCA
NAGYMEZŐ UTCA

KIRÁLY UTCA

KAZINCZY UTCA

CSAK A ▼
JÓ SÖR

TÉR UTCA
ALMÁSSY UTCA

▼ KADARKA

▼ APROPÓ

LIEBLING ▼
LÁRM ▼

SZÉKELY MIHÁLY UTCA
VASÁRI PÁL UTCA

ANKER'T ▼

INSTANT ▼

MAZEL
TOV ▼

BARCSAY UTCA
KERTÉSZ UTCA

PAULAY EDE UTCA
MIHÁLY UTCA

DOB UTCA

KLAUZÁL
SQUARE MARKET ■

KÁDÁR ▼

WOMBATS CITY
HOSTEL BUDAPEST ■

Klauzál
tér

WESSELÉNYI UTCA

ERZSÉBET KÖRÚT

GHETTO
MEMORIAL
WALL ★

KÖLEVES
KERT ▼

FEKETE
KUTYA ▼

NEW YORK
CAFÉ ●

ELLATÓ ▼
KERT

DIÓFA UTCA

KAZINCZY STREET
★ SYNAGOGUE

Klauzál UTCA

GOZSDU
COURT

KÖLEVES ▼

LÉHÚTÓ ▼

FRÖHLICH ▼

Kéthly
Anna tér

NEW YORK
PALACE

TELEP ●
ROOMBACH
HOTEL ■

DOBLÓ ▼

DOBOZ ▼

BARACK &
SZILVA ▼

RÁKÓCZI ÚT
KÖRÚT

RUMBACH STREET
SYNAGOGUE ★

RUIN BARS
★

KARAVAN ▼
SZIMPLA KERT ★

Blaha
Lujza tér
M

HOLLÓ UTCA
KAZINCZY UTCA

DOB UTCA

WESSELÉNYI UTCA

SZIMPLA
DESIGN ▼

▼ PRINTA

MY LITTLE
MELBOURNE ●

HUNGARIAN
JEWISH MUSEUM
AND ARCHIVES ■

BORS
GASZTRO
ÁBÁR ▼

JEWISH
QUARTER

RÓDODENDRON ●

DOHÁNY STREET
★ SYNAGOGUE

SZPUTNYIK ●

RÁKÓCZI ÚT

SZIMPLY ●

MAGYAR
PÁLINKA
HÁZA ■

Astoria
M

© MOON.COM

51

Hungarian Parliament Building

In the hall under the dome, you'll see the Hungarian Crown Jewels, which once belonged to the canonized King Stephen, the first monarch of Hungary. The crown has led an adventurous life over the past 1,000 years—it has been lost, stolen, and was locked up in Fort Knox at one point until its return to Hungary in 1978. It resided in the Hungarian National Museum until 2000, and then found a new home under the iconic dome.

The tour will take you into the Lobby Room, where you'll spot statues dedicated to Hungarian shepherds, doctors, and theologians. You'll then enter the Session Hall and the north gallery overlooking the Danube. Make sure you take some time in the final exhibition room, where you'll find interactive screens and curious information about Budapest and the Parliament Building. (For example, there are no chimneys on the structure, and the central heating actually comes from a boiler room in a nearby building—hot air is funneled through a series of shafts and tunnels. And cold air from ice wells under the square was once used as an early form of air-conditioning.) You can also see the original red star that was on top of the building in the Communist era.

CHAIN BRIDGE

A symbol of a unified city, the Chain Bridge (Lánc híd) is Budapest's oldest permanent stone bridge. This suspension bridge features two vaulted,

Chain Bridge

classical-style pillars connected by large iron chains. Count István Széchenyi financed its construction, and it took almost 50 years to build.

The Germans blew up the bridge in 1945 following the Siege of Budapest, and it was rebuilt in the late '40s. Today, it's one of the most romantic spots to cross the Danube, especially at night when thousands of lightbulbs come on. Make sure you stop to look at the stone lions created by sculptor János Marschalkó that flank the entrances to the bridge. Local legend says the sculptor forgot to carve the tongues and jumped into the Danube after being mocked for it. However, it's just hearsay, as the sculptor lived for decades after the bridge was built, and the lions have tongues—they can be seen from above but not from the sidewalk.

At the time of writing, the Chain Bridge was scheduled for 24 months of renovations starting in late 2019. But you can still get great views from the promenade on both sides of the river, or from above at the top of Castle Hill.

SHOES ON THE DANUBE

Set on the embankment just in front of the Hungarian Parliament, the Shoes on the Danube memorial, envisioned by sculptor Gyula Pauer and filmmaker and poet Can Toga, is a poignant reminder of the horrors of the Holocaust. Sixty pairs of iron shoes face the river bank to commemorate the Jews shot into the river by the fascist Arrow Cross Party in the 1940s. Sadly, this was not the only location in Budapest where executions like these happened. The shoes—men's, women's, and small children's—were modeled after 1940s designs, with the iron creased and folded like leather.

Shoes on the Danube is a memorial to the Jews shot into the river by the fascist Arrow Cross party.

To get here, follow the stairs down the side of the Parliament, take the crossing over, and walk back toward the Chain Bridge.

LIBERTY SQUARE (Szabadság tér)

This green patch in the heart of the city, enclosed by grand buildings housing banks, embassies, and offices, was once the location of an 18th-century Austrian barracks. Today, statues and memorials can be found all around the square. The Soviet War Memorial, an obelisk topped with a gold star, was erected in 1946 by the Soviet army. It stands directly over the resting place of the Russian soldiers who died during the city's liberation from the Germans. Considering Hungary's communist history, it's controversial, but Hungary signed an agreement to protect the monument. On the other side of the square, a newer memorial to the "Victims of German Occupation" appeared in 2014. The memorial has been criticized by some

53

BUDAPEST BY BOAT

the view of Buda Castle from a boat on the Danube

Budapest is best seen from the Danube, especially on hot summer days when there's a refreshing breeze to keep you cool. The water is generally calm. From the perspective of a boat, you can really appreciate the differences between Buda and Pest and get close to monuments like the Hungarian Parliament Building in a way you can't on land.

RIVER CRUISES

Options in this category include a classic sightseeing cruise, speedboat tour, or amphibious bus:

- **Legenda** (Dock 7 Jane Haining rakpart, tel. 06/1-317-2203, www.legenda.hu, HUF 4,200) offers a classic 70-minute-long sightseeing cruise with a glass of

for whitewashing Hungary's collaboration with the Nazis. A moving **protest memorial** made up of candles, personal memorabilia, and letters by those whose families died in the Holocaust can be visited just a few feet away.

POSTAL SAVINGS BANK

Postatakarék, Hold utca

Just behind Liberty Square is the former Postal Savings Bank. It is not open to the public but is worth passing by. Designed by Ödön Lechner and completed in 1901, this striking example of Hungarian Art Nouveau is an

architectural symphony of Hungarian folk ornamentation, with sprouting flowers and ceramic bees "flying" up to a ceramic beehive. The design culminates with a tapestry-like rooftop made from glazed green-and-yellow octagonal tiles, topped with serpents, angel wings, and dragon tails.

For an excellent view of the Postal Savings Bank, head across the street to the rooftop terrace of the Hotel President. In the summer, you can sip a coffee on the terrace café, but if you're around in the winter, come up for the rooftop ice rink and a cup of mulled wine.

sparkling wine, beer, or soft drink included. The boats fit 150-180 people and they are adaptable to the weather. If you're interested in knowing more about the various sites, audio guides are available. Otherwise, just sit and relax. Once you get to Margaret Island, you can get off the boat for 90 minutes before being picked up, or you can decide to stay on board.

- **RiverRide** (Széchenyi István tér 7-8, tel. 06/1-332-2555, www.riverride.com, HUF 9,000) operates an amphibious bus tour. After taking an on-road tour through the Inner City, you'll see the Danube on a water bus. The tour takes around 95 minutes and starts on Széchenyi István tér near the Chain Bridge.

- **Dunarama** (tel. 06/70-942-2613, www.dunarama.hu, HUF 39,000-72,000 for 25- or 50-minute cruises without a guide) is a speedboat tour down the Danube. This luxury water limousine fits only 10 people in its closed cabins and open platform, so this is an option if you're traveling with a small group or you're really feeling fancy.

CRUISING ON A BUDGET

From March through October, public **BKK** boats run from Kopaszi gát in the south to Margaret Island, or even as far as Rómaifürdő in the north. The route (HUF 750, or free with a city transport pass on weekdays) takes two hours. These boats stop at a variety of docks en route, including the Castle Garden Bazaar, the Hungarian Parliament Building, and on weekends Margaret Island.

A word of caution: these boats can be unreliable (i.e., not on schedule), and if the boat is already full, it won't dock. Your best bet is to embark at one of the first ports of call, like Kopaszi gát, the National Theatre, or Rómaifürdő, if you want a good seat and a guarantee to board.

Boats are packed on weekends, but weekday mornings are quiet (for locals, it's not the fastest commute). The boats are a little rustier than the touring boats, but the view is still the same. If you're lucky, there is a working bar or toilet on board.

One thing that public boats have over the sightseeing cruises (other than the price tag) is that they go further than the central part of the river, taking you down into the Millennium Quarter and the Kopaszi Dam to the south, and up past Margaret Island and Óbuda Island to the north—beyond the usual sites like Buda Castle, the Parliament, and the Chain Bridge. The boat north passes offbeat sites like the Óbuda Gas Works, which looks more like a turreted castle than an old factory.

HUNGARIAN HOUSE OF ART NOUVEAU (Bedő House)

Honvéd utca 3, tel. 06/1-269-4622, www.magyarszecessziohaza.hu, Mon-Sat 10am-5pm, HUF 2,000 for the museum

From the outside, the Hungarian House of Art Nouveau (also known as Bedő House) looks like it was piped out of a bag full of icing. Designed by Hungarian Art Nouveau architect Emil Viador for the Bedő family, the building has a style more in line with French, Belgian, or German Jugendstil than Lechner's orientalist creations. Although residential apartments and offices occupy most of the building, the rest is a shrine to all things Art Nouveau. You'll find a café and museum filled with period furniture, ceramics, and artwork. The space is more like a curious antique shop than a curated museum. It offers a fascinating collection for anyone wanting a glance into a past world and the way the Hungarian upper middle class lived in the early 1900s.

GRESHAM PALACE

Széchenyi István tér 5

The building that is now the **Four Seasons Hotel** was once a block of luxury apartments and offices, built between 1905 and 1907 by

Budapest's yellow trams make it easy to navigate the city, and some lines even offer the perfect sightseeing vantage point. Hop on the number 2 tram, beginning at Jászai Mari tér near **Margaret Bridge.** The tram will take you past the Hungarian Parliament Building, down the Danube banks past the Chain Bridge, the Vigadó (a gorgeous concert hall), and the city's most famous bridges. Get off at Fővám tér by the **Central Market Hall,** or continue to the **Bálna cultural center** or the Müpa-Nemzeti Színház stop for the **Millennium cultural complex.** Around Christmas, the tram may be dressed up with thousands of festive fairy lights.

the London Gresham Insurance Company, which used the building as its headquarters. The gently undulating façade is typical Art Nouveau style, with ceramic accents, intricate wrought ironwork, friezes, and floral motifs. Take a peek into the lobby at the intricate curved arcade made with tiles of lead glass, and the beautiful mosaic flooring.

✪ ST. STEPHEN'S BASILICA

Szent István tér, www.bazilika.biz, Mon-Fri 9am-5pm, Sat 9am-1pm, Sun 1pm-5pm, HUF 200 recommended donation. Viewing Platform daily 10am-4:30pm Nov-Mar, 10am-5:30pm Apr, May, Oct, 10am-6:30pm June-Sep, HUF 600. Treasury 10am-6:30pm July-Sep, 10am-4:30pm Oct-Jun, HUF 400.

It took half a century to build this basilica, partly because its iconic dome collapsed halfway through construction, and the work began again almost from scratch. Today, this impressive neoclassical cathedral stands at the same height as the Hungarian Parliament. (Both are the tallest buildings in downtown Budapest.) You can scale over 300 stairs (or take an elevator) to the viewing platform outside

St. Stephen's Basilica

the rooftop of the Royal Postal Savings Bank by Lechner

Ödön Lechner may be known as the Hungarian Gaudí, but the architect who defined **Hungarian Secession** (or Art Nouveau) created his most extravagant buildings a couple of years before Gaudí built his most colorful creations. Searching for a style that he could call uniquely Hungarian, and rebelling against the architectural norms of the Habsburg styles, Lechner turned to Hungarian folk art expressed through embroidery and wood painting. He also turned toward the East—following the anthropological theory popular at the time that the Hungarians were an Asiatic race. His architecture blended Indian and Persian influences, Hungarian folk art, and modern technological innovations like iron, steel, fortified concrete, and colorful glazed ceramics and tiles from the Zsolnay factory in Pécs. (Zsolnay was one of the first porcelain, ceramics, and tile manufacturers to develop pyrogranite, a durable type of ornamental ceramic fired under high temperature that could withstand the elements, like frost, making them perfect for architectural details and roof tiles.)

Lechner is regarded as the master of Secession and the father of modern Hungarian architecture. His work was a departure from the traditional Habsburg style visible all across Central Europe (which draws its inspiration from Rococo, Baroque, and Western Historicism). Hungarian Secessionism followed the Art Nouveau trends popping up in Europe, but it applied its own Eastern accent, whether in floral motifs inspired by embroidery or in the intricate details from Islamic architecture. His work, which can look like it's been made from gingerbread, is characterized by glazed ceramics and tiles in greens, blues, and yellows. His most beautiful buildings can be found in Budapest, including the former **Postal Savings Bank,** the **Museum of Applied Arts,** and the **Geological Institute of Hungary.**

the dome for 360-degree views of Budapest's most famous sites.

The interior of the cathedral—laid out in a Greek cross—is intricate, with frescoes adorning the gold-accented walls. In the chapel on the right-hand side from the entrance, head over to see a mummified relic: the holy right hand of St. Stephen, which is kept inside a gilded box. It gets taken for a yearly "walk" on August 20, during the St. Stephen's Day procession. Throw a coin in the slot, and the gilded box will light up so you can see the relic in its full glory.

Why is there a mummified limb in the basilica? Legend has it that when the Hungarian king was canonized in 1083, part of making him a saint involved exhuming his body; his right arm was found as fresh as the day he was buried (although apparently not the rest of him). His right arm was chopped off and preserved as a Catholic relic. The hand has traveled to Bosnia, Dubrovnik, Vienna, and Salzburg. (A priest from the American army returned it to Budapest in 1945.)

Outside the entrance, opposite the stairs heading up to the dome, you can take the elevator to the treasury to see some of the fine silver, gold, and textiles that are the property of this opulent cathedral.

If you want to get to know the basilica better, take a guided tour between 10am and 3pm, but you need to book in advance on the phone (06/1-338-2151). Guided tours in English cost HUF 12,700 for a group of one to five persons.

If you're fascinated with the huge pipe organ inside, you can hear it in action (www.organconcert.hu) on Monday nights (HUF 3,500) and Friday nights (HUF 4,500-7,000).

JEWISH QUARTER
✪ DOHÁNY STREET SYNAGOGUE

Dohány utca 2, tel. 06/1-413-5585, www.jewishtourhungary.com, Sun-Thu 10am-6pm, Fri 10am-4pm Mar-Oct, Sun-Thu 10am-4pm, Fri 10am-2pm Nov-Feb, HUF 4,500 (with guide), metro 2, tram 47, 49

Above Károly körút at the intersection with Dohány utca is the Grand Synagogue, more colloquially known as the Dohány Street Synagogue. Its twin towers, topped with onion-shaped domes (covered in intricate gold leaf), rise over 42 meters (140 feet).

The Grand Synagogue is Europe's largest. The architecture deviates from traditional synagogues—the architects were not Jewish, and the

the Grand Synagogue

inspiration for the building came from Christian basilicas. It includes a stunning rose window, a cluster of stars made out of stained glass; an orientalist Moorish twist symbolizes both the Jews' Eastern origins and the Neolog interest in integrating into the local community.

German-Austrian architect Ludwig Förster, along with Hungarian architect Frigyes Feszl, built this 3,000-seat synagogue in the 1850s. Inside, the seating is divided in two, with the men taking the ground floor (gilded with golden columns) and the women meant to sit in the gallery above, beneath dripping chandeliers.

The arcaded garden outside was a makeshift cemetery during the Holocaust. The 2,000 bodies buried here are commemorated with graves and memorials. Beyond, the Heroes' Temple, also known as the Winter Synagogue, is used for weekday services. In the courtyard before the exit, you'll find the **Raoul Wallenberg Holocaust Memorial Park,** dedicated to the Swedish diplomat who saved tens of thousands of Jews during World War II. You'll see the profound metallic sculpture of a weeping willow by Imre Varga, which was placed directly above a mass grave; victims' names and tattoo

Unlike Prague, Venice, or Krakow, Budapest has never had an exclusively Jewish neighborhood. Jews have lived side by side in Hungary with non-Jews. (The most famous Jewish area in the VII District received the name "Jewish Quarter" after becoming a ghetto in the 1940s.)

The story behind the Jews of the VII District ties in with the segregation rules of the 18th century—Jews could not even spend the night in the Inner City at that time. So the community grew outside the city walls. Many Jews worked as merchants, typically trading grain, cattle, leather goods, and textiles in the market just outside, in today's **Deák Ferenc tér** (a large downtown central square bordering on the Inner City where three metro lines meet).

As the community prospered in the 19th century, Budapest's Jews split into

the Star of David at Dohány Street Synagogue

two factions: **Neolog Jews,** a socially liberal group inclined toward integrating into Hungary that preferred to speak Hungarian over Yiddish, and the **Orthodox** community, a conservative group that resisted the modern and secular leanings of the Neolog community.

Budapest's Jewish population peaked following World War I. At that time, there were 125 synagogues and over 200,000 Jews in the city. Tragically, nearly 50 percent of the city's Jews died in the Holocaust, and the community never fully recovered.

Today, a walk around this district reveals signs of Jewish heritage. But you won't find signs of Jewish life only in this district. In the **VIII District, XIII District,** and in **Buda** today, you'll find active synagogues and prayer houses with tightly knit Jewish communities. Some synagogues are visible from the outside, like the **Grand Synagogue** on Dohány utca, or they may be tucked away in a private apartment, like the prayer house on Teleki tér in the VIII District.

numbers glint on the sculpture's dangling metal leaves. You'll also find the **Hungarian Jewish Museum and Archives** (Dohány utca 2, tel. 06/1-462-0477, www.milev.hu, Sun-Thu 10am-6pm, Fri 10am-4pm Mar-Apr and Oct, Sun-Thu 10am-8pm, Fri 10am-4pm May-Sep, Sun-Thu 10am-4pm, Fri 10am-2pm Nov-Feb, HUF 4,000). It includes a collection of objects from religious and daily Hungarian Jewish life.

KAZINCZY STREET SYNAGOGUE

Kazinczy utca 29-31, tel. 06/1-351-0524, Sun-Thu 10am-6pm Mar-Oct, Fri 10am-1pm Mar, Fri 10am-4pm Apr-Oct, Sun-Thu 10am-4pm, Fri 10am-1pm Nov-Feb, HUF 1,000

The Kazinczy Street Synagogue, also known as the Orthodox Synagogue, stands in the corner of the cobbled portion of Kazinczy utca. You need to look up to see the Hebrew lettering on the ashlar above the exposed brick façade. The Secessionist-style interior, drawing influences from Hungarian folk art (such as the Transylvanian wood carvings and Hungarian floral motifs), is surprising—it is the heart of Orthodox Jewry in Budapest. The complex, designed by Béla and Sándor Löffler in 1912-1913, expands into a courtyard where there is a kosher restaurant and a shop.

RUMBACH STREET SYNAGOGUE

Rumbach Sebestyén utca 11-13, metro 1, 2, 3, tram 47, 49

A few blocks away from the Kazinczy and Dohány utca synagogue, the minaret-like spires of the Rumbach Street Synagogue tower over the design shops, vibrant street art, and avant-garde underground theaters that characterize the Jewish Quarter today. This Moorish-style synagogue, designed by Viennese architect Otto Wagner in 1872, is a museum and cultural hall.

Inside the synagogue, seven striking rose windows in a kaleidoscope of colors can be seen in its domed ceiling, and the walls are covered in ornate lavender-, fuchsia-, and lapis-toned friezes. The synagogue fell into disuse following the war and then stood as a semi-derelict, pigeon-infested ruin after a partial reconstruction in the late 1980s and early 1990s. (The work had to be aborted when the private corporation that bought the building went bankrupt.) But at the time of this writing, it's now back in Jewish hands and is being restored to its former glory.

GHETTO MEMORIAL WALL

15 Király utca

In the winter of 1944, more than 50,000 Jews were moved into the ghetto, an area fortified with wooden fencing and stone walls topped with barbed wire. A local conservation group working to protect the Jewish Quarter's cultural heritage has reconstructed the original ghetto wall as a memorial. Take a walk down Király utca and peek through the bars of the gate at number 15 to see it—it's at the back of a courtyard of residential houses. The memorial was constructed from stones from the original ghetto wall and is topped with barbed wire.

AROUND ANDRÁSSY AVENUE

✪ HUNGARIAN STATE OPERA

Andrássy út 22, tel. 06/1-814-7100, www.opera.hu, metro 1

As you're strolling down Andrássy Avenue, stop to admire the Hungarian State Opera House, one of the world's most beautiful opera houses. This neo-Renaissance structure was built in 1884 by Miklós Ybl, with the financial support of Emperor Franz Joseph I. Its exterior is decorated with stone sphinxes, muses between the columns, and images of famous opera composers on the roof terrace. Marble columns, vaulted ceilings, and chandeliers adorn the interior. The gold-covered auditorium seats over 1,200, and at the time of this writing, the building is undergoing a major renovation to improve its acoustics and staging, allowing it to compete with other great European opera houses. (It's expected to reopen in 2020.) If you can't catch a show, you can still join one of the daily tours (HUF 2,990) at 2pm, 3pm, or 4pm. The tours include a mini concert at the end.

HOUSE OF TERROR

Andrássy út 60, tel. 06/1-374-2600, www.terrorhaza.hu, Tue-Sun 10am-6pm, HUF 3,000, metro 1

This infamous four-story apartment block on a corner of Andrássy Avenue was once the headquarters of the secret police and a place where many were held captive, tortured, and killed. Today, its imposing roof with the word "TERROR" punched out in the metal overhang dominates this part of the

the Hungarian State Opera on Andrássy Avenue

avenue. Inside is a unique museum—a monument to the victims of Hungary's fascist and communist regimes—that opened in 2002. The interactive museum contains chilling reconstructed prison cells in the basement, rooms lined with propaganda posters, and installations from the darkest moments in Hungarian history. The museum spreads from the basement to the second floor, and it's worth taking two to three hours to go through, especially if you watch the poignant interactive video displays, where you can listen to firsthand stories of victims and survivors.

How did the infamous number 60 turn into a tourist attraction? In late 2000, the Public Foundation for the Research of Central and East European History and Society bought the building and spent a year reconstructing the interior to create a memorial and museum to the victims of the regimes.

CITY PARK AND AROUND

VAJDAHUNYAD CASTLE

Városliget, tel. 06/1-422-0765, Tue-Fri 10am-5pm, HUF 2,100 combined ticket for museum and towers, metro 1

The spires of Vajdahunyad Castle may look like something out of *Dracula* (it has been a film location in an adaptation). But look closely and you'll notice that this castle, built at the end of the 19th century, is an eclectic mixture of architectural styles. Medieval towers share space with Baroque statues. You get the best views from the gate tower (enter through the door on the left as you go through the gate) or the Apostle's Tower, which is accessible from inside the Museum of Agriculture with a guide. The interior of the castle is just as spectacular, with ornate rococo ballrooms, crystal chandeliers, Renaissance-inspired frescoes in hues of blue and maroon, and stained-glass windows.

City Park

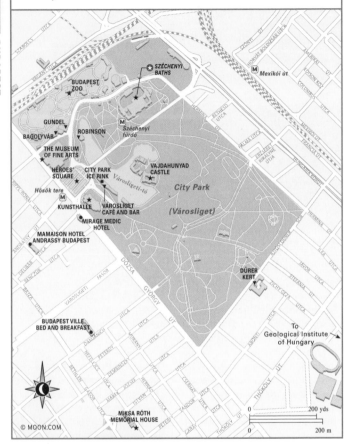

- SZÉCHENYI BATHS
- Mexikói út
- BUDAPEST ZOO
- GUNDEL
- BAGOLYVÁR
- ROBINSON
- Széchenyi fürdő
- THE MUSEUM OF FINE ARTS
- HEROES' SQUARE
- CITY PARK ICE RINK
- Városligeti-tó
- VAJDAHUNYAD CASTLE
- Hősök tere
- KUNSTHALLE
- City Park
- (Városliget)
- VÁROSLIGET CAFÉ AND BAR
- MIRAGE MEDIC HOTEL
- MAMAISON HOTEL ANDRASSY BUDAPEST
- DÜRER KERT
- BUDAPEST VILLE BED AND BREAKFAST
- To Geological Institute of Hungary
- MIKSA RÓTH MEMORIAL HOUSE

© MOON.COM

0   200 yds
0   200 m

Vajdahunyad Castle in City Park

The interior of the castle houses the **Museum of Agriculture** (www.mezogazdasagimuzeum.hu), which showcases the history of Hungarian agriculture with reconstructed yurts and dwellings, antique plows, farming equipment, and an impressive collection of taxidermy and antlers. Upstairs, next to the intricate staircase, is an interesting photographic exhibition displaying the architectural inspirations for the castle.

The castle grounds are free of charge to roam. You can even go up to the hooded statue of Anonymous, the unknown chronicler who penned the history of the early Magyars in the court of King Béla III, and rub the bronze pen for literary inspiration.

BUDAPEST ZOO

Állatkerti körút 6-12, tel. 06/1-273-4900,
www.zoobudapest.com, daily 9am-sunset,
HUF 3,300, metro 1

Founded in 1866, Budapest Zoo is one of Europe's oldest zoos. Located near City Park, the zoo is a vast complex with two artificial mountains, 500 species of animals, and 4,000 plant species. You can explore greenhouses dedicated to Madagascar and an Australia section where kangaroos hop right past you. Pay a visit to the turn-of-the-20th-century palm houses built by the Eiffel Company in Paris; they feature a replica rainforest complete with sprinkler-generated "rain." The neighboring butterfly house is also a great stop.

The main highlights of the zoo include the "Magic Mountain" set inside a hollow, artificial rocky outcrop where you'll find a life-school made up of an aquarium, games, educational experiments, and 3D documentary screenings. The Art Nouveau elephant house, another highlight, is a spectacular piece of architecture, with mosque-like domes covered in scaly turquoise Zsolnay tiles.

On the way in and out, notice the gate of the zoo, created by the architect who designed the elephant house. It's flanked by elephants, topped with polar bears, and decorated with intricate botanical murals. (The zoo's Art Nouveau buildings have been listed as national landmarks.)

THE MUSEUM OF FINE ARTS (Szépművészeti Múzeum)

Dózsa György út 41, tel. 01/469-7100,
www.szepmuveszeti.hu, Tue-Sun 10am-6pm,
HUF 2,800, metro 1

The Museum of Fine Arts, which resembles a Greek temple, lies on the northern side of Heroes' Square. After three years of construction work, it reopened to the public in the fall of 2018. The permanent collection spans five floors, so expect to spend over three hours if you want to explore the whole museum—and that's without the temporary exhibitions thrown in.

Start in the basement for the museum's exquisite collection of Egyptian art and Classical antiquities. The collection features bronze statuettes of Egyptian gods, painted pottery, colorful sarcophagi, Hellenic sculpture, and Roman glass, which could keep any history lover occupied for a couple of hours.

The ground floor is exciting because this is where you will find the Romanesque Hall—which was closed to the public for 70 years after a bomb damaged the museum in 1945—a stunning hall designed to showcase Hungarian Romanesque art. The Romanesque Hall is covered wall-to-wall with colorful frescoes inspired by the art from medieval churches with a vibrant cast of characters like kings and angels, and mythological figures such as dragons, painted in hues of royal reds, lapis blues, wood green, and accents of gold leaf. It had been built to house medieval plaster casts, but now the hall itself is an exhibition in its own right.

The first floor is now home to European art from 1250 to 1600, with work from Europe's greatest Renaissance and Baroque masters like Raphael, Titian, Tintoretto, van Dyck, Holbein, El Greco, and Goya. However, if you're passionate about sculpture, head to the second floor to the display of European sculpture 1350-1800, including a statue of a horse attributed to Leonardo da Vinci.

Level three is dedicated to Hungarian Baroque art from 1600 to 1800. This collection was originally housed in the Hungarian National Gallery, in the Royal Palace in Buda, and now gets a new home here in the museum.

KUNSTHALLE

Műcsarnok, Dózsa György út 37,
tel. 06/1-460-7000, www.mucsarnok.hu,
Tue-Wed, Fri-Sun 10am-6pm, Thu noon-8pm,
HUF 2,900 (combined ticket
for all exhibitions)

Since the 19th century, the Kunsthalle has been the main hub of contemporary art in Hungary.

Flanking Heroes' Square, opposite the Museum of Fine Arts, the Kunsthalle looks more like a Greek temple than an exhibition hall, with gold-gilded Corinthian columns. Kunsthalle is one of Budapest's largest exhibition spaces focusing on visual and contemporary art. Top international exhibitions change with the seasons—examples include photography from Steve McCurry and Sandro Miller.

HEROES' SQUARE

Heroes' Square, marked by the towering pillar topped by the angel Gabriel holding the holy crown, can be seen all the way down Andrássy Avenue. The square itself was erected in 1896 to celebrate the millennium of the conquest of the Carpathian Basin. (The rest of the work on the square was completed in 1929.) The features of the square are packed with Hungarian symbolism,

Heroes' Square

The Miksa Róth museum showcases the work of the famous stained-glass artist.

Miksa Róth (1865-1944) was one of Hungary's most prolific and famous artists. Working for half a century, he became a master of stained glass and mosaic art. Róth's style evolved through the Secession and beyond with the Renaissance of stained-glass art at the end of the 19th century. Following World War I, his art declined while Hungary suffered social and economic challenges.

Róth was Jewish, and his work suffered again during World War II. Although baptized as a Roman Catholic in 1897, Róth still struggled under the anti-Semitic law passed in 1939 that limited Jewish public and economic life. Eventually, he closed his workshop and transferred his house and possessions to his Roman Catholic wife. He died of natural causes in Budapest in 1944 at 89.

His stained-glass art can be found as far away as Oslo and Mexico City, but only in Budapest is his craft embedded into the architectural landscape of the city. Look for his work in the stained-glass windows of the **Hungarian Parliament Building** and inside the stairwell of the **Gresham Palace** building housing the Four Seasons Hotel. Beyond stained glass, Róth also created architectural mosaics, like those in the **Liszt Ferenc Music Academy** and adorning the dome inside the intricate entrance of the **Széchenyi Baths.**

from the chieftains of the seven Magyar tribes at the base of the pillar to the two semicircular colonnades featuring bronze statues of Hungarian kings and leaders. You'll find statues of Hungarian heroes like Lajos Kossuth, a revolutionary who struggled for independence from Austrian rule during the 1848 uprising against the Habsburgs.

You can get up close to the monuments, including the tomb of the unknown soldier, a cenotaph remembering the soldiers from multiple wars. Next to the tomb is a cast-iron manhole covering (originally made out of wood) for the first thermal water well used for a thermal bath that once stood on the square.

Today, you'll only find locals on Heroes' Square during protests and marches, like Budapest Pride, or for public events like the National Gallop, a large Hungarian cultural festival centered on horse racing. Otherwise, the square is filled with tourists.

MIKSA RÓTH
MEMORIAL HOUSE

Nefelejcs utca 26, 06/1-341-6789, www.
rothmuzeum.hu, 2pm-6pm Tue-Sun, HUF 750

Tucked inside a courtyard in the outer VII District, the Miksa Róth Memorial House is a fascinating and underrated museum dedicated to the life and work of stained-glass artist Miksa Róth. The entrance from the street will bring you into the courtyard. Take the door on the left to get into the museum.

The former Róth residence occupies part of the museum here, so you'll get a glimpse into the way the Róth family lived. The top floor of the building contains an exhibition of Róth's work, with beautiful panels of stained glass and stunning Art Nouveau mosaics. Sometimes the museum closes for August.

GEOLOGICAL INSTITUTE
OF HUNGARY

Stefánia út 14, email one week in advance to
visit the geological museum and the interior:
muzeum@mbfsz.gov.hu, free entrance, bus
5, 7, 110, 112

It's worth going off the beaten track to see the Geological Institute of Hungary, arguably one of Ödön Lechner's most spectacular buildings. Its two-toned blue tiled roof is topped with four Atlas figures holding up a terrestrial globe. Fittingly, the building incorporates geological elements: the roof represents the Thetis Sea, and the building is embedded with fossil-shaped ceramics. Emperor Franz Josef I approved the founding of the institute, but Lechner, who won a competition for the commission, began work on the building in 1896, finishing in 1899. The institute features the typical Lechner qualities, including folk motifs in the architectural ceramics and flowers carved into the windows.

The institute also houses a geology museum, which can be visited by appointment.

Geological Institute of Hungary

MARGARET ISLAND
AND AROUND
WATER TOWER

Margitsziget, tel. 06/20-383-6352, lookout
platform open daily 11:30am-7pm May-Oct,
HUF 600, bus 26

Towering above trees and grassy lawns, the Water Tower on Margaret Island is visible from both Buda and Pest. A beautiful piece of architecture embodying the Hungarian Secessionist style, the tower was also one of the first structures of its kind in Europe that employed innovative ferro-concrete engineering. Designed by Szilárd Zielinski and built by architect Rezső Vilmos Ray in 1911, it reaches over 55 meters (180 feet) into the air.

The tower can be admired from most spots on the island, whether you're relaxing with a book or riding a quadracycle. To get into the tower you must buy a ticket at the ticket office (which is also the box office for the

Margaret Island

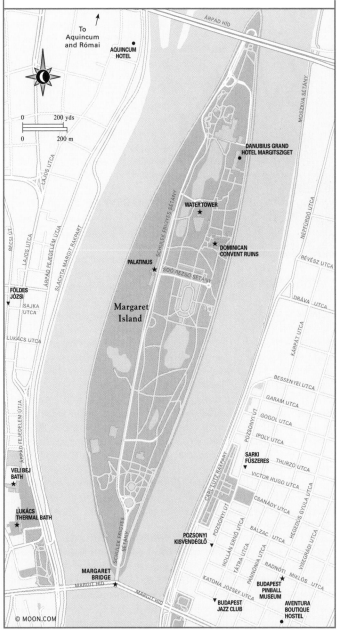

To
Aquincum
and Római

**AQUINCUM
HOTEL**

ÁRPÁD HÍD

MOSZKVA SÉTÁNY

0   200 yds
0   200 m

**DANUBIUS GRAND
HOTEL MARGITSZIGET**

NÉPFÜRDŐ UTCA

WATER TOWER ★

SCHULEK FRIGYES SÉTÁNY

REVÉSZ UTCA

★ **DOMINICAN
CONVENT RUINS**

PALATINUS
★

SOÓ REZSŐ SÉTÁNY

DRÁVA UTCA

**FÖLDES
JÓZSI**
▼

SAJKA
UTCA

KÁRPÁT UTCA

Margaret
Island

LUKÁCS UTCA

BESSENYEI UTCA

GARAM UTCA

ÁRPÁD FEJEDELEM ÚTJA

GOGOL UTCA

POZSONYI ÚT

IPOLY UTCA

**SARKI
FŰSZERES**
▼

CARL LUTZ RAKPART

THURZÓ UTCA

**VELI BEJ
BATH**
★

VICTOR HUGO UTCA

POZSONYI ÚT

CSANÁDY UTCA

HEGEDŰS GYULA UTCA

**LUKÁCS
THERMAL BATH**
★

HOLLÁN ERNŐ UTCA

BALZAC UTCA

VISEGRÁDI UTCA

SCHULEK FRIGYES
SÉTÁNY

**POZSONYI
KISVENDÉGLŐ** ▼

TÁTRA UTCA

PANNÓNIA UTCA

RADNÓTI MIKLÓS UTCA

**MARGARET
BRIDGE** ★

MARGIT HÍD

KATONA JÓZSEF UTCA

**BUDAPEST
PINBALL
MUSEUM**

MARGIT HÍD

▼ **BUDAPEST
JAZZ CLUB**

**AVENTURA
BOUTIQUE
HOSTEL** ●

© MOON.COM

LAJOS UTCA

BÉCSI ÚT

ÁRPÁD FEJEDELEM ÚTJA

SLACHTA MARGIT RAKPART

open-air theater in the area). Then you can hike up 153 steps to the lookout platform for 360-degree views across the island, the river, and the city.

The Margaret Island Water Tower has become a symbol of the island.

DOMINICAN CONVENT RUINS

Margitsziget

King Béla IV is responsible for this convent's construction. He promised God he would build a convent on the island and send his daughter Margaret there if Hungary survived the Mongol invasion in 1241. The Mongols withdrew, and his daughter, then nine years old, became a nun. She was later canonized.

The ruins of the Dominican Convent still stand on Margaret Island, and they consist mostly of excavated stone walls with a few Gothic features. The ruins are available for public view for free, so anyone can stroll among them. Margaret's remains were taken off the island when the nuns fled the Turkish invasion in the 16th century, but you can still see her sepulcher marked by a slab of red

marble. Nearby, a memorial enclosed in red bricks contains pictures of the saint, and you'll likely see candles left behind by devout Catholic locals. There are metal lookout points positioned among the ruins that allow a better overview of the former convent's layout.

If you're interested in medieval history, there are more ruins scattered on the island. Just north of the convent, there is the reconstructed **Romanesque Premonstratensian Church**, dating back to the 12th century.

BUDAPEST PINBALL MUSEUM

Radnóti Miklós utca 18, www.flippermuzeum. hu, Wed-Fri 4pm-midnight, Sat 2pm-midnight, Sun 10am-10pm, HUF 3,000

Over on mainland Pest, the Budapest Pinball Museum (officially Europe's largest ongoing interactive museum dedicated to pinball machines) draws visitors from the world over. Tucked away in a 400-square-meter (4,300-square-foot) basement, the museum's 130 vintage pinball machines are are not just for show; they are available for play. There is no need to bring any coins—playing on the machines is included in the museum's admission price. The oldest pieces in the collection are bagatelles from the 1880s, a 1920s table hockey game, and a Humpty Dumpty game from the 1940s (one of the first pinball machines to include flipper bumpers).

MARGARET BRIDGE

Margaret Bridge is Budapest's second permanent bridge, built in 1876 by French engineer Ernest Gouin. The iron structure painted in pale yellow is suspended on seven stone pillars with statues of winged, bare-breasted

The Turks ruled over the city of Buda for 150 years (1541-1686), and you'll find plenty of Ottoman relics in Budapest today. The Turkish baths are the most famous Ottoman contribution to the city—but look closely and you'll find turban-topped tombstones around **Buda Castle,** or Islamic elements left behind in Christian churches, like the mihrab (a niche in the mosque wall indicating the direction to Mecca) in the **Inner City Church** next to the Danube in Pest. On the hill overlooking the Danube in north Buda, there is also the octagonal tomb of the dervish **Gül Baba,** who legend has it bought roses to Hungary.

Turkish influences still linger in the language, with words like *dohány* (smoke) and *kávé* (coffee) in the Hungarian lexicon. **Paprika,** an ingredient

Only traces of the occupation can be found in Budapest, like the baths.

synonymous with Hungarian cooking, arrived in the country during the Ottoman era and became part of peasant cooking after the Turks were seen spicing their stews with the red powder.

women (created by French sculptor Adolphe Thabard). This bridge doesn't stretch across the river in a completely straight line; it stands at angles to converge with Margaret Island's southern tip. It begins from the edge of the Grand Boulevard and goes over to Buda, where the middle prong (which was added in 1900) also runs down to the island. You can take tram 4 or 6 to the middle of the bridge and stroll down to the island.

GÜL BABA'S TOMB

Mecset utca 14, tel. 06/1-618-3842, www.gulbabaalapitvany.hu/en/ gul-babas-tomb, daily 10am-6pm, free

Despite some 150 years of occupation, few Ottoman buildings are left in Budapest. Beyond the Turkish baths, one of the most interesting sites from this period is the tomb of the 16th-century dervish Gül Baba. It is the northernmost site of pilgrimage for Muslims. Legend has it this Islamic saint brought roses to Hungary

(the local neighborhood's name means "Rose Hill" in Hungarian). When Gül Baba died in 1541, Sultan Suleiman the Magnificent commissioned this tomb, which was completed in 1548, and named the dervish the saint of Buda.

It's worth hiking up to the tomb for its rose gardens and views over the Danube. The mausoleum is a classic octagonal Ottoman structure with the sarcophagus inside covered in silk cloth, surrounded with plush carpets. If the mausoleum is closed, you can peek through the window to see the coffin. The complex has a lovely garden with a colonnade and a few lookout towers.

Make sure you go to the museum—just take the stairs down inside the building, left of the gate or the elevator. You'll get some historic context into life in Ottoman Buda, with artifacts like ceramics, engraved silver cups, and waxworks of Turkish figures in traditional dress. An exhibition

The top of Gellért Hill has some of the best views of Budapest.

room in the back often features contemporary Turkish artists.

SOUTH BUDA
✪ GELLÉRT HILL

Gellért Hill, a green, rocky outcrop on the banks of the Danube, is named for martyred Venetian bishop St. Gellért, who, according to legend, was thrown down the hill in a barrel full of nails during the Great Pagan Rebellion of the 11th century. His statue still towers above a man-made waterfall, surrounded by columns (with stone pagan Magyars by his feet) opposite Elizabeth Bridge.

You can take the stairs going past the waterfall and the statue of the saint, and then follow a labyrinth of paths to the top of the hill and the Citadel, or you can hike up alternative routes, like the path up by the Danubius Hotel Gellért and the Thermal Baths. Winding trails thread through the woodland covering the hillside, with incredible views through the trees over the river and

the castle. Both routes take 15-20 minutes to walk.

If you want the view without the hike, take the number 27 bus from Móricz Zsigmond körtér to the Búsuló Juhász (Citadella) stop for a gentle stroll to the Citadel. Stop at the lookout point on the left for amazing views of the city.

Philosopher's Garden

Halfway up Gellért Hill—if you turn right at the statue rather than take the path to the Citadel—you'll find the Philosopher's Garden, named for sculptures representing figures like Gandhi, Jesus, and Lao-Tsu, among others. It's a peaceful patch of green with views over Buda Castle and the river. On the weekends, you'll find people on picnicking and maybe practicing yoga here.

The Citadel

The Citadel fortress crowns the top of the hill. This dramatic structure was built by the Habsburgs after the

South Buda

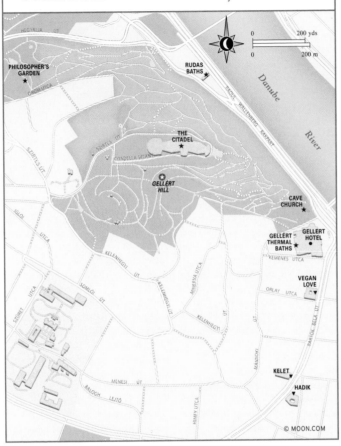

0   200 yds
0   200 m

HLGYALJA UT
PHILOSOPHER'S GARDEN
CROWA UTCA
RUDAS BATHS
Danube River
SZIRTES UT
THE CITADEL
CITADELLA SETAN
GELLÉRT HILL
IGLOI UTCA
SZIRTES UT
CAVE CHURCH
GELLÉRT THERMAL BATHS
GELLERT HOTEL
KEMENES UTCA
KELENHEGYI UT
MINERVA UTCA
SOMLOI UT
KELENHEGYI UT
VEGAN LOVE
ORLAY UTCA
KELENHEGYI UT
SZIRT UTCA
BARTOK BELA UT
MANYOKI UT
MENESI UT
HIMFY UTCA
KELET
BALOGH LEJTO
HADIK

© MOON.COM

1848-1849 War of Independence and became obsolete by the time it was built. Although the museum in the Citadel has closed indefinitely, it's worth the hike up for the views over the Inner City. This is the highest point in downtown Budapest, and you're rewarded with panoramas over the Danube, Buda Castle, and the bridges.

Then wander over to the **Liberty Monument,** which dominates the skyline with its bronze female figure clasping a palm leaf above her head. The monument, a tribute to the Soviet soldiers who died liberating the city, is one of the few Soviet relics in the city center.

CAVE CHURCH

Szent Gellért rakpart 1/a,
tel. 06/20-775-2472, Mon-Sat
9:30am-7:30pm, HUF 600

Facing the entrance to the Gellért Baths on a rocky outcrop is the cavernous entrance to the Cave Church.

There's evidence that the cave was inhabited as far back as 4,000 years ago, but the earliest known inhabitant was a hermit named Iván, who resided in the Middle Ages and helped cure the sick with the bubbling thermal waters that now fill the pools of the Gellért Baths. The church's rocky interior became a home to Paulite Monks, Hungary's only homegrown monastic order, in 1926. The monks expanded the cave to make way for further chapels and attached a neo-Gothic monastery to the side of the hill looking over the Danube in 1934. The Cave Church led an active life in the 20th century: it sheltered Polish refugees in World War II, and in the 1950s it was seized by the Communists, who briefly walled up the entrance with concrete.

Today the church is functioning again. Outside Mass hours (daily 8:30am, 5pm, and 8pm; Sunday 11am), the church is open to visitors. You can explore the caverns, which lead into the turreted monastery on the outside.

A cemetery for old communist statues can be found in the Memento Park.

✪ MEMENTO PARK

Balatoni út-Szabadkai utca sarok,
tel. 06/1-424-7500, www.mementopark.hu,
daily 10am-dusk, HUF 1,500

Memento Park is a cross between an open-air museum and a graveyard for Communist statues and street propaganda. Following the fall of the regime, all the statues and propaganda were removed from the city and relocated to this plot of land, which was transformed into a public outdoor museum in the early 1990s. It's a trek to reach, but the excursion up into the XII District's Buda Hills is worth it. Take the shuttle bus from Déak Ferenc Square, a central transport hub on the border of the Inner City and the Jewish Quarter (daily 11am Apr-Oct, Mon and Sat Nov-Mar, HUF 4,900 round-trip including entry, HUF 3,900 if you book online), which returns at 1pm. Or take the 150 bus from Újbuda or the Kelenföld train station.

It's impossible to miss the imposing gate marking the entrance—a monumental red-brick structure that looks like a socialist caricature of a Greek temple. As you approach the ticket office, socialist songs and communist hymns blast out from the small kiosk. Beyond the kiosk, the walled park contains bronze statues and placards of propaganda. Statues of Hungarian Communist leaders stand side by side with the likes of Lenin and Soviet soldiers. István Kiss's "Republic of Councils Monument" is a behemoth of a sculpture inspired by an avant-garde propaganda poster meant to encourage military recruitment. (The figure looks as if he is sprinting.) On your way out of the park, stop by the time-traveling phone booth, where you can dial in the year and listen to the voices of Communist leaders like Stalin and Béla Kun.

Opposite the park, a replica of the

gigantic boots once belonging to a statue of Stalin hold a place on a giant grandstand. Inside, there is a bunker with a few statues and busts of Lenin. Between the statue park and Stalin's boots, there is a barracks-style building with a museum inside, dedicated to the history and the fall of communism in Hungary. To the right of the entrance, you can sit down to watch a subtitled movie screening of secret police training films from Hungary's Communist era, with interesting insights like how to equip a handbag with a hidden camera.

INNER CITY AND SOUTH PEST

CENTRAL MARKET HALL

Nagyvásarcsarnok, Vámház körút 1-4,
tel. 06/1-366-3300, Mon 6am-5pm, Tue-Fri
6am-6pm, Sat 6am-3pm, metro 4, tram 2,
47, 48, 49

As the biggest market in the city, Central Market Hall may attract its fair share of tourists snapping shots of dried paprika and cured sausages, but it's still one of the best markets for locals. This vast, cathedral-like hall with steel beams, iron girders, exposed red brick, and large windows opened in 1897. Goods were once delivered by barges that sailed into the market thanks to special docks. That capability has disappeared from the structure, but you can still stroll past the baked goods, meat, cheeses, vegetables, and stalls specializing in Hungarian delicacies. Head up to the top floor to find stands selling folk art, such as embroidery and painted woodwork, and to sample Hungarian dishes like *lángos*. Even if you have no intention to buy, you should visit the market for its grand architecture and the energy you'll experience there.

Central Market Hall

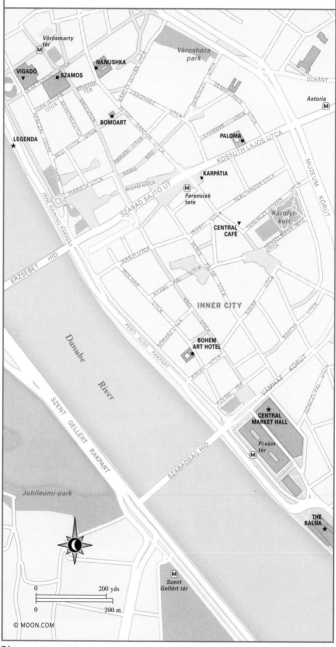

Inner City and South Pest

Vörösmarty tér

Ⓜ

VIGADÓ

SZAMOS

NANUSHKA

Városháza park

DOHÁNY

BOMOART

Astoria Ⓜ

LEGENDA ★

PALOMA

KOSSUTH LAJOS UTCA

MÚZEUM KÖRÚT

KARPÁTIA

Ⓜ

Ferenciek tere

Károlyi-kert

CENTRAL CAFÉ

SZABAD SAJTÓ ÚT

ERZSÉBET HÍD

JANE HANING RAKPART

INNER CITY

Danube River

BOHEM ART HOTEL

PEST ALSÓ RAKPART

SZENT GELLÉRT RAKPART

VÁMHÁZ KÖRÚT

CENTRAL MARKET HALL ★

Fővám tér Ⓜ

SZABADSÁG HÍD

Jubileumi-park

THE BÁLNA ★

Ⓜ Szent Gellért tér

0   200 yds
0   200 m

© MOON.COM

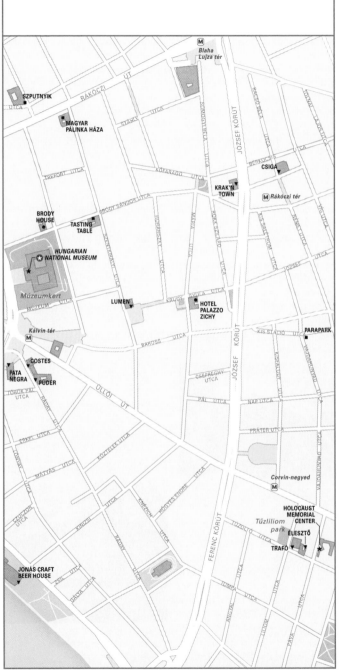

SZPUTNYIK

MAGYAR PÁLINKA HÁZA

Blaha Lujza tér

RÁKÓCZI ÚT

STÁHLY UTCA

SOMOGYI BÉLA

BACSÓ BÉLA UTCA

JÓZSEF KÖRÚT

TREFORT UTCA

KŐFARAGÓ UTCA

BÉRKOCSIS UTCA

CSIGA

KRAK'N TOWN

Rákóczi tér

BRÓDY HOUSE

TASTING TABLE

BRÓDY SÁNDOR UTCA

MÁRIA UTCA

GUTENBERG

HORÁNSZKY UTCA

KIS SALÉTROM UTCA

HENTER

JÓZSEF UTCA

HUNGARIAN NATIONAL MUSEUM

Múzeumkert

SZENTKIRÁLYI UTCA

LUMEN

KRÚDY GYULA UTCA

HOTEL PALAZZO ZICHY

MÚZEUM UTCA

Kálvin tér

BAROSS UTCA

KIS STÁCIÓ

PARAPARK

JÓZSEF KÖRÚT

KISFALUDY

VICTOR HUGO

COSTES

PÁTA NEGRA

PÜDER

TÖRÖK PÁL UTCA

BRÓDY UTCA

ÜLLŐI ÚT

CSEPREGHY UTCA

PÁL UTCA

NAP UTCA

PRÁTER UTCA

ERKEL UTCA

KÖZTELEK UTCA

MÁTYÁS UTCA

KÁLVIN UTCA

KINIZSI UTCA

TŰZOLTÓ UTCA

LEONARDO DA VINCI

Corvin-negyed

HOLOCAUST MEMORIAL CENTER

Tűzliliom park

ÉLESZTŐ

TRAFÓ

FERENC KÖRÚT

JÓNÁS CRAFT BEER HOUSE

TŰZOLTÓ UTCA

TOMPA UTCA

ANGYAL UTCA

ZSIL UTCA

PÁVA UTCA

THE BÁLNA

Fővám tér 11-12, 06/30-619-2052,
www.balnabudapest.hu, Sun-Thu 10am-8pm,
Fri-Sat 10am-10pm

From the other side of the river, it's impossible to ignore the *Bálna* ("whale" in Hungarian), a glass structure that's become the poster child of regeneration of the once-dilapidated IX District. Back in the 19th century, this part of the city buzzed with trade, as barges traveled up and down the Danube to the capital and public warehouses in the area stored wheat and other produce. Many of these red-bricked buildings fell into disrepair by the beginning of the 21st century but soon saw innovative regeneration. The Bálna found new life when Dutch architect Kas Oosterhuis embarked on creating a new complex from the four buildings standing in proximity to the Danube. Oosterhuis added the glass roof, keeping the old buildings' original brickwork.

modern building of the Bálna

Today, this unique cultural and shopping center has become a main landmark on the southern part of the river. In the summer, the restaurants, bars, and cafés open up their terraces, and the design and art galleries inside are open all year round. Antique shops and flea markets stand in the base of the "Whale." On the top floor, you'll find exhibitions in the New Budapest Gallery as well as great views over the river through the glass rooftop. The futuristic structure once stood in for NASA Headquarters in Ridley Scott's *The Martian.*

✪ HUNGARIAN NATIONAL MUSEUM

Magyar Nemzeti Múzeum, Múzeum körút
14-16, tel. 06/1-338-2122, www.mnm.hu,
10am-6pm Tue-Sun, HUF 2,600, metro 2, 3,
tram 47, 49

The Hungarian National Museum rises up like a Greek temple. It is Hungary's largest museum, dedicated to the history of the Carpathian Basin from prehistory until the fall of communism in the country. This museum once played a part in Budapest's history: revolutionaries gathered on its steps on the first day of the 1848 Revolution against the Habsburgs.

An extensive archaeology exhibition can be found on the ground floor; it features excavated artifacts that chart Hungarian history before the Magyar tribes arrived, including relics from the Celts and Romans—like a Scythian gold stag and a statue of Heracles cast in bronze. This exhibit also features artifacts left behind by

The Hungarian National Museum is the location where the 1848 Revolution began.

the first Huns and the Magyar tribes that came later.

In the basement, explore Hungary's Roman history in the incredible lapidarium, filled with mosaics, sculptures, carved headstones, and medieval stonework. The first floor of the museum is a work of art in itself, with colorful frescoes with flecks of gold leaf under a dome. Here, the exhibition splits into two parts—Hungary from the Middle Ages up to the Ottoman occupation, and from the 18th century to the Communist era.

HOLOCAUST MEMORIAL CENTER

Páva utca 39, tel. 06/1-455-3333, www.hdke. hu, 10am-6pm Tue-Sun, 1,400 HUF

The powerful Holocaust Memorial Center charts the history of the Holocaust in Hungary, from the dehumanization of the Jews to their extermination at Auschwitz and other concentration camps. It's an interactive multimedia museum where you'll find personal artifacts such as children's dolls, pens, clothing, and eyeglasses left behind. You can watch and listen to personal and family stories on interactive screens. The exhibition ends inside a beautifully renovated synagogue that was originally built in the 1920s.

ZWACK UNICUM MUSEUM

Dandár utca 1, tel. 06/1-476-2383, www.zwackunicum.hu/en/zwack-muzeumok/ zwack-muzeum-es-latogatokozpont/ bemutato, Mon-Sat 10am-5pm, HUF 2,400

You need to go off the beaten track to find this fascinating factory museum in the heart of the IX District, just one street off the Danube. You'll need a guide to visit the distillery, but once you reach the museum, you can explore on your own. The order of the tour can vary, but the first part is usually a guided tour around the distillery, where you'll learn a few of the secret ingredients in Hungary's iconic drink. You'll begin in a room filled with vats of cardamom pods, chamomile, ginger root, licorice, and peppercorns you can touch and smell. Then, you'll descend into the cellar to see the distillation process before trying a shot of Unicum straight from the red and black barrels. Back in the visitor center, you can watch a documentary about the Zwack family. The museum is filled with Unicum memorabilia, including the largest collection of miniature bottles in the world. (There are about 17,000 inside glass cabinets.)

KEREPESI CEMETERY

Fiúmei út 16-18, tel. 06/1-896-3889, http://fiumeiutisirkert.nori.gov.hu, daily 7am or 7:30am-5pm Jan, Feb, Oct-Dec, 7am-5:30pm Mar, 7am-6pm Sep, 7am-7pm Apr and Aug, 7am-8pm May-July, free

Located near the Keleti train station, this walled cemetery, established in 1874, contains roughly 3,000 graves and mausoleums amid lush parkland. The most impressive sepulchers belong to key Hungarian figures—revolutionary heroes, politicians, and prime ministers, including János Kadár, Hungary's socialist leader for three decades, and József Antall, who was the first democratically elected prime minister following the Communist era. Beyond the statesmen, you'll also find the graves of Hungary's most beloved poets, writers, scientists, artists, architects, and music hall performers. Notable figures in this cemetery include Attila József, Ödön Lechner, and Mihály Munkácsy. The graveled paths lead past columned arcades to angel-guarded tombstones and memorials and grand, neoclassical mausoleums.

ALL ABOUT UNICUM

Go into any Hungarian bar and you'll see a dark-green glass bottle with a gold cross on a red background. The concoction inside, called Unicum, is made from more than 40 herbs and spices from all over the world. Its recipe is a tightly guarded secret, passed down through the Zwack family. Dr. József Zwack, an imperial physician to the Habsburg court, invented the drink that helped soothe the digestion of Emperor Joseph II, who (legend has it) christened the drink by exclaiming *"Das ist ein unikum!"*—"This is unique!" The Zwacks decided to bottle and sell the drink on a commercial scale in 1840.

Discover the Hungarian spirit Unicum at the factory where it all started.

The Zwack family was Jewish but converted to Catholicism in 1917. Despite becoming devout Catholics, they had to hide out in cellars protected by the Swedish Embassy when members of the fascist Arrow Cross Party came looking for them. Their factory, now the location of the **Zwack Unicum Museum,** suffered bombing damage in the war; in 1948, the government confiscated and nationalized the factory, and the family fled to the US, taking their recipe with them. For decades, the Unicum produced in Hungary was inferior, until Peter Zwack returned to Hungary in the 1980s and got the business back.

For many, Unicum is an acquired taste. The almost-black liquor is served as an aperitif and digestive. If you find it too bitter, try the fruity-tasting Unicum Szilva, which is aged on a bed of dried plums.

Most spectacular is the resting place of Lajos Kossuth, a revolutionary and the governor-president during the 1848 revolution against the Habsburgs. If you wander over to plot 21, you'll find graves belonging to those who died in the 1956 Uprising.

Pick up a free map at the cemetery entrance to locate the noteworthy graves. There is also a small museum offering insight into the Hungarian approach to death and burials. If you want to see tradition in action, come on November 1 when the graves are lit up with tea lights and candles.

THE MILLENNIUM QUARTER

Take tram line 2 to the penultimate stop, Müpa-Nemzeti Színház, on the southern part of the Danube banks in Pest, and you'll come to a cultural corner built between 2001 and 2006 as part of an urban regeneration project. The Millennium Quarter is not only a cultural power hub—where you'll find the National Theatre, the Palace of Arts, and the Ludwig Museum in one spot—it's probably Budapest's most adventurous location for experimental modern architecture. You'll find a statue of a submerged "Greek" temple in the lake and a ziggurat overlooking the river.

Palace of Arts

Müpa, Komor Marcell utca 1,
tel. 06/1-555-3000, www.mupa.hu

The Palace of Arts complex is the most important building in the Millennium cultural complex, award-winning for its cutting-edge design and simplicity. It kind of looks like a windswept box on the outside, and the interior blends a Herculean sense of space with lots of glass. It's like a cultural shopping mall, home to some of the city's most important cultural venues, including the cavernous Béla Bartók National Concert Hall, the Festival Theater, and the Ludwig Museum. The Palace of Arts has some of the best acoustics and sound technology in Europe, and its consistently impressive musical lineup is booked far in advance.

Ludwig Museum

Komor Marcell utca 1, tel. 06/1-555-3444, www.ludwigmuseum.hu, Tue-Sun 8am-10pm, HUF 1,600

The Ludwig Museum is inside the Palace of Arts. This contemporary art museum showcases Hungarian and international works. You'll find an impressive Pop Art collection here, including pieces by Andy Warhol and Roy Liechtenstein, but most of the focus is on Central and Eastern European art. If you're passionate about modern art, it's worth the tram ride to this museum.

National Theatre

Nemzeti Színház, Bajor Gizi Park 1, tel. 06/1-476-6800, www.nemzetiszinhaz.hu

The National Theatre exudes architectural drama before you even step inside. There is a small ziggurat between the main building and the Palace of Arts; you can wander up its spirals for views over the river. When viewed outside from the front, you'll notice the theater sits on the bow of a ship, which rises above a man-made moat—look for the submerged Grecian temple. You'll also see statues of Hungarian actors on the park grounds. Inside, the setting is a bit more humble compared to the dramatic exterior (but it's probably better not to get distracted while you're watching a play).

ÓBUDA

AQUINCUM

Szentendrei út 133-135, tel. 06/1-250-1650, www.aquincum.hu, Tue-Sun 9am-6pm Apr-Oct, open otherwise in dry conditions, HUF 1,900

Although Roman ruins are scattered around Óbuda, the main ruins are enclosed in the archaeological site of Aquincum, a Roman city built around AD 100, whose citizens numbered between 30,000 and 40,000 by the end of the 2nd century. Allegedly, Roman Emperor Marcus Aurelius penned part of his famous philosophical "Meditations" here in this Roman settlement.

You can follow in the footsteps of Roman society, winding through the excavated ruins, including a reconstruction of a painter's house, the hypocaust systems that once warmed bathhouses, and the worn-down stones once paving the marketplace and the forum. Stroll into the lapidary (with walls lined with stone carvings and tablets). Close to the entrance is a modern museum hall set in a former electrical transformer house, which contains excavated mosaic flooring, frescoes, statues, and dolphin-adorned fountains. The museum's most famous piece is the Aquincum organ, dating back to the 3rd century, on display 75 years after its excavation.

KISCELLI MUSEUM

Kiscelli utca 108, tel. 06/1-250-0304, www.kiscellimuzeum.hu, Tue-Sun 10am-6pm Apr-Oct, Tue-Sun 10am-4pm Nov-Mar, HUF 1,600

It's a significant hike to get to the Kiscelli Museum, which is located in a former 18th-century monastery. This canary-yellow building functioned as a barracks and a military hospital before being bought up by an antiques

The name Óbuda means "Old Buda," which is fitting, since this part of the city has its roots in antiquity. The Roman settlement of **Aquincum** is the most famous reminder of pre-Magyar Budapest, and you'll find Roman ruins scattered around Óbuda. Close to Flórián tér, hidden under unsightly overpasses, are the monumental ruins of the **Roman baths** (Flórián téri aluljáró, Tue-Sun 9am-6pm Apr-Oct, open otherwise in dry conditions, free) once belonging to the Roman military camp, accessible from the underpass. Travelers can also head over to the **Hercules Villa** (Meggyfa utca 21, Wed-Sun 11am-6pm Aug-Oct, HUF 500), named for the imported mosaic featuring the villa's namesake hero. The villa was discovered in the 1950s when workmen were digging foundations to build a school. There are seven rooms in the villa, accessible via a raised platform so you can get a good look at the mosaics, and there is also a museum and a garden where you'll find ancient ruins. Other ruins in Budapest include the **amphitheater** close to Kolosy tér that once had the capacity for an audience of 15,000. There are also a few stones of **Contra-Aquincum,** the former Roman military camp in Pest, just below Elizabeth Bridge. Roman Hungary came to an end with Attila the Hun in the 5th century, five centuries before the Magyar tribes led by Árpád conquered the Carpathian Basin.

dealer whose final wishes were for the property to become a museum. The eclectic collection includes 19th-century trade signs and the contents of an entire apothecary once located in Pest. Life in 18th to early 20th century Budapest is depicted through antique furniture, sketches of the city, and Art Nouveau stained glass. Attached to the building is the shell of an old church, used for contemporary exhibitions.

Kiscelli Museum

BUDA HILLS
CHILDREN'S RAILWAY
Gyermekvasút, tel. 06/1-397-5394,
www.gyermekvasut.hu, Tue-Fri 9am-4pm
in winter, daily 8:45am-5:45pm in summer,
HUF 800

This small railway line chugs along for just under 12 kilometers (7 miles) from Széchenyi-Hegy to Hűvösvölgy with stops in between. With the exception of the drivers and engineers, all the jobs on the railway line are staffed by school children aged 10 to 14, who sell and check tickets, signal, and salute passengers as the train pulls in and out of the station. The railway is a relic from the Communist era, built in 1951 to encourage a good work ethic. Today, the tradition continues but without the propaganda. The schools work together with the railway, permitting students with a good academic record to miss the odd day of school to work here. Riding from one end to the other takes 45 to 50 minutes; the trip goes through the woods and around the Buda Hills. Buy a ticket and go from one end to the other, enjoying the view, or get off along the way and hike a bit.

To reach each end of the railway, either take the 56 or 61 tram to the end of the line at Hűvösvölgy and take the steps up to the station, or opt for the scenic route by taking the cogwheel railway (tram 60, which runs on the public transportation line) up

The Children's Railway is one of the top sites up in the Buda Hills.

into the hills to Széchenyi-Hegy from Városmajor.

ELIZABETH LOOKOUT

Daily 8am-8pm, free

Hike up the highest point in Budapest, János Hill (János-hegy), which rises about 520 meters (1,700 feet) above sea level. At the top of the hill you'll reach the Elizabeth Lookout point, a neo-Romanesque tower with 134 steps leading to incredible views across Budapest and surroundings. If it's a clear day, you might even spot the Tatra Mountains in Slovakia in the distance. Should the tower look familiar, that's because it was designed by the same architect who constructed Fisherman's Bastion in the Castle District.

To get here, get off from the Children's Railway at the János-Hegy stop, or if you're feeling adventurous, take the 291 bus from Nyugati train station to the final stop, Zugliget-Libegő, and take the chairlift (HUF 1,200 one-way, HUF 1,600 round-trip) to the base of the tower (expect to queue on sunny weekends). The climb takes around 15 minutes, and you can use the chairlift year-round from 10am until dusk (3:30pm in the winter to 7pm in the high summer).

Note that on Mondays on even-numbered weeks, it's closed for maintenance (with the exception of public holidays).

Thermal Baths

TOP EXPERIENCE

Budapest's thermal baths are a perfect antidote for its wild nightlife. They are a must-do item on any visit to Budapest.

At least one section of a bath complex must be filled with natural thermal water to qualify as a thermal bath. Each bath has thermal pools at different temperatures, ranging from cool plunge pools to hot pools (placards recommend staying in for less than 10 minutes), and then a main pool that's usually around body temperature (the recommended bathing time is usually 30-40 minutes). Some thermal baths will also have a swimming pool, saunas, and a wellness area. Massages are offered for an extra charge.

You'll find two categories of baths in Budapest—the baths built by Turks when Hungary was occupied by the Ottoman Empire, and the grand baths built in the late 19th and early 20th centuries. The Turkish baths (also called Ottoman Baths) are similar to those you'd find in Turkey, with pin-pricked cupola domes and octagonal pools; but unlike the *hamams* in Istanbul, the Budapest baths have a plunge pool rather than a marble slab where you're scrubbed down,

Gellért Thermal Baths

soaped, and massaged. These baths date back as far as the 16th century. The later **19th-20th century baths** followed hot on the heels of Central Europe's bathing cure craze; consider Baden-Baden in Germany, or Carlsbad (Karlovy Vary) in the Czech Republic. Their grandiose baths have complexes indoors and outdoors, often ornamented with neoclassical statues or Art Nouveau tiling, and you'll find large swimming pools, sauna complexes, and bathing terraces.

THE BATH EXPERIENCE

A few things are smart to bring with you to the baths:

- Bring your own **swimsuit** to Budapest. If you forget your swimsuit, some complexes allow you to rent them, along with towels and bathrobes.
- It's a good idea to pack a pair of **shower slippers** for hygienic reasons, but if you forget them, most baths rent them out as well.

- If you plan to use the swimming pools attached to the baths, make sure you wear a **swimming cap,** which you can usually buy at reception, or bring your own (even a shower cap will do).

When you buy your ticket, you'll get a wristband that lets you into the bath complex and is used to open and close your locker or cabin (so you can change and lock up your things in the same place). Some baths may offer different ticket packages, like a basic ticket that's only for the thermal section or the swimming pool, while others may charge a surplus for the sauna. Massages, on the other hand, require an appointment, so if you want one, ask when you're buying your ticket.

Make sure you shower before dipping into the pools and relaxing in the steam, whether you're indoors or outdoors.

Apart from the Rudas baths on weekdays (which is women-only on Tuesdays, and men the rest of the week), the baths are open for both

CHOOSING A BATH

It's no accident Budapest has earned the nickname "City of Spas." Below the city are over 100 geothermal springs, each with its own mineral profile. There is a bath in Budapest for everyone's taste, whether you want to bathe in a historic monument or go where the locals go.

MOST FAMOUS
The **Széchenyi Baths** is Budapest's largest and most famous thermal bath complex. Go for the stunning columned outdoor pools. Stay because you find out there are even more pools indoors (page 84).

LOCAL FAVORITE
Laid-back **Lukács** is popular with locals for its understated turn-of-the-century elegance, pump room, and the healing properties of the water (page 85).

BEST FOR FAMILIES
Open-air and seasonal, the **Római Open-Air Baths** are popular with kids thanks to the jungle of waterslides there (page 87).

MOST OPULENT
The **Gellért Baths** are an Art Nouveau architectural treasure (page 86).

BEST BATHING IN THE BUFF
If you go to the **Rudas** on weekdays, the bath is single-sex, and although you won't need a swimsuit, you will be given a loin cloth you need to wear. (The bath is now trying to cut down on full nudity.) Women's days are Tuesdays and men's are Mondays, Wednesdays, Thursdays all day, and Friday mornings (page 86).

QUIETEST TURKISH BATH
You can easily miss the entrance to the **Veli Bej** because you have to enter a hospital to get to this hidden Turkish bath, newly renovated for the 21st century (page 85).

BEST BUDGET OPTION
If you want a simple thermal bath experience, the **Dandár** is a great choice if you're pinching pennies (page 87).

men and women. And although there is no hard and fast rule, they are not recommended for anyone under the age of 14.

Unless you're at one of the infamous spa parties (also known as "Sparties," which are usually ticketed and take place Saturday night at the Széchenyi Baths), Budapest's thermal baths are a place of healing, so try not to be too noisy or splash about, unless you're in one of the outdoor swimming pools.

The best time to go is first thing in the morning before breakfast, as the baths are the cleanest at this point, and you'll miss out on most of the crowds. Some of the quieter baths, like the Veli Bej, are cozy on a winter's evening.

If you have any health concerns, like a heart condition, it's best to consult your healthcare provider about taking the waters in Budapest.

CASTLE DISTRICT
KIRÁLY BATH
Fő u. 84, tel. 06-1-202-3688,
http://en.kiralyfurdo.hu, daily 9am-9pm,
HUF 2,400-2,900, tram 41, 19, bus 9, 109
Built by the Turks over 450 years ago, Király Bath is Budapest's oldest operational thermal bath. Its cupola covers an octagonal pool surrounded by crumbling plaster and exposed brickwork. While the Király Bath is in desperate need of a renovation (the last one was completed in the 1950s to fix

the damage from World War II), it still merits a visit. Steam hovers above its three thermal pools and its icy immersion pool. A coating of mineral deposits covers the rim of the main bath from decades (perhaps centuries) of mineral water, which pours out of a vintage iron tap in the central pool. Rich in calcium, magnesium, hydrogen-carbonate, and sulfate, with a dash of sodium and the odd fluoride ion, the water is said to soothe conditions such as degenerative joint disease and chronic arthritis.

Following the reoccupation of Buda from the Ottomans, the König family acquired the bath at the end of the 18th century. It's smaller and grittier than the other baths, but many love it for its authenticity. It's the cheapest of the historic baths, so it draws in a more local crowd, mixed with a few tourists. The Király Bath is open to both men and women, and it's a good alternative to the Rudas Baths, which are single-sex on weekdays.

(At the time of writing, there were plans to close the Király Baths for renovation, so they may not be open during your visit.)

CITY PARK AND AROUND

✪ SZÉCHENYI BATHS

Állatkerti körút 11, tel. 06/1-363-3210,
www.szechenyibath.hu, daily 6am-7pm,
HUF 6,200 weekends, metro 1

Canary-yellow walls accented by Ionian columns and sculptures of bathing nymphs and youths riding dolphins surround the large turquoise pools of the Széchenyi Baths. Built between 1909 and 1913, it's one of the largest bath complexes of its kind. Once you've explored the 13 indoor pools and the labyrinthine changing rooms above and below the three outdoor pools, it's easy to see

Széchenyi Baths

why this elegant and relaxing place is so popular.

There are three public entrances to the baths. One main entrance faces the zoo and the circus and has a Rococo-inspired entrance hall; the second faces the park and shows off even more opulence, with gold-tipped frescoes and Secessionist ceramics. The third entrance is hidden on the side by the metro. All three entrances are part of the same ticket, but the type of cabin varies, as the baths were initially built with the interior side and its entrance for the aristocracy and upper classes, and the exterior part for the masses.

The complex also includes luxury massage facilities. The all-inclusive Palm House spa (HUF 34,500) can be found in the rooftop greenhouse. There is even a beer spa (HUF 15,700 combined ticket for a beer spa and entry to the baths) where you can lie in a wooden tub filled with hops, malt, yeast, and aromas—and pull your own pints from a separate keg as you soak.

MARGARET ISLAND AND AROUND

LUKÁCS THERMAL BATH

Frankel Leó út 25-29, tel. 06/1-326-1695, http://en.lukacsfurdo.hu, daily 6am-10pm, HUF 4,100 weekends, HUF 800 Sauna World supplement, tram 4, 6, 17, 19, 41, bus 9, 26, 91, 109, 191, 226, 296

Although it may lack the grandeur of the Széchenyi and Gellért baths or the history of the Turkish Baths, this tranquil 19th-century thermal bath is the place locals come to relax with a dose of old-world nostalgia.

To enter the complex, take a stroll through the garden that's next door to the Orfi Hospital, past the placards on the walls from grateful patients whose ailments were cured by the mineral rich water.

Once past the turnstiles, a tiled labyrinth links to the changing rooms and down to a courtyard where you can plunge into two frigid swimming pools. In another courtyard, a warm activity pool bubbles from massaging jets and a circular current.

Indoors, the thermal baths are compact, with dark marble columns and neoclassical statues. Each pool is heated to a different temperature. The water is piped in from one of the world's largest thermal water caves, located just across and under the road, and the pools give off a slight sulfurous whiff. For HUF 600 on weekdays and HUF 800 on weekends, you can access "Sauna World," which includes several types of saunas, a salt cabin, a steam room, and cooling pools where fresh ice is dropped in periodically thanks to a handy automated slide.

VELI BEJ BATH

Árpád Fejedelem útja 7, tel. 06/1-438-8587, daily 6am-noon, 3pm-9pm, HUF 3,100, tram 17, 19, 41, bus 9 and 109

From the street, it's easy to miss this Turkish bath, as it's hidden behind the glass windows of a rheumatological hospital. The entrance to the bath is through the hospital. Once inside, you'll see a sign that looks like a number counter, which is used when the bath is full (usually on weekend afternoons). If you have the patience to wait around 15-20 minutes, pick a number and wait in the café by the ticket counter. The waiting list system ensures that the bath will never be overcrowded.

Once you're through the ticket office and the changing room, the hospital corridors will lead you into the historic bath complex, built in the 16th century by the Turks. What's different about the Veli Bej Bath is that it's been recently renovated; in place of crumbling stone walls, you'll find fresh paint in clean white and salmon tones. The main octagonal pool is flanked by four chambers, each with a single pool at different temperatures. Pop outdoors between the bath and the hospital to the sauna cabins, where you'll see the original Turkish bath structure in its glory, or head to the corridor on the side to view remains of Ottoman excavations.

SOUTH BUDA

RUDAS THERMAL BATHS

Döbrentei tér 9, tel. 06/1-356-1322, http://en.rudasfurdo.hu, daily 6am-10pm Turkish bath, daily 8am-10pm wellness, HUF 4,300 Turkish bath weekends, HUF 6,500 combined ticket for Turkish bath, wellness, and swimming pool weekends, tram 19, 41, 56, bus 7, 8E, 108E, 110, 112

Out of all the Turkish Baths, the Rudas Thermal Bath is indisputably the most popular. The complex is composed of three parts: the 16th-century bath built by the Ottoman Turks, the 19th-century colonnaded swimming pool, and the 21st-century wellness center. The old Turkish part of the bath is "nudist," but you will get a loin cloth you need to wear to cover your private parts, and it's single-sex bathing only on weekdays (Tuesdays for women, others for men), but on the weekend and Fridays after 1 pm when the bath is mixed, swimsuits are compulsory. Expect long queues if you go on the weekends. Bathing under the cupola, with light shining through its stained glass, it's easy to see why this bath has become so popular.

On the other side, a beautiful swimming pool (filled partly with thermal water) looks more like a Roman bath than a place to take a few laps. The wellness center uses the same water as the Turkish part, from the slightly radioactive Juventus spring, which is said to have anti-aging properties. The pools downstairs are clean, modern, and can be less crowded than the Turkish baths. (And they are open to both sexes throughout the week.) The main draw is the rooftop whirlpool tub that overlooks the Danube.

GELLÉRT THERMAL BATHS

Kelenhegyi út 4, tel. 06/1-466-6166, www.gellertbath.hu, daily 6am-8pm, HUF 6,100 weekends, metro 4, tram 19, 41, 47, 48, 49, 56, bus 7, 133E

On the southern slopes of Gellért Hill, the Gellért Thermal Baths capture the grandeur of Budapest's golden age at the turn of the 20th century. The bath complex may be smaller than the vast Széchenyi, but there's plenty on offer both inside and outside.

The main pool lies enclosed in an atrium with Roman-style columns and a glass rooftop. Inside the thermal baths, steam drips off the aquamarine Zsolnay tiles that ornament the indoor thermal pools. Of the outdoor pools, the highlight is the main pool, which still uses a wave machine on the hour (it dates back to 1927) and was one of the very first of its kind. In total there are eight thermal pools ranging from 19°C (66°F) to 38°C (100°F), as well as cool plunge pools and swimming pools.

Gellért draws its water from beneath Gellért Hill—there is a hidden tunnel (not open to the public) running under the hotel and the hill going all the way to the Rudas Baths.

Aside from the medicinal waters and Art Nouveau splendor, the baths also offer a variety of treatments for those with a medical condition—like mud baths and carbon dioxide baths, a range of massages, and more.

OTHER THERMAL BATHS

Sometimes the more popular baths can get a little crowded. If you want to escape the tourist crowds, try these alternatives.

MARGARET ISLAND AND AROUND

Palatinus

Margitsziget, tel. 06/1-340-4500,
http://en.palatinusstrand.hu, daily
8am-8pm, HUF 3,600 weekends, bus 26

The Palatinus, an open-air thermal complex surrounded by trees, was once the go-to spot during the summer on Margaret Island. Since its renovation in 2017, this Art Deco bath has extended the invitation to visitors year-round. The thermal water here comes from below the island.

SOUTH PEST

Dandár

Dandár utca 5-7, tel. 06/1-215-7084,
http://en.dandarfurdo.hu, Mon-Fri
6am-9pm, Sat-Sun 8am-9pm, HUF 2,100
thermal bath, HUF 2,600 wellness and
thermal bath, tram 2

Just behind the Unicum factory in South Pest, you'll notice a brick building on the side street. The Dandár is a small, no-frills thermal bath with two thermal pools indoors. It's popular with locals for medicinal purposes. (There are two outdoor heated pools in the garden, but they don't use thermal water.)

GREATER BUDAPEST

Paskál

Egressy út 178, tel. 06/1-252-6944,
http://en.paskalfurdo.hu, daily 6am-8pm,
HUF 3,000, bus 77, 82

The Paskál Thermal and Open-Air Bath lies far out in residential Zugló and is popular with the locals for its blend of indoor spa with thermal water and outdoor swimming pool. The most attractive feature is the bubbling activity pool that spans both the inside and outside, with the exterior part leading right to a swim-up bar.

Római

Rozgonyi Piroska utca 2, tel. 06/1-388-9740,
http://en.romaistrand.hu, daily 9am-8pm
June-Sep, 2,800 HUF weekends, HÉV 5, bus
34, 134

Római Open-Air Baths get their name from the Romans, who used the thermal water in the area to supply the baths in Aquincum. Today, this modern outdoor swimming pool also uses the lukewarm water rich in minerals, but unlike other thermal baths, this open-air seasonal bath is popular with kids, thanks to its jungle of waterslides.

Bars and Nightlife

Budapest really comes to life at night. It can be impossible to avoid costumed groups of bachelor and bachelorette parties in the Jewish Quarter, but you can escape rowdy crowds after sundown if you know where to look. Ruin bars tend to rule, but in the summer, rooftop bars, gritty "kerts," and glam Danube-side terraces become main attractions.

You'll find most of the nightlife clustered around the Jewish Quarter, which also has the nickname the *bulinegyed* ("party district") for its density of bars. Kazinczy utca is the main nightlife hub, home to Szimpla Kert and other popular bars, along with Király utca. Gozsdu Court (Gozsdu udvar), a series of interconnected courtyards filled with restaurants and bars, is another of the neighborhood's hubs.

When planning a night on the town, it's a good idea to bring plenty of cash—some of the grittier ruin bars won't take cards. (Some of the larger ruin bars like Szimpla Kert or Fogas Ház will have ATMs.) You'll only come across cover fees for club nights, concerts, or special events. But expect to have your bag searched by bouncers at the door on busy nights. (They want to make sure you're not smuggling alcohol in.)

A glass of beer will cost around HUF 500-1000 depending on the bar, beer, and size (you can get a *pohár,* a 300 ml (10 oz) glass, or a *korsó,* a large 500 ml (17 oz) beer glass). Cocktails tend to range around HUF 2,000-3,000. Some bars serve bar snacks like *pogácsa,* a savory cheese or herb scone that helps soak up the booze. Aside from beer, wine, and cocktails, popular spirits include *pálinka,* a fiery fruit brandy served as a shot, and a bitter herbal liquor called Unicum.

☼ RUIN BARS

Set inside crumbling, semi-abandoned buildings filled with eclectic furniture and local art, ruin bars are unique to Budapest. You'll find most of these bars concentrated around the heart of the Jewish Quarter but some are beyond it. Many bear the name "kert" ("garden" in Hungarian), as some ruin bars pop up in empty plots in the city, serving as urban sanctuaries during the day and party hubs at night. Ruin bars also host cultural events, like farmer's markets, movie screenings, or charitable cooking drives.

TOP EXPERIENCE

JEWISH QUARTER
☼ Szimpla Kert
Kazinczy utca 14, tel. 06/20-261-8669, www.szimpla.hu, Mon-Sat noon-4am, Sun 9am-5am

Szimpla Kert is the original and most famous ruin bar in Budapest, and it probably draws as many visitors annually as Buda Castle. It spans an entire gutted apartment block. It's like a nocturnal wonderland with fairy lights, old computer monitors, and creaking furniture painted in a kaleidoscope of colors. You can even sit in a Trabant car in the courtyard.

Instant
Akácfa utca 49-51, tel. 06/70-638-5040, www.instant-fogas.com, daily 4pm-6am

Instant once resided in the VI District,

but the super-ruin pub has moved here, with Fogas Ház taking over much of the indoor space. There are four dance floors and eight bars from the basement to the top, with music catering to different tastes. The main dance hall features pixel cloud hangings and surreal wall art, and the party goes on all night.

Fogas Ház & Kert

Akácfa utca 51, tel. 06/70-638-5040,
www.instant-fogas.com, daily 4pm-6pm

Fogas Ház and Kert got its name ("House of Teeth") from its residence in a former dental lab. Trees wrapped with fairy lights brighten the courtyard next to the main bar area, which is tucked beneath a circus tent. Since Fogas became housemates with Instant, partygoers have flocked to this ruin bar complex for hedonism until dawn.

Ellató Kert

Kazinczy utca 48, tel. 06/20-527-3018,
Mon-Sat 5pm-4am, Sun 5pm-midnight

Just off Kazinczy utca, Ellató Kert is hidden behind a plastic tent flap that brings you into an open courtyard with covered rooms to the side. The murals draw influence from Aztec art, which goes well with the taco booth at the back of the bar. Out of all Budapest's ruin bars, Ellátó Kert is probably the most popular with locals.

Kőleves Kert

Kazinczy utca 37-39, tel. 06/20-213-5999,
www.koleves.com, weekdays 1pm-midnight,
weekends 1pm-1am, summer only

In the summer, this garden comes to life with hammocks, fairy lights, and laughter. Kőleves Kert ("Stone Soup") occupies a plot where a house once stood. There is a bar at the front in a small wooden pavilion where you'll

The Szimpla Kert is one of the most popular ruin bars in Budapest.

SPARTIES

Spend a Saturday night doing something you can do only in Budapest: go to a **Sparty** (www.spartybooking.com, from €50, over 18s only). These watery nights of hedonism take place in Budapest's famous spas every Saturday, usually in the outdoor pools at the Széchenyi or the Lukács Baths. It's a mix of thermal water with DJs, atmospheric lighting, and poolside bars. The demographic usually skews toward travelers in their 20s, and the parties can get pretty wild, with plenty of poolside drinking and some nudity (against the rules). Make sure you buy a ticket in advance from the website—these parties sell out fast.

have to get your own beer and stroll over the gravel back to your brightly painted bench or table.

AROUND ANDRÁSSY AVENUE
Anker't
Paulay Ede utca 33, tel. 06/30-360-3389,
Wed 6pm-1am, Thu-Sat 6pm-2am
From the outside, Anker't is just another dilapidated apartment block. But inside, this large complex has been stripped back to its foundations, and its courtyard regularly fills with crowds drinking under hanging lanterns and an open sky. At the back of this minimalist complex, you'll also find a covered bar and a dance area.

BARS AND PUBS

There's more to Budapest bar life than ruin bars, whether set on rooftops or in cozy corners.

JEWISH QUARTER
Telep
Madács Imre út 8, tel. 06/30-633-3608,
Mon-Thu noon-midnight, Fri-Sat noon-2am
You can spot Telep by the stickers plastered all over the windows and the hip crowd spilling into the street outside. Part art gallery, part bar, Telep has become one of Budapest's core urban meeting points. It's your chance to hang out with the cool crowd in Budapest.

Liebling
Akácfa utca 51, tel. 06/1-783-8820,
Mon-Sat 6pm-4am
Liebling is a cozy bar in the Instant-Fogas Ház ruin bar complex. Below the huge lips on the rooftop, Liebling is decked out in brick and wood. The spiral staircase takes you up to a hidden terrace that's popular in the summer. This bar is a good alternative for a drink if you're not in the mood for the hedonism of its ruin bar neighbors.

Fekete Kutya
Dob utca 31, tel. 06/30-951-6095,
Mon-Wed 5pm-1am, Thu-Sat 5pm-2am,
Sun 5pm-midnight
A cozy pub loved by the locals, Fekete Kutya is found under the arches on Dob utca. The bar is a little on the shabby side but has a welcoming atmosphere and a great beer collection on tap. Make sure you try their chive *pogácsa!*

AROUND ANDRÁSSY AVENUE
✪ Boutiq'bar
Paulay Ede utca 5, tel. 06/30-554-2323,
www.boutiqbar.hu, Tue-Thu 6pm-1am,
Fri-Sat 6pm-2am
One for the cocktail lovers—Boutiq'bar can mix up any drink you desire. Try one of their creative concoctions like Bombay Nights (gin with mango masala and yogurt), or Hello Tourist, made with aged apple

pálinka, wine, and a hint of pastis with cinnamon and apple. You can ask the award-winning bartenders to prepare you something unique with seasonal ingredients.

✪ The Studios (Brody Studios)

Vörösmarty utca 38, tel. 06/1-266-3707, www.brody.land/thestudios, see website for events and hours

The Studios, formerly known as Brody Studios, embraces the ruin bar aesthetic and frequently hosts parties and cultural events. This members' club may require you to ring a doorbell, but not all nights are members-only (see their website or Facebook page to check the program). It's best to check out the events online before going. It's worth visiting for its bohemian look and atmosphere.

360 Bar

Andrássy út 39, tel. 06/30-356-3047, www.360bar.hu, Mon-Wed 2pm-midnight, Thu-Sat 2pm-2am, Sun noon-midnight

360 Bar lives up to its name with panoramic views over Budapest's famous landmarks. You can reach the rooftop terrace with the elevator at the side entrance of the Párizsi department store. In the summer, enjoy drinks al fresco; in winter, the bar sets up transparent igloos so you can still enjoy views over the Hungarian Parliament Building and St. Stephen's Basilica.

WINE BARS

Wine is a big part of Hungarian culture, and at Budapest's wine bars you can find a wide range of grape varieties from different regions across the country.

LIPÓTVÁROS
DiVino

Szent István tér 3, tel. 06/70-935-3980, www.divinoborbar.hu, Sun-Wed 4pm-midnight, Thu-Sat 4pm-2am

DiVino serves exclusively Hungarian wines at its downtown location right next to the Basilica. If you want to try the best wines from up-and-coming Hungarian winemakers, look no further. Recommended by Michelin, this wine bar is always a hotspot of activity. DiVino has another branch in Gozsdu Udvar (Király utca 13).

JEWISH QUARTER
✪ Dobló

Dob utca 20, tel. 06/20-398-8863, www.budapestwine.com, Sun-Wed 2pm-2am, Thu-Sat 2pm-4am

Dobló specializes in Hungarian wine and *pálinka*. You can either take a table or sit up at the mahogany bar in the brick-walled, chandeliered tasting room. There are various tasting packages available, such as ones based on terroir or grape type.

AROUND ANDRÁSSY AVENUE
Kadarka

Király utca 42, tel. 06/1-266-5094, www.kadarkawinebar.com, daily 4pm-midnight

This sleek wine bar on Király utca embodies a character different from the surrounding ruin bars. Their impressive wine list features wines not only from Hungary but neighboring countries like Romania as well. You'll get a small plate of *pogácsa* (savory scones) before tasting begins. Kadarka fills up on the weekends and evenings, so you'd be wise to make a reservation.

Apropó

Király utca 39, tel. 06/30-193-3000,
Mon-Wed 8am-midnight, Thu-Fri 8am-2am,
Sat 10am-2am

This stylish wine bar embodies an industrial chic aesthetic, complete with exposed brick and Edison bulbs dangling from the ceiling. It serves a range of wines from Hungary, France, and Italy. They also serve Hungarian food.

CRAFT BEER

Hungary's reputation for wine has grown significantly in recent years, and Budapest's beer scene is not far behind. The recent surge in microbreweries and craft beer bars has made it easier than ever for beer lovers to enjoy great Hungarian beer. Try some locally brewed beers like Keserű Méz, a bitter, unstrained lager from the Fóti Brewery, or a really good IPA called Távoli Galaxis. If you like sour beers, try Rafa from the Fehér Nyúl brewery.

JEWISH QUARTER

Csak a Jó Sör

Kertész utca 42-44, tel. 06/30-251-4737,
www.csakajosor.hu, Mon-Sat 2pm-9pm

Csak a Jó Sör (literally meaning "good beer") lives up to its name. Although it looks like a small shop, it carries a wide range of rare and specialty beers, such as smoky stouts or brews accented with coriander. There are four types on tap if you want to drink some good beer while you're out in the Jewish District, but you can also pick up some great bottles to go.

Léhűtő

Holló utca 12-14, tel. 06/30-731-0430,
Tue-Thu 4pm-2am, Fri-Sat 4pm-4am,
Sun-Mon 4pm-midnight

You'll find Léhűtő in a brick-walled basement. This spot is popular with local beer connoisseurs, as it carries a top selection of craft beers. Six taps change regularly to showcase the best Hungarian craft beers. In addition, they have 30 local and international beers, including IPAs, stouts, and wheat beers from the best Hungarian breweries.

INNER CITY AND SOUTH PEST

✪ Élesztő

Tűzoltó utca 22, tel. 06/70-336-1279,
www.elesztohaz.hu, Mon-Sat 3pm-3am,
Sun 3pm-midnight

Élesztő was one of the first craft beer places to open in Budapest. It occupies a former glassworks factory and sports a ruin bar aesthetic, but it's unique in that it focuses on craft beer. The main bar has 21 Hungarian beers on tap, and across the courtyard you'll find imported beers.

✪ Jonás Craft Beer House

Fővám tér 11-12, tel. 06/70-930-1392,
Mon-Thu 11am-midnight, Fri-Sat 11am-2am,
Sun 11am-11pm

Jonás Craft Beer House is aptly named for its location in the Bálna (Whale). It serves not only wonderful beers but also *pálinkas* and other drinks, and you can't beat the view over the river from its Danube-side terrace. Jonás regularly changes its Hungarian beers on tap, and there is always an interesting range to try.

Krak'n Town

József körút 31a, tel. 06/30-364-5658,
www.krakntown.com, Mon-Fri
4pm-midnight, Sat-Sun noon-midnight

With ship portholes, hot-air balloons hanging from the ceiling, and plenty of brass accents, Krak'n Town may make you feel like you've wandered into a steampunk fantasy. The Hungarian beers on tap change regularly. The food here is a British-Hungarian fusion and worth trying as well.

LIVE MUSIC
Dürer Kert
Ajtósi Dürer Sor 19-21, tel. 06/1-789-4444,
www.durerkert.com, Mon-Sat 5pm-5am,
Sun 5pm-midnight

Part ruin bar, part concert venue, Dürer Kert by City Park is worth the visit if you're into rock, metal, or alternative music. Relax outdoors in the pebbled garden for a few pre-gig beers, or to talk about music till dawn. There are concerts almost daily. The cover fee depends on the event, as low as HUF 500 or up to HUF 6,500 for better-known international acts.

Barba Negra
There are two venues here: Barba Negra Music Club (Prielle Kornélia utca 4, tel. 06/20-563-2254, www.barbanegra.hu) and Barba Negra Track (Neumann János utca 2), which lies around the corner from its sister club. The former is a large indoor club that hosts rock gigs and all-night parties; the outdoor Track is only open in the summer, with loud music, enthusiastic crowds, and plenty of beer on tap.

Budapest Jazz Club
Hollán Ernő utca 7, tel. 06/1-798-7289,
www.bjc.hu, Mon-Thu 10am-midnight,
Fri-Sat 10am-2am

Budapest Jazz Club is in a converted Art Deco cinema and features a bar in the lobby. The music offered here is a diverse range of local and international jazz acts. This elegant jazz club is known for its high-quality sound and state-of-the-art equipment.

CLUBS
LIPÓTVÁROS
Ötkert
Zrínyi utca 4, tel. 06/70-330-8652,
www.otkert.hu, Thu-Sat 11am-5am,
Sun-Wed 11am-11pm

Like many venues in Budapest, Ötkert has many facets: it's a restaurant and cultural space early in the evenings and a party venue with live music and top DJs at night. The building has a capacity of up to 1,000 people. You may even spot the occasional movie star in the crowd.

They have a strict dress code—no metal or punk looks, no neck tattoos.

JEWISH QUARTER
Doboz
Klauzál utca 10, tel. 06/20-449-4801,
www.doboz.co.hu, Wed-Sat 10pm-6am,
Sun 10pm-5am

Doboz fits in with the Jewish District ruin bar look. It occupies an old apartment block. A giant metallic gorilla climbs the 300-year-old tree in the courtyard. Here, DJs work by genre in different rooms, with hip-hop in one and house in another.

LÄRM
Akácfa utca 51, tel. 06/1-783-8820,
www.larm.hu, Sun-Wed 10pm-4am,
Thu 10pm-5am, Fri-Sat 11pm-6am

LÄRM is a club that looks like a black box. It's dedicated to techno lovers, hidden inside the Instant-Fogas Ház complex. Despite being surrounded by the city's most popular bars, it keeps its underground feel. It's simple and all in black, with top audio equipment to keep even the most die-hard techno lovers content in these gut-shaking surroundings.

SOUTH BUDA
✪ A38

Petőfi híd, tel. 06/1-464-3940, www.a38.hu,
Mon-Sat 7:30am-11pm, Sun 12:30pm-11pm

A38 is certainly one of Budapest's most unusual venues. This former Ukrainian stone-carrying ship is permanently moored on the banks of the Danube. The bar and restaurant reside upstairs in the boat section. The stairs descend into a subterranean chamber beneath the Danube. A38 usually hosts indie and alternative concerts and club nights. The cover fee depends on the event (some are free), so check the program.

Performing Arts

CONCERT VENUES
Budapest Park

Soroksári út 60, tel. 06/1-434-7800,
www.budapestpark.hu, event days
6pm-dawn, tram 2

Budapest Park is one of Budapest's largest open-air venues that has a music-festival feel. It stretches over 11,000 square meters (118,000 square feet), making it ideal for large concerts and parties. It may seem like a bit of a trek to get to (especially as you have to take the number 2 tram to the end of the line beyond Rákóczi Bridge), but it's worth coming out for the buzzing atmosphere. Check the website for up-to-date listings.

Akvárium Klub

Erzsébet tér 12, tel. 06/30-860-3368,
www.akvariumklub.hu, Wed-Sat
noon-4:30am, Sun-Tue noon-1am

Akvárium Klub lies beneath an artificial lake at the heart of the city. The glass roof reflects the water into the venue, so it feels as if you are inside an aquarium. There is one large concert hall (1,300 capacity) and a smaller one (fits 700). In the evenings, you'll find local and international bands here. The music is pretty eclectic, ranging from rock and metal to jazz, pop, and electronica. Although events tend to run in the evenings, the bars—especially the terrace in the summer—are open during the day.

PERFORMING ARTS AND CONCERT HALLS

Hungary, and Budapest in particular, has a solid foundation in classical music, opera, and musical theater. Famous Hungarian composers and musicians are known the world over, and within Budapest alone you can find top classical music venues and theaters dedicated to the performing arts.

LIPÓTVÁROS
Vigadó

Vigadó tér 2, tel. 06/1-328-3340,
www.vigado.hu, tickets HUF 1,000-3,500

Budapest's second-largest concert hall takes up impressive residence on the Danube. It's in a beautiful Romantic-style building with huge arched windows. The Vigadó also houses exhibitions on the upper floors, but it's most popular for classical concerts. It may not have the best acoustics in the city, but it's worth visiting for the architecture alone.

BUDAPEST'S BROADWAY

Budapest Operetta and musical theater

Intersecting Andrássy Avenue, **Nagymező utca** is a lively street lined with cafés with street-side terraces, museums, and, above all, theaters. Footprints belonging to Hungarian stage and screen stars line the sidewalk outside the Budapest Operetta Theater, a candy-pink building with echoes of belle Époque grandeur.

In its heyday in the early 1900s, Budapest, along with Paris and Vienna, was considered one of the most important cities for operetta theater, and even today the Operetta is among the most popular theaters in the city, staging around 500 shows a year, from traditional Hungarian operettas to international musicals. An operetta is a light opera, characterized by fun melodies and comedic storylines, and you'll find shows here from the most famous Hungarian composers like Ferenc Lehár and Imre Kálmán.

Even if the ambience is more lighthearted than the Hungarian State Opera around the corner, people still like to dress up for a show, so it's best not to turn up in sneakers and jeans. Head across the road to the Komediás Kávéház for a pre- or post-show drink or dinner; you'll pass a bronze statue of Imre Kálmán (one of Hungary's most beloved operetta composers), sitting with a cigar in hand. The entire street is densely packed with theatrical history. Even the cafés on Nagymező utca capture the grandeur, and it's easy to picture an era when divas would come to dine or sip coffee between shows.

AROUND ANDRÁSSY AVENUE
Hungarian State Opera

Andrássy út 22, tel. 06/1-814-7100,
www.opera.hu, metro 1, bus 70, 78, 105

This is one of the most beautiful opera houses in Europe, and it's budget-friendly, too. If you have the chance, try to make it to an opera. With recent (and ongoing) renovations, you can expect acoustics to match the stunning architecture. Check the current program of shows on the website. Offerings range from well-known operas by Puccini, Verdi, and Mozart to more obscure work by Hungarian or contemporary composers. There are ballet productions as well. You can get cheap tickets for the top tier. (If you do, you'll need to go through the entrance on the left-hand side to go up. Note: there's no elevator.) Some seats have limited visibility. Make sure you dress up for the occasion.

The less impressive **Erkel Theater** (II János Pál pápa tér 30, tel. 06/1-332-6150, www.opera.hu) steps in for productions when the Hungarian State Opera House needs to close for renovations.

Budapest Operetta Theater

Nagymező utca 17, tel. 06/1-312-4866, www.operett.hu, tickets HUF 1,100-8,000, metro 1, bus 70, 78, 105

Alongside Vienna and Paris, Budapest is famed for its operetta, and the Budapest Operetta Theater is one of the best places to sample this unique aspect of Hungarian culture. From the outside, the Operetta looks like a pink-frosted cake; inside, it's gilded with stained glass, chandeliers, and plenty of gold. Shows are in Hungarian but subtitled in English.

Liszt Ferenc Music Academy

Liszt Ferenc tér 8, tel. 06/1-462-4600, www.lfze.hu, tickets free-HUF 12,000

The Liszt Ferenc Music Academy stands in a stunning Art Nouveau building on a square between Andrássy Avenue and Király utca, and it's worth a visit for the 50-minute guided tour (1:30pm, HUF 3,500), even if you can't make a concert. Some of Hungary's best composers and musicians have played at this ornate concert hall, and today you can still attend regular classical concerts from local and international orchestras.

INNER CITY AND SOUTH PEST
Trafó

Liliom utca 41, tel. 06/1-215-1600, www. trafo.hu, tickets range HUF 2000-2500 HUF

You'd expect a theater housed inside a former electrical transformer building to be different, and Trafó delivers. If you're looking for avant-garde theater and dance, this is the place for you. (Just prepare yourself for nudity and other surprises.)

Festivals and Events

Budapest often has something big going on, whether it's food or wine festivals or art fairs. It also plays host to one of the most important music festivals in Europe.

Sziget Festival

Május 9 Park, Óbudai-sziget, www.szigetfetival.com, Aug., €325 7-day pass, €79 day ticket

For one week in the middle of August, thousands of festival-goers (mostly 18- to 40-year-olds) flood the city for the Sziget Festival, which takes place all the way out on Óbuda Island. Sziget features an eclectic lineup with

international pop and rock acts plus world and classical music, along with nonmusical attractions in the comedy tent and circus tent. Past acts have included Muse, Lana del Rey, and Rihanna. Visitors come to the festival from over 100 countries.

Sometimes called a European Burning Man, Sziget is about more than music. Over the course of the week, Sziget becomes an "Island of Freedom," which can mean getting creative at one of the art camps, doing some yoga by the Danube, or partying late into the night after the concerts are over.

You can buy tickets months in advance (the price is also lower then—a day ticket costs €65 if you buy them before the end of December), but tickets do sell out quickly, so it's best to buy them by June at the latest.

Art Market Budapest

Millenáris Cultural Center,
tel. 06/1-239-0007
www.artmarketbudapest.hu, Oct., free entry

Central and Eastern Europe's leading art fair, Art Market Budapest takes place every October, showcasing art from the Central and Eastern European regions in addition to an invited guest country, like Israel or Brazil. Paintings, installations, sculpture, and photography are on display in the Millenáris Cultural Center, where art lovers can talk to the gallery owners and purchase high-end fine art.

Budapest Design Week

Various venues, www.designweek.hu, Oct.

Come and see why Budapest has earned UNESCO's Creative Cities "City of Design" title. For a week in the first half of October, the Hungarian capital transforms into an open showroom for Hungarian contemporary fashion, art, and design, with exhibitions, workshops, and events during Budapest Design Week, which takes place all across the city. Check out the program online (or download the booklet) for events to choose from, like parties, fashion shows, brunches, movie screenings, and open studios. You can download a design map, which you may find useful, even if you don't make it to the events. Most events are free, but they may require advance registration as space is limited.

Buda Castle Wine Festival

Buda Castle, tel. 06/1-203-8507,
www.aborfesztival.hu, Sept.,
day tickets at the door HUF 3,900

Go on a tasting trip around Hungary with the Budapest Wine Festival. This four-day wine fest takes place around the first week of September on the terrace of Buda Castle, which provides perfect views over the city.

Make sure you buy tickets in advance: Not only are they cheaper (HUF 2,990 before mid-August), but also the weekend dates tend to sell out. With entry, you'll get a glass and free entry to the Budapest History Museum. Entry does not include the wine, which you pay for as you drink—and with around 200 wineries, you have plenty to choose from. Aside from wine, there are concerts and cultural programs, but the best thing is sipping a glass of wine on the Buda Castle terrace with the view over the Danube.

Budapest 100

Various venues, www.budapest100.hu,
May, free

Go behind the scenes in May at Budapest 100 when certain buildings, such as private residential buildings (that are usually out of bounds), are opened to the public. The event is free, and it gives you a different way to see Budapest—from hidden courtyards and staircases. This is a must for any architecture lover who's looking for something different. Download a map on the website (or pick up a booklet from one of the venues) and simply wander to the buildings that are interesting for you. Some tours are offered, but they are in Hungarian, so it's best to create your own itinerary and just get out to explore.

Christmas market in front of St. Stephen's Basilica

Markets pop up across Central Europe as Christmas draws near, usually running from the middle or end of November to January 1. Budapest's entire downtown area, in addition to the squares in smaller neighborhoods, will fill up with stands selling trinkets and mulled wine. The most famous is the one down at **Vörösmarty tér** (www.budapestchristmas.com, 10am-8pm Sun-Thu, 10am-10pm Fri-Sat), which has 28 cottage-style wooden stalls where you'll find over 100 vendors focusing exclusively on local Hungarian designers. You can pick up all kinds of things like hand-bound notebooks, lavender cosmetics, bags, leatherwork, artisanal jams, chocolate, and cheeses. Make sure you get a steaming hot cup of mulled wine to keep you warm as you wander around in sub-freezing temperatures. At the heart, there is a large gastro terrace where you can sample some seasonal delights like roast goose thigh with braised red cabbage or roast pork knuckle. It can get crowded, especially on the weekends, so do keep an eye on your belongings at all times.

Falk Art Forum
Falk Miksa utca, tel. 06/20-944-9155, www.falkart.hu, May, free

Falk Miksa utca already has a reputation for its antique shops and art galleries, but for one day around May 5, more than 50 galleries in the area open up for exhibitions (showcasing, for example, Art Deco furniture or Japanese kimonos) or for stage performances. There's everything from music and theater to roundtable discussions and culinary delicacies. If you prefer to go antiquing later, the shops extend their hours, so you won't run out of time to visit.

Recreation and Activities

PARKS

Budapest has a lot of green spaces, from the woods in the Buda Hills to more mainstream spots like Margaret Island and City Park.

City Park
(Városliget)

City Park branches out from the end of Andrássy Avenue and Heroes' Square and extends for more than a kilometer (about a mile) to Ajtósi Dürer sor on the other end. The park itself has evolved over history, along with its name, and is still transforming today with the city's plans to install a new museum quarter (scheduled to open in 2020). It's a popular place for recreation, with the Széchenyi Baths, the zoo, a circus, a lake that's open for boating in the summer and ice skating in the winter, and its own castle, Vajdahunyad Castle. The surrounding area is residential—you'll find romantic turreted villas and Art Nouveau wonders around Stefánia út.

Margaret Island

The island, 2.5 kilometers (1.5 miles) long, is mostly made up of parkland. Apart from a couple of hotels, ruins, thermal baths, and swimming pools, the stretch is populated with green lawns, wooded areas, and spots that are perfect for a small tennis or soccer match with friends. There is a small Japanese garden to the north and a rose garden in the middle. If you want to find a good picnic spot, take the 4 or 6 tram to Margit Sziget, walk the bridge to the musical fountain, and set your blanket down there. The great thing about the island is that any spot is wonderful for lounging in the grass with friends.

BEACHES

Hungary might be a landlocked country, but it makes the most of its water. The Danube is no exception. Although the Danube is dangerous to swim in due to the powerful undercurrents (and it's illegal in most parts as well), you can still relax by the water and spend an afternoon at the beach. If you take a boat up the Danube, further up the Danube Bend, you'll see small, private beaches with one or two people who got there by canoe or bicycle. But you don't need to seek out isolated spots to enjoy Danube beaches; check out the venues listed here.

Római Part

Head out to the north part of Buda in the summer to Római Part, a stretch of embankment with pebbly beaches

Margaret Island

99

leading gently into the river. Locals bring beach towels and have picnics. There are cordoned-off paddling areas to enjoy (the net will stop you from going further into the river). You'll find bars, street food, and riverside cafés along this leafy stretch of the Danube. You can take the 34 or 106 bus over from Lehel tér (you can reach this by metro 3). In the summer, take the BKK boat service from any of the downtown docks, like Battyány tér, Várkert Bazár, or Kossuth Lajos tér (or head to the beginning of the line like Kopaszi gát or the National Theatre) for HUF 750.

Kopászi Dam is popular for water sports and beaches.

Kopászi Dam

On the other end of Buda, far south from Római Part, Kopászi Gát (Kopászi Dam, tram 1) is a small stretch of land that juts out, dotted with parkland and cafés and bistros. There is a sandy beach in the bay area of the dam, and while it's protected from the main flow of the Danube, swimming can still be risky here. It's closer than Római Part to the city center, so it's more convenient if you don't want to head far into the Óbuda suburbs. I personally like this beach area for its unique setting—the walk down

the dam is beautiful, with trees, trendy modern bistros, and a view overlooking the enclosed bay where you can see little boats sailing under the shadow of the old power station. Kopászi Gát looks its best at the golden hour just before sunset.

Lupa Tó

Lupa Tó (lake) lies outside Budapest toward the town of Szentendre. In the past couple of years, it's been the go-to beach for Budapest denizens. This lake has crystal-clear water and has been revamped with sandy beaches and palm trees. In the VIP Lupa Beach section you can rent a waterside curtain-draped double sunbed with pillow from HUF 4,000, where you can sit back and sip a cocktail. Another part of the lake, known as Öböl Beach, is simpler and better if you're on a budget. On the weekends entrance to Öböl Beach is HUF 1,500 (weekdays HUF 1,000); for the VIP Lupa Beach area, HUF 3,900 (HUF 2,900 weekdays).

HIKING

Get out of the chaos of the city and explore a side of Budapest that's a world away from the ruin bars.

Kecske Hegy

Take the 11 bus to the end of the line (the ride lasts 25 minutes from Batthyány tér) for hikes up around Kecske Hegy (Goat Hill). Get off at the final stop, Nagybányai út, and you should see trails marked on the trees—take the one that looks like a green arrow in a circle, which indicates a round-trip. One of the most popular sites on this trail is the Lion's Rock (Oroszlánszikla), which resembles a lion. Nearby is the rock-covered Goat Hill (Kecskehegy), which makes for some great active hiking with some boulder climbing thrown in. Make sure you stop and look back, because the panorama is spectacular. This moderate hike is approximately 4 kilometers (2.5 miles) and can last 2-3 hours.

Elizabeth Lookout

Take the 21 or 21A bus for approximately half an hour from Széll Kálman to Normafa for hikes up to Elizabeth Lookout Tower, the highest point in the city. It's an easy 2.5-kilometer (1.5-mile) hike and takes about half an hour to reach. Around the lookout, you'll find another trail that leads you down to Tündér Szikla (Fairy Rock). Or you can continue along the ridge past the lookout tower to the neighboring hill by following the trail. If you feel a little lazy after climbing up to the lookout tower, go back to town by taking either the chairlift down (HUF 1,200, free with the Budapest Card) or the **Children's Railway.**

Sas Hegy

Nature lovers should head south to Sas Hegy (tel. 06/30-408-4370, www.sas-hegy.hu), which is a nature reserve complete with a visitor center and gentle and wheelchair-accessible hiking trails. It's the closest nature spot to the city center, as you can get bus 8 from Keleti train station to Korompai utca and head up the hill (following Korompai utca uphill once you get off the bus). The route from the bus stop to the lookout point is around 750 meters (half a mile). On the way up, the visitor center will be signposted on wooden arrows with a green dot—and you can learn about the species of plants that have survived on the hill since the last Ice Age. While you're here, make sure you head up to the lookout point for one of the best spots to overlook the city.

CYCLING

For the best cycle-side views, head over to the 27-kilometer (17-mile) bike trail running along the Danube to the picturesque town of Szentendre (page 152). Margaret Island is also a good spot to take a bike—cars are banned from most of the island. You can pick up a MOL BuBi bike on the Buda or Pest side and ride to the island. There are numerous paved paths on the island you can use for cycling.

BIKE SHARING AND RENTALS
MOL BuBi

https://molbubi.bkk.hu

Budapest is popular with cyclists. Anywhere in the center, you may notice lime green MOL BuBi bike stations. You can operate the MOL BuBi system by simply using your cell phone. At a MOL BuBi station, follow the instructions to buy a ticket. Your credit card will be charged the rental fee, along with a HUF 25,000 deposit (released when you return your bike). Once you've bought your ticket, you will get a PIN code on your phone (see the website for complete instructions). Return the bike at any of the docking

MOL BuBi bikes

stations in the city. You have the option of buying a ticket for 24 hours (HUF 500), 72 hours (HUF 1,000), or one week (HUF 2,000), which gets you 30 minutes free cycling time. Beyond that there are usage fees that go up the longer you use the bike (60 minutes HUF 500, 2 hours HUF 1,500—see the website for full fares).

Bringohintó

Hajós Alfréd sétany 1, www.bringohinto.hu
If you're in a group, renting a quadracycle is a fun way to explore Margaret Island. Bringohintó can rent them on a half-hour (HUF 2,880) or hourly basis (HUF 4,280).

CAVE TOURS AND SPELUNKING

Because of an abundance of underground water, Budapest has a secret subterranean world, making the Hungarian capital the world's only city with numerous natural caves running beneath it. There are around 200 caves under Budapest. You can pay a visit to the show caves in the Buda Hills, or go underneath Buda Castle to the labyrinth below—but if you want to get down and dirty, you can also slide through honeycomb-like holes and tunnels on a spelunking expedition. If you plan on visiting the caves, it's a good idea to wear layers (it's around 12°C/54°F in the caves) and closed-toed shoes with a grip.

CAVE TOURS

The Pálvögyi Caves and Szemlőhegyi Caves are located relatively close to one another and can be visited on a combined ticket (HUF 3,100). **Caving Under Budapest** (www.caving.hu) provides private English-language walking tours (HUF 6,000) of these two caves as well.

Pálvögyi Caves

Szépvölgyi út 162, tel. 06/1-325-9505, www. dunaipoly.hu/hu/helyek/bemutatohelyek/ pal-volgyi-barlang, Tue-Sun 10am-4pm, tours at quarter past the hour, HUF 1,950
Located in the Buda Hills, the Pálvögyi cave system takes you through a labyrinth of chambers filled with stalactites and stalagmites, going as deep as 30 meters (98 feet) underground. You can only visit the caves on the 45-minute walking tour, which is given in Hungarian, but it's possible to request a sheet with information in English, and guides can answer questions in English. While much of the show cave is paved, there are times when it will be necessary to scale up a ladder. (But you won't need to get on your hands and knees and get dirty.)

Szemlőhegyi Caves

Pusztaszeri út 35, tel. 06/1-325-6001, www. dunaipoly.hu/hu/helyek/bemutatohelyek/ szemlo-hegyi-barlang, Wed-Mon 10am-4pm, tours on the hour, HUF 1,950
Floret-like mineral and crystalline deposits coat the cave walls here (created by thermal water coming in from below), which has earned this cave system the nickname "Underwater Flower Garden." It is the most accessible out of Budapest's caves. The lower level is sometimes used as a respiratory sanitorium because of its pure air. It needs to be visited on a guided 35- to 45-minute walking tour in Hungarian, but most guides speak English and can answer questions. No climbing or tight spots with this one.

SPELUNKING AND CAVE DIVING

For subterranean diving, head out to the submerged part of the former Kőbánya stone mine and beer factory and go on a 40-minute dive with

Paprika Divers (www.paprikadivers. com/en, €50 not including gear rental).

Mátyáshegy Caves

162 Szépvölgyi út, www.caving.hu

Opposite the Pálvölgy Cave system, just on the other side of Szépvögyi út, is the Mátyáshegy cave network. You'll need a guide to explore these caves, and you'll also need to change into a caving suit and wear a hard hat with a built-in lamp. Caving Under Budapest will take you on a three-hour subterranean adventure (HUF 10,000 pp), where you can expect tight squeezes and rock climbing, as well as lots of wriggling on the cave floor. Make sure you book in advance. Although tours run daily, they can fill up quickly, and there is an age limit of 10 to 55.

Molnár János Cave

www.mjcave.hu/en

Just a few feet away from the Lukács Baths and the Danube is the Molnár János Cave, which is the largest known active thermal water cave, stretching over 6 kilometers (4 miles); it's filled with water that reaches 27°C (80°F) in places. If you want to take it to another level and you're a qualified cave diver or you have an open-water diving certificate, you can dive here from €60 (for the 50-minute cave intro dive, not including dive gear rental). It's only possible to visit these caves on the diving tour.

BOATING
City Park Lake

Olof Palme sétány 5, tel. 06/1-261-5209, www.mujegpalya.hu, daily 10am-9pm

In the summer, the lake in City Park turns into a pleasure lake where you can rent a rowboat (HUF 1,800 for 30 minutes), a canoe (HUF 1,800 for 30 minutes), or a water bicycle (HUF 2,600 for 30 minutes) for up to four people, and you can gaze at the turrets of Vajdahunyad Castle. Bear in mind that opening hours depend on the weather, and if you're coming between seasons, check the website or give them a call. You'll find a mix of families, friends, and couples boating on the lake on hot sunny days. (Note that the water is unfit for swimming and life jackets are not provided.)

ICE SKATING
City Park Ice Rink

Olof Palme sétány 5, tel. 06/1-363-2673, www.mujegpalya.hu

In the winter, the lake in City Park freezes over and becomes one of Europe's largest open-air ice rinks. With the romantic Vajdahunyad Castle as the backdrop, it's probably one of the most beautiful ice rinks, too. If you're visiting Budapest between December and February, it's a fun place to spend an hour or two. You can buy tickets (HUF 1,500 weekdays, HUF 2,000 weekends) online to skip the queue, and you can also rent skates (HUF 1,800) on-site.

Hotel President Ice Rink

From the ice rink on top of the Hotel President, you can see the Postal

In the winter the lake in City Park becomes a popular ice rink.

Savings Bank and the Hungarian Parliament Building in the distance. Entrance to the terrace costs HUF 900 (free for hotel guests), and you can rent skates (HUF 490) on the rooftop. The 110-square-meter (1,200-square-foot) ice rink is made of synthetic ice—good if you're a novice skater. You'll find a mix of locals with kids skating along-side hotel guests. Between skating sessions, grab some mulled wine and a *beigli* (a rolled Hungarian pastry filled with walnuts or poppy seeds) from the wooden hut beside the ice rink and just take in the view from one of the tables at the terrace.

ESCAPE ROOMS

Escape rooms (live-action games where you have an hour to get out of a locked room using teamwork and logic) have exploded in popularity across the globe, and they were created in Budapest. Since ParaPark set up the first live room-escape game, dozens of game rooms have opened in basements and apartments, sometimes even under ruin bars. They're great for groups who are up for the challenge of solving logical puzzles as the clock ticks down. You will usually have to book the room in advance, typically done via the game's website.

ParaPark

Vajdahunyad utca 4, www.parapark.hu, HUF 9,900 per 2-6 person group

ParaPark is a place of pilgrimage for escape-room lovers. There is a selection of rooms in the basement of an VIII District ruin bar, like the Community Cube Factory game inspired by the Hungarian Rubik's Cube, or a crime scene scenario. The damaged walls and creaking doors of the basement add atmosphere to the game, but once you're locked in, you won't

have time to look at the décor—you'll be on your hands and knees looking for clues, turning dials, and opening hidden doors trying to get the key.

TOURS
Budapest Free Walking Tours

www.triptobudapest.hu

Familiarize yourself with the city with a free walking tour with Budapest Free Walking Tours. The tours have a number of interesting themes, like Communist Budapest, and there's one of the Jewish Quarter.

Taste Hungary

www.tastehungary.com,
$79-110 for culinary tours

Tours with Taste Hungary whet the appetite by exploring the culinary side of Budapest through food and culture walks. There's plenty to choose from, whether you want a market tour, dinner walk, or something more niche, like their coffeehouse walk or Jewish culinary tour.

Context Travel

www.contexttravel.com,
$59-66 to join a group tour

Context Travel caters to the intellectual traveler. The company offers tours of Budapest given by historians and academics, providing alternative insight into the city and covering specific topics like architecture, politics, conflict, and culture. They also provide more general orientation tours of the Jewish Quarter and the Castle District.

Budapest Flow

www.budapestflow.com, €45 pp per tour

If you want to explore an alternative side of the city, Budapest Flow takes you around the ruin bars or through the more interesting, nontouristy parts of the city, like the heart of the gentrifying VIII District.

CLASSES
ChefParade Cooking Budapest
www.cookingbudapest.com
Learn all about Hungarian cooking hands-on with ChefParade Cooking Budapest. First, you'll visit the Central Market Hall to buy the best produce. Then, you'll learn how to cook three Hungarian dishes. Courses (including the market tour) last around 4.5 hours and cost around €100 per person.

Shopping

UNESCO awarded Budapest the Creative Cities title of City of Design. To get a taste for Budapest's artistic innovation, start by visiting the city's shops and showrooms. Within basements, on side streets, and hidden in tea room mezzanines, you can find vintage stores selling clothes and accessories from bygone days, and often at a bargain.

SHOPPING DISTRICTS

Váci utca or Andrássy út both offer great high-end shopping. In some of the more exciting neighborhoods, like the Jewish Quarter or the VIII, IX, and XI Districts, you'll find independent boutiques and designers around the downtown streets. Antique lovers flock to Falk Miksa Street for its row of galleries and antique stores. There are around 20 shops just on the row, which comes to life in May during the Falk Art Forum (www.falkart.hu). The event turns antique shopping into a street party with exhibitions, culinary bites, and performances.

Any fashion fiend would do well to head to Deák Ferenc utca. Between Váci utca and Deák Ferenc tér, this small street is replete with luxury boutiques from international designers like Hugo Boss, Tommy Hilfiger, Lacoste, and Massimo Dutti. The street is also lined with luxury hotels and bistros.

MARKETS

While Central Market Hall is the most famous out of Budapest's markets, there are plenty of others to explore, whether you're looking for antiques or artisanal cheese.

JEWISH QUARTER
Gozsdu Court

Gozsdu Court (Gozsdu udvar) is a set of interconnected courtyards lined with restaurants and bars that fill up with a hip, young crowd in the evenings, but on the weekends, it turns into a curious market with antiques, work from local designers, and more. You can find communist badges and soldiers' helmets on one table, prints from local artists on another, jewelry made from cut-out 100-year-old letters, or necklaces made from tiny globes of glass filled with copper wire. It can be hard to deal with the crowds to look at the stalls, but if you do get tired, fortunately there are plenty of cafés offering refuge.

Klauzál Square Market
Klauzál tér 11, tel. 06/1-785-4770, www.antikplacc.hu, Sun 10am-5pm
At the heart of the Jewish Quarter,

BEST SOUVENIRS

Uniquely Hungarian items are known as Hungaricum and some make great gifts. You can pick up food and drinks to take home, or folk art, porcelain, or antiques.

FOOD AND DRINKS

- **Paprika:** You can find packs of powdered paprika from Szeged (a Hungarian town in the south) in places like the Central Market Hall, or in smaller souvenir shops or open-air markets like the farmers market at Szimpla Kert on Sunday morning. Hungarian paprika comes in two varieties: sweet (*édes*) and hot (*erős*). If you can pick up a pack of paprika in a cute embroidered or patterned cheesecloth bag, these make great gifts. Bags can range between HUF 1,500 and 3,700 depending on the size and if any extras like wooden serving spoons are included.

- *Pálinka:* This strong fruit brandy can be found in most wine shops, but a good place to pick up a bottle is the **Magyar Pálinka Háza.** You can get this fruit brandy in a variety of flavors: plum, apple, pear, apricot, cherry, grape, and rarer types like raspberry and elderflower. I personally like the Rézangyal Brand (HUF 3,590-6,490), but you can always ask for recommendations when you go to a specialist shop.

- **Unicum:** This bitter herbal liquor makes a good gift if you want something uniquely Hungarian. You can find Unicum (HUF 3,199-5,000 depending on the size) pretty much everywhere, including supermarkets and cigarette shops. If you want to take home a bottle that is less bitter, try the Unicum Szilva (HUF 3,199-5,000 depending on the size), which has been aged on a bed of dried plums.

- **Wine:** Hungary is gaining recognition for its wine, so why not take home a bottle? You can get wine at all price ranges, from HUF 500 to well beyond HUF 10,000, but you can find something in between that makes the perfect gift. Head to a wine shop like **Tasting Table** where the staff can help you find something quality. If you want something special, pick up a bottle of Tokaj; if you're partial to reds then a good bottle of Egri Bikavér is the way to go.

ART AND DESIGN

- **Herend porcelain:** Herend porcelain stands out because of its delicate motifs, whether in a tea set, tableware with birds and flowers, or hand-painted figures of carnival workers or horses. You can get Herend porcelain for anywhere between HUF 20,000 and 85,000, although rarer pieces can cost hundreds (if not thousands) of dollars. Do note that there are a lot of fakes on the market, so be careful where you buy. To ensure authenticity, head to one of the official Herend stores (József Nádor tér 10-11).

- **Zsolnay ceramics:** This is a unique type of porcelain that originated in the Hungarian town of Pécs. Zsolnay doesn't just produce architectural ceramics—they also create vases and dinnerware. What make Zsolnay different from Herend are the vibrant colors, and almost metallic hues and unique designs. There are a few Zsolnay stores (Rákoczi út 4-6) in Budapest, with prices ranging from as low as HUF 8,000 for small figurines to thousands for larger, rarer items.

- **Folk Art:** Embroidery makes a wonderful gift, whether on a tablecloth or stitched onto a shirt. You can find unique folk art in the **Central Market Hall** in the form of embroidery and lacework. Expect to pay around HUF 10,000-15,000 for quality items, and considerably less for smaller items like doilies.

- **Antiques:** Antiques are great gifts if you're looking to take a piece of history home, whether you pick up some Communist memorabilia from **Ecseri Market** or something more valuable on **Falk Miksa utca,** like a painting, an elegant dinner set, or a wall mirror.

Esceri Market in the suburbs of Pest is a treasure trove of antiques and odd items.

Klauzál tér market reopened in 2015 following a renovation. On Sundays, this old red-brick building turns into an antique market with a difference—you can find not only classic antiques but also those that have been given a revamp by local designers. You'll find repainted and upholstered furniture, old watches fitted with new straps, or restrung jewelry.

Szimpla Farmers Market
Kazinczy utca 14, tel. http://en.szimpla.hu/
farmers-market, Sun 9am-2pm
Szimpla Kert may be best known as a ruin bar, but every Sunday morning till 2pm it turns into an extravagant farmers market with artisanal cheeses, loaves of spelt bread, and seasonal vegetables—and you can listen to live jazz or Hungarian folk music. There is also a charity cookoff in the back of the bar. For a donation, you can get some freshly cooked gulyás (a spicy beef-paprika soup) or stew.

INNER CITY AND SOUTH PEST
Ecseri Market
Nagykőrösi út 150, tel. 06/1-348-3200,
Mon-Fri 8am-4pm, Sat 5am-3pm,
Sun 8am-1pm
Getting to Ecseri Market is an adventure that requires a long bus ride out into the suburbs on bus 54 or 55 to Nászod utca (Használtcikk piac). Then you have to cross the bridge over the highway—but once you're here, this fascinating antiques market is a sight. It's a labyrinth of curiosities, from grand serpentine fountains taken from Buda villas to vintage porcelain, old cameras, gramophones, and portraits of communist political leaders. Even if you're not looking to buy, it's worth visiting just for the experience.

DESIGN SHOPS
CASTLE DISTRICT
FIAN Koncept
Fortuna utca 18 and Úri utca 26-28,
daily 10am-6pm
You'll find the FIAN Koncept design

shops in the Castle District between the colorful houses on Úri utca and Fortuna utca 18. Both spaces are open-concept and modern, with exposed brick and all-white shelving, which is different from other souvenir shops filled with bags of embroidered paprika and postcards. Look for pieces by Romani Design (www. romani.hu), founded by two Roma sisters who wanted to incorporate traditional Romani designs into contemporary fashion.

LIPÓTVÁROS
Rododendron
Semmelweis utca 19, tel. 06/70-419-5329, www.rododendronart.com, Mon-Fri 10am-7pm, Sat 10am-5pm, Sun 11am-3pm

Rododendron Art and Design showcases work from around 30 local designers in its ground-floor shop split between Semmelweis utca and Röser courtyard. The main focus is on art and jewelry, but you'll find other bits and pieces in its changing collection.

JEWISH QUARTER
Printa
Rumbach Sebestyén utca 10, tel. 06/30-292-0329, www.printa.hu, Mon-Sat 11am-7pm

Printa is a shop that doubles as a gallery and coffee shop. This trendy

Printa

silkscreen print studio also carries its own eco-friendly clothing made out of upcycled material. Many of their products also feature Budapest in some way. If you want a silkscreen print to take home or a trendy bag, Printa is your place.

Szimpla Design
Kazinczy utca 14, Wed-Sat noon-7pm

Szimpla Design is set in the front of its namesake ruin bar. It's an Aladdin's Cave of items, with purses, postcards, and handwoven beanie dolls amongst curious pieces of antiques and upcycled items. It embodies the aesthetic of the ruin bar next door, but it offers you the chance to bring home a little of the Budapest ruin chic aesthetic.

INNER CITY AND SOUTH PEST
BomoArt
Régiposta utca 14, tel. 06/20-594-2223, www.bomoart.hu, Mon-Fri 10am-6:30pm, Sat 10am-6pm

BomoArt is a must for anyone who loves stationery. Their hand-bound diaries and notebooks with leather and prints displaying vintage hot-air balloons, aviaries, and old-fashioned pictures of Budapest make unique souvenirs. They have a second location at the Castle Garden Bazaar, and you can find their products in many shops across town.

FOOD AND WINE
Hungarian food and wine can make good souvenirs, so why not take a packet of paprika or a bottle of Hungarian wine home with you? While somewhere like Central Market Hall is the obvious choice, you can pick up some bites to take home in these shops, too. You can also pick up some Hungarian products from local

chain stores like Príma or Spar, but the quality and packaging may not make them ideal for gifts.

LIPÓTVÁROS
Szamos
Deák Ferenc utca 5, tel. 06/30-570-5973, www.szamos.hu, Mon-Sun 10am-9pm

Nothing makes a better souvenir than a box of marzipan chocolates. You'll find Szamos shops and patisseries all over the city, but the most beautiful is on Vörösmarty tér. You can also buy decadent cakes (although these probably won't last the flight home), so why not treat yourself to a Dobos cake (a chocolate cake topped with hardened caramel) and a coffee in the café? Then you can peruse the boxes of chocolates with pictures of the city or Hungarian embroidery to take home.

INNER CITY AND SOUTH PEST
Tasting Table
Bródy Sándor utca 9, tel. 06/30-720-8197, www.tastehungary.com/tasting-table-budapest, daily noon-8pm

For great Hungarian wines, head to Tasting Table. If you want to try before you buy, they organize a few wine tastings. You can book these for 3pm or 6pm daily via the website ($39-$54 per person). The people in the shop are friendly, speak English, and can help you find the right bottle. There's a great selection of Tokaj wines here. For something special, try a bottle from Oremus (prices range from HUF 4,800 for wines from 2010 to HUF 150,000 for rare vintages from the 1950s). You'll also find other wines from Hungary and surrounding regions like Egri Bikavér (Bull's Blood), or sparkling wine from Somló near Lake Balaton.

Magyar Pálinka Háza
Rákóczi út 17, tel. 06/30-421-5463, www.magyarpalinkahaza.hu, Mon-Sat 9am-7pm

Magyar Pálinka Háza, which translates as the "Hungarian House of *Pálinka*," offers this Hungarian spirit in a vast selection, not only in the type of fruit available but also its distilleries. This large shop stocks hundreds of bottles, so deciding may be difficult. You can't taste before you buy, but the staff will help you make the right choice. Most locals will pick up a bottle from the supermarket (or make their own *pálinka*), the huge selection appeals to connoisseurs of the fiery fruit brandy and tourists looking for a special souvenir.

CLOTHING AND ACCESSORIES
LIPÓTVÁROS
Nanushka
Bécsi utca 3, tel. 06/70-394-1954, www.nanushka.com, Mon-Sat 10am-8pm

Nanushka is perhaps Hungary's best-known fashion brand, with boutiques in over 30 countries. The headquarters can be found in downtown Budapest. Nanushka's designs are characterized by lush fabrics and playful cuts designed for the urban woman. Prices are on the high side, with most clothes costing a few hundred euros, but still priced less than international designers.

INNER CITY AND SOUTH PEST
Paloma
Kossuth Lajos utca 14, tel. 06/20-961-9160, Mon-Fri 11am-7pm, Sat 11am-3pm

Paloma is a collective of designers hidden away in a Budapest courtyard in the Inner City. The series of shops on the first floor up from the winged courtyard staircase showcases work from 40 local, young, up-and-coming designers, with jewelry, bags, clothing, and shoes.

JEWISH QUARTER
Szputnyik

Dohány utca 20, tel. 06/1-321-3730, www. szputnyikshop.hu, Mon-Sat 10am-8pm, Sun 10am-6pm

Szputnyik mixes a large range of vintage clothing and accessories with newer, quirky bags, shoes, clothing, and jewelry, plus altered and revamped vintage items. It's a popular shop for fashion-forward, trendy Hungarians skewing more to the alternative, boho crowd. Prices won't break a midrange budget.

Retrock

Anker köz 2-4, tel. 06/30-472-3636, Mon-Sat 11am-9pm, Sun 11am-8pm

Pick out unique creations made by Hungarian and international designers from used and recycled materials, or secondhand items and accessories. Retrock is a treasure trove of bijoux and unusual fashion items, such as mountain man-style bags, Gothic alien-inspired fashion lines, and handmade cycling accessories.

Food

Hungarian food is heavy. Portion sizes are large, meals center around meat, and of course, you'll get plenty of paprika accenting the dish to give it a slight kick. You won't leave a restaurant hungry, but if you're on a diet or vegetarian, you may want to visit an international or specialty restaurant.

Breakfast is usually a big deal. Hotels will ply you with cold cuts, chopped vegetables, and plenty of bread in the morning. Fried eggs with bacon or sausage is a typical Hungarian breakfast.

CASTLE DISTRICT
HUNGARIAN
21 Magyar Vendéglő

Fortuna utca 21, tel. 06/1-202-2113, www.21restaurant.hu, daily 11am-midnight, HUF 3,680-5,680

Magyar Vendéglő literally means "Hungarian restaurant," but this chic bistro up in the Castle District applies an innovative and lighter twist on traditional dishes, like its paprika chicken made with a paprika reduction and served with homemade dumplings. You may want to try one of their special seasonal dishes like farm duckling breast with cottage cheese potato dumplings. Beyond the creative cuisine, this restaurant stands out for friendly service. (Plus, they bottle their own wine.)

Mandragora

Kacsa utca 22, tel. 06/1-202-2165, www.mandragorakavehaz.hu, Mon-Sat 11am-11:45pm, HUF 3,100-4,500

Mandragóra (named after the mandrake, a humanoid-looking root used in witchcraft in the past) evokes images of magic and the occult, but this family-run restaurant employs its magic in the kitchen with its contemporary, seasonal takes on Hungarian classics, like paprika pike perch served with cottage cheese noodles and crumbles of bacon, or creative

traditional Hungarian fried bread *Lángos*

ENTRÉES

- *Gulyásleves* (Hungarian goulash): Hungarian goulash is known the world over, but it's a soup and not a stew as commonly believed. This rich beef soup made with chunks of potato and peppers is accented with quality red paprika powder, which gives the soup its crimson color.

- *Halászlé:* Similar to *gulyásleves* but made with fish instead of meat (called *halászlé*). This fisherman's soup comes from the south of the country, around Szeged.

- Chicken *paprikás:* A creamy chicken dish made with oodles of powdered paprika (which gives it a salmon hue), served with thin dumplings called *galuska* or *nokedli* and a side of sour cucumber salad.

- Mangalica pork: Keep an eye out for mangalica on the menu. This unique Hungarian breed of pig is not only rare for its woolly coat (that kind of looks like a sheep's), but it's dubbed to be the "Kobe beef of pork." It's a fatty meat that's loved for its marbled texture and superb taste.

For flavoring, **paprika** is a staple in the Hungarian kitchen, with locals reaching for bottles of sweet or spicy powdered paprika in place of pepper at times.

STREET FOOD
Lángos is a deep-fried savory dough similar in texture to a donut that usually comes topped with cheese and sour cream. You'll find this calorific street treat sold in kiosks and food trucks, mainly in parks, festivals, street food courts, and around metro stations.

WINE
Wine plays a big part in Hungarian meals, as the country is home to numerous wine regions (including the famous golden Tokaji dessert wines). Hungarians also like to sip spicy reds from the southern part of the country, such as **Szekszárd** and **Villány**, crisp whites from Lake Balaton's Badacsony region or nearby Somló, and the iconic **Bikavér** (Bull's Blood) red cuvée from Eger.

SPIRITS

- *Pálinka:* A famous fruit brandy distilled from local fruits like plum, pear, apple, quince, and apricot, which is often drunk with heavy Hungarian meals. Locals swear *pálinka* is a cure for digestive problems, colds, stomach aches, and even heart pains.

- Unicum: A bitter liqueur made from a secret recipe of 40 herbs and spices, which is said to help digestion.

additions like the coffee spicing up their duck breast served with yellow beetroot. However, what makes Mandragóra really stand out are the desserts, especially the homemade chocolate cake, which is so good that they sell the cake to order so you can take it home.

✪ Csalogány 26

Csalogány utca 26, tel. 06/1-201-7892, www.csalogany26.hu, Tue-Sat noon-3pm and 7pm-10pm, entrées HUF 2,400-6,000 or tasting menu HUF 16,000

Csalogány 26 offers inspiring dishes made from local, seasonal ingredients—like a spiced peasant consommé with homemade udon noodles or cottage cheese mousse with sea buckthorn. Some say this restaurant run by a passionate father-and-son team is one of the best in Budapest. Go all-out with their lavish degustation menu, or try the budget-friendly three-course lunch menu for just HUF 3,100.

INTERNATIONAL
Zóna

Lánchíd utca 7-9, tel. 06/30-422-5981, www.zonabudapest.com, Mon-Sat noon-midnight, HUF 3,900-7,700

Zóna embraces a modern, urban aesthetic and prepares creatively executed international dishes. The menu offers an eclectic selection from gourmet burgers to an elegant degustation menu that changes seasonally but may feature dishes like guineafowl goulash and lamb rump served with sweet potato, kale, and panna cotta (yes, the Italian dessert). Zóna focuses on international fusion, mixing up Italian-inspired dishes with street food, along with tastes from Israel and Hungary thrown in.

Arany Kaviár

Ostrom utca 19, tel. 06/1-201-6737, www.aranykaviar.hu, Tue-Sun noon-3pm and 6pm-midnight, HUF 4,900-18,900

This Russian restaurant embodies the principles of fine dining in an intimate setting and with beautiful food presentation. If you're a fan of fish eggs, try their caviar menu (they have more than five types) accompanied by traditional Russian blinis and *smetana* (sour cream). If you fancy a splurge, go for their tasting menu (HUF 21,000-30,000), but their three-course lunch menu (HUF 5,900) gives you a chance to try their fine Russian dishes without breaking the bank. Apparently Brad and Angelina came here on a date night once, so you may want to people-watch if you visit.

BISTRO AND BRUNCH
✪ Pierrot

Fortuna utca 14, tel. 06/1-375-6971, www.pierrot.hu, daily 11am-midnight, HUF 3,780-8,640

Pierrot is a stylish bistro on the site of a 13th-century bakery. Its kitchen focuses on Austro-Hungarian cuisine, but it's been updated for the more adventurous tastes of the 21st-century diner. Try their veal goulash or confit of duck baked into puff pastry.

Baltazár Grill and Wine Bar

Országház utca 3, tel. 06/1-300-7050, www.baltazarbudapest.com, daily noon-11pm, HUF 3,180-9,680

The bistro in this boutique hotel attracts locals and visitors. Baltazár Grill and Wine Bar serves up tantalizing brunches (including pastries), but they are best known for their charcoal-grilled meats and burgers. They also have an extensive wine collection from all around the Carpathian Basin. Another nice touch is their interesting

Baltazár Grill and Wine Bar occupies the ground floor of a boutique hotel.

gin selection with tailored garnishes that go toward making the perfect gin and tonic.

VEGAN AND VEGETARIAN
Édeni Vegán
Iskola utca 31, tel. 06/20-337-7575,
www.edenivegan.hu, daily 8am-8pm,
HUF 690-1,490
You can find Édeni Vegán at the base of Castle Hill, in an old townhouse just off Batthyányi Square. This vegan restaurant serves hearty dishes made with organic ingredients, from burgers to salads and raw desserts. Gluten- and sugar-free options are also available.

CAFÉS AND CAKE
Ruszwurm
Szentháromság utca 7, tel. 06/1-375-5284,
www.ruszwurm.hu, Mon-Fri 10am-7pm,
Sat-Sun 10am-6pm, HUF 420-720
Ruszwurm, Budapest's oldest functioning café and confectionary—dating back to 1827—is in a pistachio-green Baroque-style house. The interior is minimal, and the cakes are displayed in a wooden apothecary-style cabinet. Try the café's signature cake, the Ruszwurm Cream Pastry, a custard- and cream-based dessert topped with layers flaky dough. (In the high season, you may find it hard to find somewhere to sit!)

Budavári Rétesvár
Balta köz 4, tel. 06/70-408-8696,
www.budavariretesvar.hu, daily 8am-7pm,
HUF 310
It might take a while to find the Budavári Rétesvár, a hole-in-the-wall discoverable under a dark archway in the Castle District, but worth the exploration just for the strudels. You can find variations of the Hungarian strudel, known as *rétes*, with fillings including sweet poppy seed, plum, or apple, plus savory dill and cottage cheese.

LIPÓTVÁROS
HUNGARIAN
✪ Zeller Bistro
Hercegprímás utca 18, tel. 06/30-651-0880,
www.zellerbistro.hu, Tue-Sun noon-midnight,
HUF 3,200-6,500
Zeller Bistro specializes in contemporary Hungarian cooking using fresh and seasonal ingredients from local farmers, producers, and small Hungarian wineries. The restaurant is in a cozy downtown setting and blends rustic with industrial chic. I recommend the duck liver brûlée with carrot and mango or the daily fish that comes straight from the market with a side of risotto. The carrot cake is also one of the best in town.

FINE DINING
✪ Onyx
Vörösmarty tér 7-8, tel. 06/30-508-0622,
www.onyxrestaurant.hu, Tue-Fri
noon-2:30pm, Tue-Sat 6:30pm-11pm,
tasting menus HUF 33,900
Try the two-Michelin-starred take on Hungarian food at Onyx with its six-course (or more) tasting menu that documents the evolution of Hungarian cuisine with creative dishes like goose liver paired with coffee and almond, or catfish bacon fish soup. Their

"Beyond Our Borders" tasting menu has seasonal takes inspired by continental European cooking, featuring dishes like saddle of lamb with summer truffles. Onyx is more than just a meal out—it's a dining experience that can last for hours. Opt for the simpler three- or four-course lunch menu (HUF 19,900-27,900) if you just want a taste.

Borkonyha

Sas utca 3, tel. 06/1-266-0835,
www.borkonyha.hu, Mon-Sat noon-4pm
and 6pm-midnight, HUF 3,500-7,950

The menu is always changing at this contemporary Hungarian restaurant headed by Chef Ákos Sárközi. Borkonyha earned its Michelin star for its innovative menu, drawing inspiration mostly from the Transylvanian kitchen, while playing with international ingredients and modern cooking techniques. Try the foie gras wrapped in flaky pastry, and anything that is made with mangalica pork. If you go for a tasting menu, invest in the wine pairing—there is a reason why this restaurant is called "Wine Kitchen" in Hungarian.

INTERNATIONAL
Baraka

Dorottya utca 6, tel. 06/1-200-0817, www.
barakarestaurant.hu, Mon-Sat 11am-3pm
and 6pm-11:30pm, HUF 7,500-17,500

If you love fine dining and Asian and French food, you'll love Baraka. Since Baraka opened its doors and presented Asian-French fusion with a fine-dining, seasonal slant and a Hungarian accent, it's been a hub for foodie lovers. Seafood dominates the menu, with creative dishes such as bouillabaisse made with steamed-fish gyoza, capers, and seaweed.

There are options for meat eaters and vegetarian diners here, with degustation menus and à la carte choices available. East-meets-West flavors combine in dishes like togarashi with beetroot, or Hungarian wild boar with ume shiso.

Da Mario

Vécsey utca 3, tel. 06/1-301-0967,
www.damario.hu, daily 11:30am-11pm,
HUF 2,000-7,000

For authentic Italian cuisine, Da Mario is the place to go. This Italian-owned restaurant offers classic pasta and pizza, as well as seafood and meat dishes made with the best ingredients sourced from Italy, plus Italian wines. The atmosphere is relaxed and friendly, and the setting is stylish.

BISTRO AND BRUNCH
✪ Szimply

Károly körút 22 Röser Udvar,
www.szimply.com, Mon-Fri 8am-4pm,
Sat 9am-4pm, HUF 1,800-2,900

It's hard to get a table in this small breakfast bistro (which does not accept reservations), but Szimply is worth it if you can grab a spot. With a choice of savory and sweet seasonal specials, you can be sure to get fresh and beautifully presented breakfast dishes, from favorites like avocado toast to more innovative ones like zucchini pancakes.

Kispiac

Hold utca 13, tel. 06/1-269-4231,
Mon-Sat noon-10pm, HUF 2,300-3,950

Kispiac Bisztró can be found in one of the shopfronts of the Belvárosi market hall, and the staff serves up hearty Hungarian dishes with generous portions. Ingredients come straight from the market so everything is fresh, and even the preserved ingredients like jams, bread, and pickled vegetables are handcrafted by the restaurant. Each day they put up six dishes to choose from, as well as regular Hungarian specials. (Take note: this bistro only seats 20, so you might have stiff competition for a table.)

CAFÉS AND CAKE
Gerbeaud

Vörösmarty tér 7-8, tel. 06/1-429-9001,
www.gerbeaud.hu, daily noon-10pm,
HUF 1,150-4,990

Gerbeaud is an institution in Budapest's café and confectionary culture. Founded in 1858, it eventually became the most fashionable spot in the city for the elite. Today, its palatial interior with rococo friezes, silk drapes, and crystal chandeliers invites guests to sit at the marble-topped tables to sip coffee and take bites from decadent cakes.

JEWISH QUARTER
JEWISH

Jewish food in Budapest frequently overlaps Hungarian food, but there are some distinguishing markers. You won't find the pork-heavy recipes you'd get elsewhere. Instead, you'll find beef, lamb, or chicken. Hungarian-Jewish dishes like *cholent* (a bean stew) or goose feature heavily on menus. Not all restaurants are kosher. The only one that gets kosher approval from the Orthodox community is Hanna (in the courtyard of the Kazinczy Street synagogue), but it is not the place to go if you want an outstanding culinary experience. Other Jewish restaurants also draw influences from Israeli dishes, like hummus and tabbouleh.

Mazel Tov

Akácfa utca 47, www.mazeltov.hu,
tel. 06/70-626-4280, Mon-Fri 6pm-2am,
Sat-Sun noon-2am, HUF 1,990-5,890

What started out as the next generation of ruin pubs has morphed into a popular restaurant where a reservation is almost mandatory. Mazel Tov serves up Israeli fusion, such as pulled lamb with eggplant, tabbouleh and tahini, or classic hummus-centered dishes, and sizzling Middle Eastern grilled meat plates with spicy Moroccan sausages and marinated skewers of meat. The setting—with exposed brick, twinkling fairy lights wrapped around the tree in the courtyard, and Mediterranean-tiled bar—pulls in the crowds as much as the food. Reservations are a must.

Kőleves

Kazinczy utca 37-41, tel. 06/20-213-5999,
www.kolevesvendeglo.hu, Mon-Fri 8am-1am,
Sat-Sun 9am-1am, HUF 2,180-5,180

Kőleves ("Stone Soup") serves Jewish-inspired dishes, like *cholent*, a traditional Jewish bean stew served up with egg (or goose egg), and goose broth with a matzo ball. There are also plenty of vegetarian options, like vegetarian gratin made with black lentils, gruyere, and walnuts.

Fröhlich

Dob utca 22, tel. 06/20-913-2595,
www.frohlich.hu, Mon-Thu 9am-6pm, Fri
9am-2pm, Sun 10am-6pm, HUF 140-950

This kosher café and cake shop is a Jewish staple in the heart of the VII District. Fröhlich is famous for its *flódni*, a layered Jewish cake with apple, walnut, and poppy seed, but it's also worth trying some of their other baked goods and sweets. The interior has a faded old-world charm to it, with deep red walls and wooden lattice tables.

HUNGARIAN
Frici Papa

Király utca 55, tel. 06/1-351-0197,
www.fricipapa.hu, Mon-Sat 11am-11pm
HUF 430-1,000

For Hungarian food on a budget, Frici Papa is the place to go. Frici Papa serves up classic Hungarian dishes in generous portions at fair prices. Even though it's located in a downtown, touristy area, it's still popular with locals. Just note that all dishes are sold separately, from meat and mains to side dishes.

Kádár

Klauzál tér 9, tel. 06/1-321-3622,
Tue-Sat 11:30am-3:30pm, HUF 1,000-2,500

The gentrification of the Jewish District hasn't stopped Kádár from serving up classic retro dishes over the generations. It's a time capsule with checkered tablecloths, antique seltzer bottles, and vintage photos of celebrities on the wall. Kádár dishes up traditional Hungarian-Jewish cooking for lunch only, with plenty of boiled beef and dishes like sólet (cholent, a Jewish bean stew) on their ever-changing menu. You need to keep tabs on what you've eaten and drunk (including the slices of bread and the water from the seltzer bottle) as each item is charged individually, but prices are very budget-friendly.

Barack & Szilva

Klauzál utca 13, tel. 06/1-798-8285,
www.barackesszilva.hu, Mon-Sat
6pm-midnight, HUF 3,100-5,500

Barack & Szilva ("Peach and Plum") is a small family-run bistro serving up Hungarian provincial food fused with influences from French, Italian, and Jewish cuisines. You can go à la carte or dive into the seasonal chef's offer with a delicious tasting menu with a wine pairing option.

M Restaurant

Kertész utca 48, tel. 06/1-322-3108,
www.metterem.hu, daily 6pm-midnight,
HUF 2,400-3,600

The menu at M Restaurant changes daily and features Hungarian specials, sometimes with a French twist. It has a cozy feel in a compact setting with sketched brown paper on the walls. Reservations highly recommended.

FINE DINING
Bock Bisztró

Erzsébet körút 43-49, tel. 06/1-321-0340,
www.bockbisztropest.hu, Mon-Sat
noon-midnight, HUF 3,400-17,400

Located in the building belonging to the Corinthia Hotel, Bock Bisztró gives you the chance to try Hungarian delicacies inspired by Spanish tapas. One of the main draws is its excellent and extensive wine list—over 200 to choose from. Chef Lajos Bíró is legendary in local culinary circles, drawing Hungarians and visitors alike to this elegant establishment.

STREET FOOD
✪ Bors Gasztro Bár

Kazinczy utca 10, tel. 06/70-935-3263,
daily 11:30am-9pm, HUF 600-1,000

You'll always see waiting crowds outside this pantry-sized street food bar. Bors Gasztro Bár elevates street food with a menu that changes daily and is based on fresh, seasonal ingredients. Dishes include soups, baguettes, stews, and pasta, with innovative options like coconut-chili pumpkin cream soup or their French Lady baguette that combines emmentaler cheese and spiced

HUNGARIAN BAKERIES

Hungarians love their *cukrászda* (confectionaries serving decadent cakes and coffees). Café culture is a big part of local life and a popular tourist attraction in itself. Old Habsburg-era grand cafés serving dessert and cakes still line the boulevards of Budapest. The New York Café is cited as the most beautiful café in Europe—if not the world—with marble columns, gold-gilt mirrors, rococo-style frescoes on the ceiling, and crystal chandeliers. Other cafés, like Gerbeaud, Művész, Central, and Astoria, also carry on the Austro-Hungarian coffee traditions. New-wave cafés are percolating on the scene, too, catering to hip and trendy crowds who love their flat whites and Chemex coffees.

Look for the following desserts behind the glass cabinets of the city's beloved *cukrászdas*:

- *Dobostorta:* A chocolate cake topped with a hard caramel topping.

- *Eszterházy:* Cake made with walnuts and rum.

- *Somloi galuska:* A Hungarian-style tiramisu without the coffee.

- *Krémes:* A custard and cream cake set between layers of flaky pastry.

chicken breast, accented with rosemary red onion jam.

Karavan

*Kazinczy utca 18, tel. 06/30-934-8013,
Sun-Wed 11:30am-11pm, Thu-Sat
11:30am-1am, HUF 750-2,500*

If you want a bite to eat before grabbing drinks at Szimpla Kert, Karavan is a great choice. This open-air street food court serves up a range of snacks from its numerous food trucks, from Hungarian *lángos* (deep-fried savory pastries topped with cheese) to sausages and vegan burgers. Head in with friends, and you can each buy from a different truck and sit together.

CAFÉS AND CAKE
New York Café

*Erzsébet körút 9-11, tel. 06/1-8866-167,
www.newyorkcafe.hu, daily 9am-midnight
HUF 1,650-18,000*

Some say the New York Café is the most beautiful café in the world, and with its curved marble columns, rococo-style balconies and friezes, and generous application of gold leaf, it's certainly a candidate for the most

opulent. This is not a place you come to for the food (which could be better, to be honest). However, people do come here for the experience. Along with the coffee and tempting cakes, the café also serves up plenty of history, since it was once a popular hangout for artists, nobility, and writers. Some of the most influential newspapers around 1900 were edited up in the café gallery. One local legend has it that writer Ferenc Molnár stole the keys to the café and tossed them in the Danube so the restaurant would be forced to stay open 24/7. Although it also functions as a restaurant, most come here to have a coffee and admire the scenery. But if coffee is not your thing, try the lemonade (which is based on a 19th-century recipe). Mornings are the best time to pop by, and if you're lucky, a cellist might even serenade you. You'll find the café inside the New York Palace Boscolo Budapest Hotel right on Grand Boulevard.

My Little Melbourne

*Madács Imre út 3, tel. 06/70-394-7002,
www.mylittlemelbourne.hu, Mon-Fri*

7am-6pm, Sat-Sun 8:30am-6pm,
HUF 400-950

My Little Melbourne was one of the first new-wave coffee bars that opened in Budapest. Get quality espressos and flat whites in their tiny mezzanine café, or head next door to My Little Brew Bar where you can treat yourself to a chemical lab's worth of drip coffees, from Chemex to syphon-made coffees.

AROUND ANDRÁSSY AVENUE

HUNGARIAN
Menza

Ferenc tér 2, tel. 06/1-413-1382,
www.menzaetterem.hu, daily 10am-midnight
HUF 1,690-4,290

Menza combines retro interior design with Hungarian food classics adapted to the modern palate like gulyás soup. They also offer more contemporary dishes like duck burgers. The menu changes weekly. For a great bargain, come at lunchtime during the week for quality food for only HUF 1,490.

INTERNATIONAL
Indigo

Jókai utca 13, tel. 06/1-428-2187,
www.indigo-restaurant.hu, daily
noon-11pm HUF 1,200-4,900

Anyone from the local Indian community will recommend Indigo as the go-to Indian restaurant in Budapest. The menu focuses mostly on North Indian cuisine, cooked up by the best Indian chefs in the city. You'll find dishes from tandoor-cooked charred meats to creamy vegetarian curries. It's best to make advance reservations, but just in case you can't get a table at their Pest restaurant, they have another location in Buda (Fény utca 16).

BISTRO AND BRUNCH
Két Szerecsen

Nagymező utca 14, tel. 06/1-434-1984, www.ketszerecsen.hu, Mon-Fri 8am-midnight,
Sat-Sun 9am-midnight, HUF 2,390-5,990

This cozy bistro serves up an eclectic menu, with brunch classics such as eggs benedict and international dishes like Moroccan lamb shoulder and Thai curries. Két Szerecsen combines the classic coffeehouse vibe with a Parisian bistro environment. In the summer, there is a very nice terrace area just next to the café.

VEGETARIAN, VEGAN, AND GLUTEN-FREE
Drop

Hajós utca 27, tel. 06/1-235-0468,
www.droprestaurant.com, daily
8am-midnight, HUF 2,350-7,490

At Drop, there's a range of tasty gluten-free dishes to try, from salads and cheese plates to pasta dishes and Hungarian specialties. It's also worth popping by for breakfast, especially if you want some gluten-free bread and baked goods. Lactose-free and vegetarian dishes are also available. (Great news for those who are gluten-intolerant or allergic—everything on the menu is gluten-free.)

STREET FOOD
Pizzica

Nagymező utca 21, tel. 06/70-554-1227,
Mon-Thu 11am-midnight, Fri-Sat 11am-3am,
HUF 190-490

For great Italian street food pizza, you can't beat Pizzica. The pizza here comes on the perfect thin base, with toppings like buffalo mozzarella or truffle cream. Slices are cut with scissors and served up on wooden boards. In the mezzanine, local art is usually on display.

Eat&Meet (Danubius utca 14, tel. 06/30-517-5180, www.eatmeet-hungary.com, see website for scheduled dinners, €45 three-course meal including drinks) is no ordinary restaurant. Set in a private apartment in the XIII District (and in a garden house just outside Budapest in the summer), this unique pop-up restaurant runs regular dinners for those wanting to try authentic Hungarian food as you would have it at home.

Zsuzska Goldbach, a young Hungarian woman who speaks both English and Italian, began Eat&Meet with her parents as a passion project to showcase true Hungrian home cooking you won't find in a restaurant. The three-course meal is seasonal, made with fresh, local ingredients, and dishes are paired with Hungarian wines. Zsuzska explains everything in detail, from specific ingredients to the wines and Hungarian culinary traditions. Guests are welcomed with the family's own aged *pálinka*. Dinners are scheduled on certain dates, so contact Eat&Meet to arrange when you'd like to come.

You won't really find locals at Eat&Meet, but you feel like you're at an international dinner party where everyone is seated together. You may end the evening with a new friend or two. This restaurant is highly recommended if you're a solo traveler and fed up with dining alone. The food is fantastic and worth the price. It's made even more special by the Goldbach family's passion and attention to detail.

CAFÉS AND CAKE
Művész

Andrássy út 29, tel. 06/70-333-2116,
www.muveszkavehaz.hu, Mon-Sat
9am-10pm, Sun 10am-10pm, HUF 550-890

A classic on the Hungarian cake and café scene since the 19th century, Művész is known for its cakes, with staples like custard cream and chocolate alongside seasonal specials. Try the house special—the Művész kocka—a layered cake with nuts, chocolate mousse, cream, and sheets of dark chocolate. The café interior captures a fading old-world decadence, with silk wallpaper, marble tables, and crystal chandeliers. The Művész's proximity to the opera house and the theaters on Nagymező utca make it a good pre-theater hangout.

CITY PARK AND AROUND
HUNGARIAN
Bagolyvár

Károly út 4, tel. 06/1-468-3110,
www.bagolyvar.com, daily noon-midnight
HUF 2,500-4,900

This family restaurant located next to the zoo offers good food at a reasonable cost. Bagolyvár ("Owl Castle"), named for its former avian residents, is the sister restaurant of the fancier, fine-dining Gundel restaurant next door. Bagolyvár serves up innovative cuisine inspired by chef Károly Gundel but in a more relaxed atmosphere—and without the Gundel prices.

FINE DINING
✪ Gundel

Gundel Károly út 4, tel. 06/1-889-8111,
www.gundel.hu, daily noon-midnight,
HUF 5,500-39,000

Gundel is an institution whose founder is considered the Escoffier of Hungarian cuisine. Try the piquant goulash soup made from an in-house recipe, and the walnut pancakes accented with rum, raisins, and lemon zest—and drizzled with bitter chocolate. The extremely popular crepe-like Gundel pancake has inspired similar versions in restaurants across the country. If you want to try Gundel but it's out of your budget, head next door to the more affordable Bagolyvár.

INTERNATIONAL
Robinson

Városligeti tó, tel. 06/1-422-0222, www.robinsonrestaurant.hu, daily noon-3pm and 6pm-11pm, HUF 3,500-6,200

On a small island in the heart of City Park, Robinson is all about the location. Robinson is in a two-story glass-paneled lake house, so when you're inside, it feels like you're dining on the water. Although you'll find Hungarian dishes like Hortobágy pancakes (meat-filled pancakes topped with a creamy paprika sauce) on the menu, the focus is more on international cuisine (mostly French), along with grilled dishes and sizzling steaks.

BISTRO AND BRUNCH
Városliget Café and Bar

Olof Palme sétány 6, tel. 06/30-869-1426, www.varosligetcafe.hu, daily noon-10pm, HUF 1,990-9,990

Városliget Cáfe and Bar overlooks Vajdahunyad Castle with views of the lake (or ice rink, depending on the season). It's in a beautiful 19th-century, neo-Baroque pavilion. The food is a mix of international bistro cuisine with a few Hungarian specials like paprika chicken, stuffed cabbage, and roasted goose leg. The restaurant prides itself on its Tányérhús (slow-cooked boiled beef served over three courses, starting with beef broth, then the marrow on toast, and finally the tender meat with sides like fried potatoes, cream of spinach, and horseradish-spiked apple sauce), inspired by the Austrian Tafelspitz. Make sure you close the meal with their signature Liget Coffee, made with their house blend, roasted and ground on premises.

MARGARET ISLAND AND AROUND
HUNGARIAN
Pozsonyi Kisvendéglő

Radnóti Miklós utca 38, tel. 06/1-787-4877, Mon-Fri 9am-midnight, Sat-Sun 10am-midnight, HUF 1,100-3,050

Pozsonyi Kisvendéglő is popular with locals for its friendly, welcoming atmosphere. It's always full, and it can be a challenge to get a table, but with generous portions and budget-friendly prices, it's easy to see why. You'll find all the classic Hungarian dishes, and you may feel overwhelmed by the choices. Try the goulash or the roasted duck, or take advantage of the seasonal menu. Reservations highly recommended.

CAFÉS AND CAKE
Sarki Fűszeres

Pozsonyi út 53-55, tel. 06/1-238-0600, 8am-8pm Mon-Fri, 8am-3pm Sat, HUF 790-2,300

This retro café is a great spot for a quick brunch or sandwich. Sarki Fűszeres is both a wine shop and a delicatessen selling platters of cheese and artisanal meat cuts. Whether you have a savory or sweet palate, you can be sure to find a snack to tempt you.

SOUTH BUDA
BISTRO AND BRUNCH
Hadik

Bartók Béla út 36, tel. 06/1-279-0290, www.hadik.eu, daily noon-1am, HUF 1,600-3,600

Located on up-and-coming Bartók Béla út, Hadik delivers a mix of classic Hungarian and more experimental dishes. Hadik was once a hangout for the Buda literary elite, and it sports a more laid-back industrial chic look. Neighboring Szatyor (www.szatyorbar.com) offers the same menu and has an eclectic ruin bar feel. Both places fill up quickly in the evenings, and during the day they make a great stop for coffee.

VEGETARIAN, VEGAN, AND GLUTEN-FREE
Vegan Love
Bartók Béla út 9, www.veganlove.hu;
daily 11am-9pm HUF 1,590-1,990

For Budapest's best vegan burgers, head to Vegan Love. This street food bar offers delicious vegan options like sweet potato or BBQ tofu burgers and vegan chili dogs. The creations here are adventurous and flavorful, and they will also appeal to non-vegans.

CAFÉS AND CAKE
Kelet
Bartók Béla út 29, tel. 06/20-456-5507,
Mon-Fri 7:30am-11pm, Sat-Sun 9am-11pm,
HUF 350-1,850

This charming café, covered wall-to-wall with books, is popular with locals for its third-wave artisanal coffees and tempting snacks, like creative toasted sandwiches made with Indonesian-style peanut butter or exotic chutneys. Make sure you try their hot chocolates or drip coffees made from single-origin beans.

INNER CITY AND SOUTH PEST
HUNGARIAN
Karpátia
Ferenciek tere 7-8, tel. 06/1-317-3596,
www.karpatia.hu, Mon-Sat 11am-11pm,
Sun 5pm-11pm, HUF 3,400-7,900

Karpátia dates back to the late 19th century and is worth visiting for the frescoed interior that looks like something out of a museum. When it comes to food, Karpátia serves up classic Hungarian dishes with a range of spicy goulash soups and variations of paprika-laced meat stews made with chicken or beef. If you come in the evening, expect to dine while listening to *csárdás* (traditional Hungarian-Romani folk dance music).

INTERNATIONAL
Pata Negra
Kálvin tér 8, tel. 06/1-215-5616,
www.patanegra.hu, daily 11am-midnight,
HUF 650-2,650

Share some tapas at Pata Negra, a Spanish tapas bar featuring classics like *patatas bravas*, *croquetas*, and *jamón iberico*. This restaurant is ideal to visit with a group so you can share different dishes and a jar of sangria, or enjoy a glass of Spanish wine or sherry.

FINE DINING
✪ Costes
Ráday utca 4, tel. 06/1-219-0696,
www.costes.hu, Wed-Sun 6:30pm-midnight,
HUF 9,000-13,000

Costes was the first restaurant in Hungary to receive the much-coveted Michelin star. Chef de Cuisine Eszter Palágyi has created a fine-dining experience that marries Hungarian family recipes with international trends. The restaurant features locally sourced fish dishes and more experimental signature recipes, like wild pigeon served with beetroot and Ethiopian coffee crumbs.

BISTRO AND BRUNCH
Púder
Ráday utca 8, tel. 06/1-210-7168,
www.puderbar.hu, daily noon-1am,
HUF 1,850-3,950

Púder is an eclectic bistro and bar with a decor that combines the look of ancient Pompeii with quirky local art and dilapidation. The menu mixes up

AROUND BARTÓK BÉLA AVENUE

Running from the Liberty Bridge well into the XI District's Kelenföld Station, Bartók Béla Avenue is a lifeline on the Buda side of the river. The far end takes you past the concrete apartment blocks off the tourist route, and the first stretch until Móricz Zsigmond körtér Feneketlen tó (the "Bottomless Lake") is an exciting mixture of *fin-de-siécle* architecture, contemporary art galleries, alternative cultural centers, vegan street food, and vibrant café culture. The influx of visitors has turned the trendy Inner City areas into a tourist hub. Hip Hungarians now hang out on the other side of the river in cafés like book-lined **Kelet** or historic **Hadik** (once the hangout for the Hungarian literary elite), which has recently undergone a makeover to embrace the trending industrial chic look. Bartók Béla Avenue is the new up-and-coming district, with new cafés and galleries popping up in Art Nouveau buildings each week.

The area around Bartók Béla Avenue is one of the most happening neighborhoods in Buda.

light bites with more substantial bistro food, like pork knuckles with rosemary, or rosé duck breast with arugula mashed potato and cinnamon-plum red wine ragout.

Csiga

Vásár utca 2, tel. 06/30-613-2046,
daily 8am-11:45pm, HUF 1,500-4,000

It's almost impossible to get a seat at Csiga, which attracts a local bohemian crowd of artists and VIII District creatives due to its relaxed ambience. The menu includes soups, salads, and modern takes on Hungarian dishes. It's a great choice for vegetarians, and if you want to eat lunch on a budget, take advantage of their lunch menu that changes weekly. (Call to make a reservation.)

CAFÉS AND CAKE

Lumen

Horánszky utca 5, tel. 06/20-402-2393,
Mon-Fri 8am-midnight, Sat-Sun
10am-midnight, HUF 850-3250

Lumen is a café within the heart of the Palace District that draws in the local arts crowd with its laid-back atmosphere and exhibitions held on-site (focusing mostly on photography). This café has its own roastery. You can get some light bites if you're hungry, like soup and hummus, or daily specials on the lunch menu, like curried vegetable soup and lasagna.

Central Café

Károlyi utca 9, tel. 06/1-266-2110,
www.centralkavehaz.hu, daily 8am-midnight,
HUF 1,800-4,900

This historic coffee house opened in 1887 and was the hub of Hungarian fin de siècle literary life in the 19th and 20th centuries. Writers once gathered up on the mezzanines to scribble away or edit literary journals, but they also mingled with scientists, artists, and composers during their coffee drinking hours. Today this old world café with marble tables, frescoes, and low hanging chandeliers is an elegant spot for breakfast, coffee, or cake. If you're hungry and need fueling up for the day, try the Central 1887 breakfast plate with a substantial selection of roast beef, duck liver paté, smoked salmon, cheese, egg, and more, or you can keep things light with a freshly baked croissant. Or just pick one of the delicious cakes from behind the glass—you really can't go wrong. They also have a restaurant serving Hungarian classics like goulash.

ÓBUDA AND BUDA HILLS
HUNGARIAN
⭐ Náncsi Néni

Ördögárok út 80, tel. 06/1-397-2742,
www.nancsineni.hu, daily noon-11pm,
HUF 2,350-4,780

Náncsi Néni is worth the journey into the leafy Hűvösvölgy area, especially in the summer. It's noted for its exceptional traditional classics (like your Hungarian grandmother would cook), but there are also more creative concoctions, like duck liver marinated in sherry and served with steamed grapes, as well as a number of freshwater fish dishes and steaks. Reservations highly recommended.

Földes Józsi

Bécsi út 31, tel. 06/70-500-0222,
www.foldesjozsietterme.hu, Mon
11:30am-3:30pm, Tue-Sun 11:30am-10pm,
HUF 2,250-4,800

This simple restaurant, established by hotel chef "Joe Earthy" (*Földes Józsi*), serves excellent Hungarian homestyle dishes, with a menu that changes seasonally. *Földes Józsi* is worth the visit if you find yourself on this side of Buda. Try their paprika chicken (or if in season, their goose specials).

BISTRO AND BRUNCH
Villa Bagatelle

Németvölgyi út 17, tel. 06/30-359-6295,
www.villa-bagatelle.com, Mon-Fri 8am-7pm,
Sat-Sun 9am-6pm, HUF 890-3,990

In a beautiful bright villa in the Buda Hills, Villa Bagatelle is a special place to have brunch, well worth the excursion out of town. Make sure you try their coffee, which is made with special care using beans from a local roaster. And try their salmon breakfast, where slices of whole-grain toast are topped with avocado, smoked salmon, and a poached egg. Or go all out and indulge in the champagne breakfast.

Accommodations

Picking the right location really depends on what you are looking for. If you want to be in the heart of the action and just crawl into bed straight from the ruin bars, then stay in the Jewish Quarter. If you want a good night's sleep, avoid anything with "Party Hostel" in the name. If seclusion, nature, and peace and quiet are what you desire, you might check into the Grand Hotel on Margaret Island. Hotels in the Inner City lean toward luxury. Budget options lie further afield in neighborhoods such as the residential area around City Park or out in Óbuda, but they give you the chance to immerse yourself more fully in local life.

It's not unusual to find accommodation in formerly residential buildings (or occupying a floor in a still-residential building), which can provide a less-touristy atmosphere while you're in the city. Most hotels do offer breakfast, but some might charge for it, so double-check before booking.

CASTLE DISTRICT

UNDER €150

Baltazár

Országház utca 31, tel. 06/1-300-7051,
www.baltazarbudapest.com, €95-135 d

This family-owned boutique hotel, with just 11 rooms and suites, is located at the northern end of Castle Hill. This hotel has a bohemian feel with quirky and colorful rooms and vintage furniture. It's noted for its bistro and grill and its wine bar downstairs.

Pest-Buda Design Boutique Hotel

Fortuna utca 3, tel. 06/1-800-9213,
www.pest-buda.com, €90-140 d

One of the oldest hotels in Budapest, the Pest-Buda Design Boutique Hotel opened in 1696. The hotel was renovated in 2016, and it now blends worn wood with a touch of industrial chic and vintage sketches in its 10 individually designed rooms and suites in a three-story house. (Note: there is no elevator, only stairs.) Continental breakfast is available in the popular ground-floor bistro.

€150-250

Art'otel

Bem rakpart 16-19, tel. 06/1-487-9487,
www.artotels.com/budapest-hotel-hu-h-1011/
hunbuart, €135-189 d

This four-star hotel overlooking the Danube banks exhibits 600 works by American artist Donald Sultan, and guests can join a free tour to learn more about the artist and his work.

Art'otel occupies a modern seven-story building with a small Baroque wing inside. The main draw of the hotel is its views, some overlooking the Castle District up the hill, or overlooking the river. There are 75 rooms here, and the hotel offers disabled access and facilities.

Maison Bistro and Hotel

Országház utca 17, tel. 06/1-405-4980,
www.maisonbudapest.hu, €149-179 d

In a Baroque house built upon 15th-century foundations, Maison Bistro and Hotel captures the historical essence of the Castle District. The 17 rooms and suites feature king-size beds, with twins available upon request. Some rooms come with a private garden terrace. Guests are treated to a welcome drink upon arrival.

OVER €250

Hilton

Hess András tér 3, tel. 06/1-889-6600,
www.danubiushotels.com/en/our-hotels-
budapest/hilton-budapest, €280-450 d

The Hilton Budapest incorporates the ruins of a 13th-century Dominican monastery into its design. This Hilton is located by Fisherman's Bastion, and it has 298 rooms and 24 luxury suites, some with views over the Danube. The hotel has its own restaurant (ICON) serving Hungarian and international food, and there's a fitness center on-site. It is also accessible for travelers with disabilities.

LIPÓTVÁROS

€150-250

Kempinski Hotel Corvinus

Erzsébet tér 7-8, tel. 06/1-429-3777,
www.kempinski.com/en/budapest/
hotel-corvinus/welcome, €145-280 d

The Kempinski Hotel Corvinus is next door to the Ritz-Carlton, but it sports a different aesthetic. This modern hotel with an in-house Zen spa and gastronomic quarter puts it on the map. There are 351 rooms, including 35 suites. On-site restaurants include Nobu, an avant-garde fusion of Japanese-Peruvian cuisine, and És Bisztró, serving contemporary Austro-Hungarian cuisine, as well as the Living Room and the Blue Fox Bar.

Hotel President
Hold utca 3, tel. 06/1-510-3400,
www.hotelpresident.hu, €160-199 d
With a rooftop terrace overlooking the Royal Postal Savings Bank and the Hungarian Parliament, Hotel President has some of the best views in the city. This four-star hotel has 152 rooms and two suites, as well as a wellness center with a jet stream pool. The highlight is its rooftop, which serves as a café and a restaurant in the summer and becomes an ice rink in the winter (which is free for guests).

OVER €250
✪ Four Seasons
Széchenyi István tér 5, tel. 1-268-6000,
www.fourseasons.com/budapest, €440-640 d
The Four Seasons Hotel Gresham Palace not only ticks the box for one of the best views in town (facing the Chain Bridge and Buda Castle head-on), but it's also one of the most beautiful Art Nouveau buildings on the Danube. This five-star hotel has 160 rooms (51 of which overlook the Danube) and 19 suites in a palette of cream and ivory. In addition, there's **Kollázs Brasserie & Bar**, its own fine-dining restaurant, and a rooftop spa.

✪ Aria
Hercegprímás utca 5, tel. 06/1-445-4055,
www.ariahotelbudapest.com, €235-425 d
There is a reason that the Aria Hotel

tops numerous lists as one of the world's best hotels. This design hotel was built around an old Inner City townhouse, and it has a musical theme throughout, from its piano key-decorated lobby to its 49 rooms, each of which is named after a musician or composer. Every room comes with its own balcony, and there's a wellness center in the basement. But the real *pièce de résistance* is the rooftop bar overlooking St. Stephen's Basilica. Guests can also relax to live piano music in the lobby while sampling complimentary wine and cheese between 4pm and 6pm.

Ritz-Carlton
Erzsébet tér 9-10, tel. 06/1-429-5500,
www.ritzcarlton.com/en/hotels/europe/
budapest, €390-490 d
The Ritz-Carlton Budapest attracts guests not only with its modern take on old-world luxury, but also with its central location close to Váci utca and the few minutes' walk to the Jewish Quarter. The hotel, occupying the former Adria Palace, emulates the tones of the Danube in a palette of blues and grays. The most beautiful feature in the hotel is the stained-glass dome under the Kupola Lounge. There are 171 rooms and 29 suites. In 2016, the hotel opened a new fitness and wellness center, including a naturally lit pool.

JEWISH QUARTER
UNDER €150
Wombats City Hostel Budapest
Király utca 20, tel. 06/1-883-5005, www.
wombats-hostels.com, €20 dorm bed, €65 d
Wombats City Hostel Budapest is located in the heart of the action in the Jewish Quarter. You can either sleep in a dorm or take a private room in this modern, clean hostel. There is a

24-hour common kitchen and a laundry room, plus social areas. There is also a buffet breakfast on offer.

Roombach Hotel
Rumbach Sebestyén utca 17,
tel. 06/1-413-0253, https://roombach.
accenthotels.com, €85-100 d

Roombach Hotel stands right next to bustling Király utca and Gozsdu Court, but on a peaceful side street opposite the Rumbach Synagogue. This colorful, youthful hotel with ensuite rooms and geometric décor offers a lovely view of a quiet courtyard. This is a great budget option in the city center.

OVER €250
✪ Corinthia Hotel Budapest
Erzsébet körút 43-49, tel. 06/1-479-4000,
www.corinthia.com/en/hotels/budapest,
€125-360 d

Located on the Grand Boulevard, the Corinthia Hotel Budapest possesses a fascinating history. The original mirrored ballroom (as well as a spa) were forgotten for decades, until plans arose to build an underground parking lot. Stories abound in this grand hotel. Behind its original 19th-century façade, you'll find modern luxury, with over 400 rooms in addition to four restaurants, one bar, and a music club. In the marble lobby check out the placard that lists the names of actors, musicians, and other well-known figures who have stayed in the hotel.

New York Palace
Erzsébet körút 9-11, tel. 06/1-886-6118,
www.dahotels.com/new-york-palace-
budapest, €204-280 d

The New York Palace (formerly the Boscolo Budapest) is in an elegant 19th-century building on the Grand Boulevard—and famous for its extravagant New York Café. The hotel's 185 rooms are decorated in an Italian style, with soft, warm tones and lush fabrics. There is a wellness center on-site, with a steam bath and relaxation pool. There's also a fitness center.

AROUND ANDRÁSSY AVENUE
UNDER €150
Kapital Inn Bed and Breakfast
Aradi utca 40, tel. 06/30-915-2029,
www.kapitalinn.com, €89-149 d

This cute boutique hotel is on the top two floors of a classic old apartment block just off Andrássy Avenue. It offers five luxurious rooms with a sleek, modern design. One of the main draws is the stunning rooftop terrace. Rooms go fast at this popular hotel. (Note that there is no elevator in the building.)

€150-250
Hotel Moments
Andrássy út 8, tel. 06/1-611-7000,
www.hotelmomentsbudapest.hu, €199-244 d

Just a few steps from the Hungarian State Opera House, Hotel Moments is centrally located within walking distance of main sights. This four-star hotel has 99 elegant rooms, as well as an on-site Hungarian bistro where a buffet breakfast is served (which also includes gluten-free baked products).

CITY PARK AND AROUND
UNDER €150
Mirage Medic Hotel
Dózsa György út 88, tel. 06/1-400-6158,
www.miragemedichotel.hu, €115-160 d

The Mirage Medic Hotel is in a historic villa on the fringes of City Park. This hotel, owned by a Chinese doctor, offers in-house medical services and holistic remedies ranging from herbalism to acupuncture. The 37 rooms come with mattresses designed to work on pressure points and regulate body temperature. Disabled access rooms are also available.

This is not the usual wellness break (there are no saunas on-site), but if you book for more than two nights, you get a holistic diagnosis from the hotel's Chinese doctors. Even if you're not looking for anything to do with alternative medicine, the value and the location merits a stay.

Budapest Ville Bed and Breakfast

Damjanich utca 32, tel. 06/1-791-9962, www.budapestville.com, €45-80 d

Budapest Ville Bed and Breakfast occupies a floor in a 19th-century apartment block. It features an arched double courtyard in a quiet neighborhood next to City Park. The design follows a vintage chic look, combining modern comforts with nostalgia in its four rooms.

€150-250
Mamaison Hotel Andrassy Budapest

Andrássy út 111, tel. 06/1-462-2100, www.mamaisonandrassy.com, €150-205 d

Mamaison Hotel Andrassy Budapest is on the illustrious boulevard close to City Park. The hotel has 61 rooms and seven suites decorated in warm colors and a modern design to give it the feel of a boutique hotel. A buffet breakfast is served at the on-site La Perle Noire Restaurant for a surplus of €16.

MARGARET ISLAND AND AROUND
UNDER €150
Danubius Grand Hotel Margitsziget

Budapest-Margitsziget, tel. 06/1-889-4700, www.danubiushotels.com/en/our-

hotels-budapest/danubius-grand-hotel-margitsziget, €85-130 d

Margaret Island lies away from the bustle of the city, making sister hotels the Danubius Grand and Hotel Margitsziget relaxing places to stay. For a wellness getaway, guests can use the thermal water spa in the modern part of the hotel, and they can opt for treatments like the salt cave or doctor-prescribed health treatments.

The hotel is in two parts. The original Grand Hotel is a beautiful 19th-century hotel, one of the first in Budapest; the other is a more modern building constructed around the 1960s. The two parts are connected via an underground passage, giving guests easy access to the wellness center.

Aventura Boutique Hostel

Visegrádi utca 12, tel. 06/1-239-0782, www.aventurahostelbudapest.com, €11-14 dorms, €15-30 d per person

This laid-back, family-run hostel takes guests around the world with its themed rooms including India, Africa, and Japan (and outer space). The dorms sleep four to eight people. There are also private apartments available. The dorms link up with a common kitchen. The hostel is in the quiet Újlipót district in Pest, close to Margaret Island and the Grand Boulevard. It's noted for being LGBTQ-friendly as well.

SOUTH BUDA
UNDER €150
Shantee House

Takács Menyhért utca 33, tel. 06/1-385-8946, www.backpackbudapest.hu, €10-16 dorms, €13.50-26 yurt, €39-52 private room

This hostel located in the XI District welcomes visitors with its sense of community. Private rooms and dorms are available, as well as a yurt in the summer. There is a kitchen you can use, with free tea and coffee offered during your stay. There is also a small bar on-site, where you can pick up wine (€3 a bottle) and chilled beer (€1.50 for a 500ml bottle), and smoke some shisha (€3.50) in the garden. Bicycles and skateboards are available for rent (€10 for 24 hours), and there are hammocks in the garden to relax in.

INNER CITY AND SOUTH PEST

UNDER €150
✪ Brody House

Bródy Sándor utca 10, tel. 06/1-266-1211, www.brody.land/brody-house, €80-130 d

This illustrious townhouse in the Palace District started as an artists' studio and bohemian clubhouse before its owners converted it into a boutique hotel. There are 11 shabby-chic rooms featuring work by the artists who once painted there. Breakfast is available (€10), along with an honesty bar and other concierge services. Guests at the hotel get temporary membership to the Brody Studios members' club just off Andrássy Avenue.

Hotel Palazzo Zichy

Lőrincz Pap tér, tel. 06/1-235-4000, www.hotel-palazzo-zichy.hu, 88-150€ d

Once the residence of Count Nándor Zichy, this 19th-century mansion blends rococo stuccos and wrought-iron balustrades with contemporary design—plus a glass pyramid roof. Guests can enjoy a complimentary lavish breakfast or beverages in the lobby bar. There are 80 rooms and a sauna and gym on-site.

the Tinei Room at bohemian boutique hotel Brody House

Bohem Art Hotel

Molnár utca 35, tel. 06/1-327-9020,
www.bohemarthotel.hu, €115-290 d

The Bohem Art Hotel uses the concept of a local art gallery (featuring work by young Hungarian artists). Its 60 hotel rooms are each decorated by a different artist, and guests can choose a room based on the art they like in the building's public gallery. You can enjoy a full American breakfast here, served with sparkling wine.

ÓBUDA AND BUDA HILLS
UNDER €150
Aquincum Hotel

Árpád Fejedelem útja 94, tel.
06/1-436-4100, www.aquincumhotel.com,
€70-120 d

Located close to the historic Baroque squares in Óbuda, the Aquincum Hotel stands right alongside the Danube, overlooking Margaret Island. The hotel has a vast wellness center complex, which is complimentary for guests. It draws its therapeutic thermal water from Margaret Island. There are 310 guest rooms, along with various dining options on-site with a 15 perent discount for hotel guests.

Waltzer Hotel

Némétvölgyi út 110, tel. 06/1-319-1212,
www.hotelwalzer.hu, €35-75 d

This romantic hotel up in the Buda Hills offers the chance to get away from the busy streets of the Inner City, but it is still accessible to town. The hotel, surrounded by lush greenery and picturesque villas, resides in a castle-like building. Guests can dine on Hungarian food in its restaurant and take advantage of the sauna. There is also a wonderful garden on the property.

Information and Services

TOURIST INFORMATION

You can find Budapestinfo (Sütő utca 2, tel. 06/1-486-3300, www.budapestinfo.hu, daily 8am-8pm) Tourist Information Points in various locations in the city: in the Inner City, up at the airport terminal, and in the ice rink building at City Park. Pick up free publications and maps, buy tickets for sights, theater, or opera productions, and get some help on navigating the city from the multilingual staff. These Budapestinfo tourism bureaus are also a good place to buy a Budapest Card.

BUSINESS HOURS

Most shops in Budapest open at 10am and close at 6pm. At one point, shops were required to close on Sundays, but due to popular demand, they reopened. (Note that opening hours may be shorter, and smaller shops and boutiques may not open on Sunday.) Budapest is not a city with seasonal opening hours, unless what you want to visit is an outdoor attraction, where you may find closing time correlates with the hours of sundown.

EMERGENCY NUMBERS

Hungary's emergency number is 112. The average time to answer the phone is five seconds, and the operators speak English. However, it's not the only emergency number available. If you need an ambulance, call 104; fire brigade 105; police 107. There is also a 24-hour English-speaking medical hotline called Falck's SOS: 06/1-2000-100.

CRIME

The main crime risks for tourists are pickpockets and restaurant scams. Take care with your belongings in busy, public spaces and on public transportation. Ask for a menu with a price list when dining out or getting drinks in a bar (especially if you're going for drinks with random girls you've met in the street—this is a classic scam). If you have any problems, you can call the Tourist Police (06/1-438-8080), a 24-hour hotline with English-speaking operators.

HOSPITALS AND PHARMACIES

There are dozens of hospitals in Budapest, usually one for each district. If you're looking for a private option, the Medicover Health Center (Teréz körút 55-57, tel. 06/1-435-3100, www.medicover.hu) has English-speaking doctors and a 24-hour receptionist. FirstMed Centers (Hattyú utca 14, tel. 06/1-224-9090, www.firstmedcenters. com) accepts some US insurance, and has an entirely English-speaking staff.

You can find pharmacies all over Budapest, denoted by a green cross and the word gyógyszertár. Most of them are open for regular shopping hours and close in the evenings and on Sundays, but a few are open 24 hours, like Térez körút 41 and Fővám tér 4 in the central areas in Pest.

FOREIGN CONSULATES

If you have an emergency (like losing your passport or you need consular help), the United States Embassy (Szabadság tér 12, tel. 06/1-475-4400) is located in the city center, close to the Hungarian Parliament. The Canadian Embassy (Ganz utca 12-14, tel.06/1-392-3360) can be found in Buda, along with the British Embassy (Füge utca 5-7, tel. 06/1-266-2888) and the South African Embassy (Gárdonyi Géza út 17, tel. 06/1-392-0999). There is no Australian (Mattiellistraße 2-4, Vienna, tel. +43-1-506-740) or New Zealand Embassy (Mattiellistraße 2-4, Vienna, tel. +43-1-505-3021) in Budapest, so you will have to go to Vienna.

Transportation

GETTING THERE

AIR

Budapest has one international airport, the Ferenc Liszt International Airport (BUD, tel. 06/1-296-7000, www.bud.hu), sometimes known by its former name of Ferihegy Airport, located in the southeastern suburbs. There are two terminals, but terminal 1 has been closed since 2012, so all flights go in and out of 2A and 2B.

Airport Transportation

Getting to and from the airport is easy. For door-to-door service, the miniBUD (tel. 06/1-550-0000, www.minibud.hu, HUF 4,900 one-way to the city center) minibus service offers easy access to your hotel around the clock. miniBUD customer service counters can be found as soon as you exit arrivals. You may have to wait up to 30 minutes for a minibus; they will either call your name or your Budapest address. The journey time depends on your destination in the city, the traffic, or the number of passengers with you (the bus stops door-to-door in the neighborhood), so account for around 30 to 60 minutes for the journey into town. You can get return tickets when you buy your ticket at arrivals, or you can book online (latest: five hours before departure).

Another option is to take the 100E bus (HUF 900), which will take you directly into the city center. The buses usually run on a half-hourly basis (from 4am to 11:30pm) and take 30 minutes to get downtown.

A taxi from the airport can cost HUF 5,500-7,000 and takes around 30 minutes to reach the city center.

TRAIN

Budapest has four main train stations. Keleti (Eastern) Train Station (metro lines 2 and 4) is the main one. The others are the Nyugati (Western) Train Station (metro 3), Déli (Southern) Train Station (metro 2), and Kelenföld (metro 4). Except for Kelenföld, all are located in the city center with good transport connections by metro, trams, and buses.

There are a number of trains that go to and from Budapest and other destinations in Hungary and abroad. You can buy tickets and check timetables from MÁV (www.mav.hu) for both international and domestic connections. If you buy an international train ticket from Budapest online, you will get a code, and you'll need to print it from the ticket machine. You can go to the international desks at the Nyugati and Keleti Train Stations.

BUS

The main bus station for international journeys is Népliget Bus Station, which connects to metro line 3. Flixbus, in collaboration with the domestic Volánbusz company (http://nemzetkozi.volanbusz.hu/en), is the most reliable international bus service to other European destinations.

CAR

There are five motorways and four main roads in Hungary, with eight starting from Budapest. If you're planning to drive on the motorway, you must buy a motorway sticker (HUF 3,000 for a 10-day sticker), available at the border crossing or gas stations. The M1 motorway connects

DON'T FORGET TO VALIDATE!

Unless you have a Budapest Card or a 24-hour or longer pass, you will need to **validate your bus, metro, or tram ticket** by punching it in a slotted box. Find these boxes at metro entrances and onboard the tram and bus. Some older trams require you to put the ticket in vertically and pull it down hard so the ticket punches. **Double-check for the time stamp or punch marks,** as some machines may run out of ink and ticket validation won't be visible.

Ticket inspectors (sometimes in uniform, sometimes plain-clothed with a purple armband) check transport at random for tickets. **Keep your validated tickets with you at all times** as you can be inspected at any point—even when exiting the metro. If you are caught without a ticket, ticket inspectors can get unpleasant and charge a fine of HUF 8,000, which you can pay on the spot or at designated BKK Customer Service Centers (such as Rumbach Sebestyén utca 19-21 or Akácfa utca 22) within two days. You can also pay by bank transfer if you exceed the two-day threshold, but this will cost more (HUF 16,000).

There are a few "fake" ticket inspectors who may insist on a cash fine. If you are suspicious, insist on paying at the BKK Customer Service Centers. (Paying by transfer after two days is more expensive, but at least you'll know that you're not just giving money to someone taking advantage of the system.) If you can get to a customer service center as soon as possible, the fine should be the same as paying immediately.

If you have a pass and left it at the hotel, you can request a form and pay a reduced fine of HUF 2,000 at the BKK Customer Service Center when you prove you had a pass. Typically, inspectors will ask you for identification, and you may be asked to get off the tram/bus/metro if you don't have a validated ticket.

Budapest to Vienna and Prague. The M3 will take you out of the city toward Eger or Gödöllő and all the way to the Ukrainian border. The M7 heads toward Lake Balaton, and the M5 heads down toward the Serbian border. The Hungarian Highway Code (KRESZ) is similar to the rest of the EU, with speed limits within the cities at 50 km/h (30 mph) and on the motorways at 130 km/h (80 mph). Front and rear seat belts are compulsory, and mobile phones must be used with a hands-free kit.

GETTING AROUND

Budapest is a relatively compact city that's easy to get around on foot or with public transport operated by Budapest's public transit network, the Budapesti Közlekedési Központ (BKK, www.bkk.hu). You have plenty of modes to choose from: metro, bus, tram, and trolleybus. Just note that single-use tickets are not valid for transfers—except on the metro.

TRANSIT PASSES

You can buy transit passes at the kiosk in the metro or from purple machines next to the bus, tram, or metro. Passes can be valid for 24 hours (HUF 1,650), 72 hours (HUF 4,150), or 7 days (HUF 4,950) and can be used on all forms of transport, except the BKK boat on

entrance to Metro on Vörösmarty tér

weekends. Single tickets cost HUF 350 or HUF 3,000 for a block of 10.

METRO

Budapest has four metro lines denoted by numbers and colors. The yellow metro line 1 runs from Vörösmarty tér, traversing the entire stretch of Andrássy Avenue to City Park. The red metro line 2 passes under the Danube and the city center. The blue line metro 3 runs from the suburbs in northern Pest into the city center and up toward the airport. The newest line, green metro 4, goes between the Keleti and Kelenföld Train Stations, crossing from Pest into South Buda. You can change between metro lines at Deák Ferenc tér (lines 1, 2, 3), Kálvin tér (lines 3 and 4), and Keleti pályaudvar (lines 2 and 4). At the time of writing there were plans to construct a fifth metro line running from Szentendre to Csepel, Ráckeve. The current HÉV H5 suburban train line is being called "Metro 5" as of September 2019, but this won't affect development.

Metros operate between 4:30am and 11:30pm daily.

TRAM, BUS, AND TROLLEYBUS

The tram is the easiest and quickest way to get around Budapest. Lines 4 and 6 running along the Grand Boulevard are the most efficient for getting from Buda to Pest and take you all the way around the center—and line 6 runs all night long (most trams run at the same time as the metro, 4:30am-11:30pm). Other tram lines, like 2 or 41, are a scenic way of seeing the city. Buses and trolleybuses are less attractive for travelers, but the buses are efficient and will take you further out of the city than the tram. The red trolleybuses only really operate in Pest and tend to take you out into the more residential areas.

BOAT

In the summer, you can take BKK's public boat along the Danube, which is free on weekdays with a travel pass, or HUF 750 for a single ticket or on the weekends. There are docks all along the Danube, with some going as far as Rómaifürdő.

TAXI

Avoid hailing a taxi, as there are some rogue operators who take advantage of tourists. Instead, call a reputable taxi company, like City Taxi (tel. 06/1-211-1111), Fő Taxi (tel. 06/1-222-2222), Taxi Plus (tel. 06/1-888-8888), Taxi 6x6 (tel. 06/1-666-6666), or use an app like Taxify.

GÖDÖLLŐ

Itinerary Idea 136
Sights 137
Food 140
Transportation 141

Just outside Budapest, the town of Gödöllő (pop. 35,000) dates back to the 14th century and is famous for its beautiful Habsburg summer palace. This small town is a leafy, peaceful suburb of the capital and makes the perfect day or half-day trip. Gödöllő centers around the baroque palace that once belonged to the Austro-Hungarian emperor Franz Joseph I and his wife, Elisabeth. You'll also find a Baroque theater and a bunker from World War II hidden in the grounds of the palace. Beyond the chateau,

HIGHLIGHTS

✪ **GÖDÖLLŐ ROYAL PALACE:** This Baroque chateau surrounded by lush gardens once functioned as the summer palace for the Habsburg emperor and empress (page 137).

✪ **BAROQUE THEATER:** Tour Hungary's oldest functioning theater, located within the Royal Palace (page 139).

✪ **HORTHY'S BUNKER:** Step back into the 1940s as you descend into this secret bunker beneath the palace, built to be a military command center during World War II (page 139).

the residential town is covered with green parks, arboretums, and tree-lined streets.

ORIENTATION

Gödöllő is a compact, walkable town, and most of the sights are situated within the palace grounds.

PLANNING YOUR TIME

Gödöllő is just a half hour from Budapest, so it's easy to make it a day trip, or even a half-day trip. Note that the Baroque Theater is only open Saturday and Sunday.

You could combine the trip with Eger, which is an hour and a half from Budapest and on the same train route

as Gödöllő. However, I would only recommend doing both destinations if you're spending the night in Eger. There are no luggage storage facilities in Gödöllő station (or anywhere else in town), so only consider combining the two places if you're traveling light.

TOURIST INFORMATION

You can find a tourist information center with all the basic information you need at Tourinform (Ady Endre sétány, Royal Palace, tel. 06/28-415-402, www.tourinformgodolloikisterseg.hu, Mon-Fri 10am-4pm, Sat-Sun 10am-5pm), just next to the ticket office inside the Royal Palace.

Gödöllő is a small town and relatively easy to walk around. Although the main draw is the palace, there are a few attractive squares and public spaces.

Itinerary Idea

It's enough to spend a day or even half a day in Gödöllő. I'd recommend having a hearty brunch back in Budapest before grabbing the metro 2 to Örs Vezér Tér and then the HÉV number 8 suburban train. If you want to do the Baroque Theater (Sat. and Sun. only) and Horthy's Bunker, call the Royal Palace to find out when there are tour slots available (in peak seasons, groups get priority to visit these sites, so you may not be able to get in without a little planning, and the time slots on the website are not set in stone). Your itinerary will depend on the times of these tours, so use this as a rough guide to work around that.

ESSENTIAL GÖDÖLLŐ

1 Head straight to the **Gödöllő Royal Palace.** Buy the tickets for the museum and the guided tours at the main ticket office, and head up to the museum for a journey back into the palace's history. If you're done and need to wait for the tour, explore the chateau grounds for great views of the palace (and photo ops).

2 Pay a visit to the **Baroque Theater.** This will take 30 minutes with a guide, and you'll get some fascinating insight into this historic little theater.

3 Join the tour for **Horthy's Bunker,** which will take another 30 minutes.

4 Once you're finished with the sites at the Royal Palace, head due north

Gödöllő

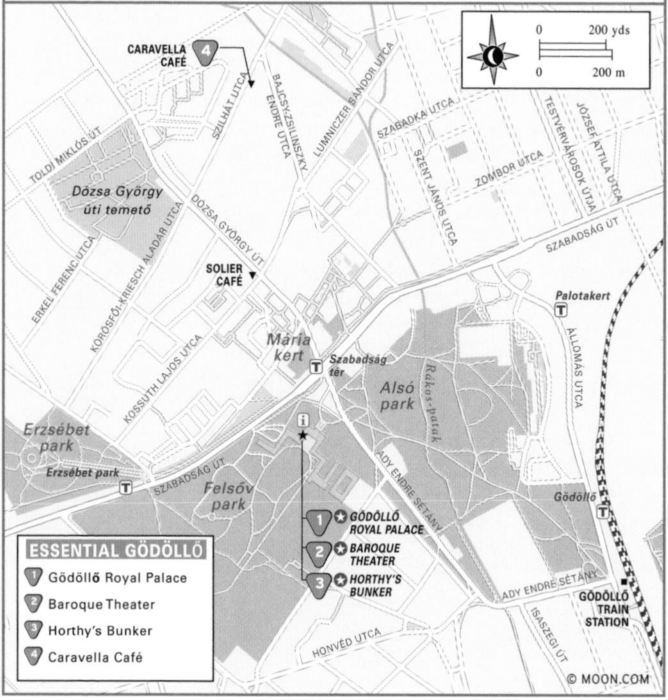

CARAVELLA CAFÉ 4

ESSENTIAL GÖDÖLLŐ
1. Gödöllő Royal Palace
2. Baroque Theater
3. Horthy's Bunker
4. Caravella Café

1. GÖDÖLLŐ ROYAL PALACE
2. BAROQUE THEATER
3. HORTHY'S BUNKER

to **Caravella Café.** It's a 15-minute walk and well worth the trek for their cakes and the magical garden. Take it easy, drink a coffee, enjoy a few cakes, and maybe pet one of the cats before you head back to the suburban train to go back to Budapest.

Sights

Note that Horthy's Bunker and the Baroque Theater can only be visited if the schedule is not full with group tours. Group tours take priority, so in peak season there is a chance you won't be able to enter. It's best to call the museum that morning to enquire about availability.

TOP EXPERIENCE

✪ GÖDÖLLŐ ROYAL PALACE

Grassalkovich-kastély 5852, Ady Endre sétány, tel. 06/28-410-124, www.kiralyikastely.hu, Mon-Thu 10am-4pm, Fri-Sun 10am-5pm Feb-Mar, Mon-Thu

10am-5pm, Fri.-Sun. 10am-6pm Apr-Nov, HUF 2,600

Gödöllő Royal Palace was one of the many summer residences for Emperor Franz Joseph and his wife, Elisabeth, aka Sisi. Sisi loved Hungary and championed the Hungarians' cause for their rights within the Austrian Empire. Gödöllő was the one of Sisi's favorite places. The palace is one of the most important monuments in Hungary, and it predates its celebrity Habsburg owners. Count Antal Grassalkovich built the chateau in the 18th century, but once the male line of the family died out it passed into royal hands and became the official Hungarian residence for the Austro-Hungarian emperors. Under the Soviet communists, it functioned as an old people's home. It reopened to the public as a museum in the 1990s.

You enter the palace from the leafy Ady Endre sétany, up the winged steps that lead to the white entrance peppered with the odd bit of gold leaf. The ticket office is on the right. Once you've got your ticket, take the main stairs up to see the permanent collection. You walk through the old apartments once belonging to Franz Joseph and Sisi, a network of 23 colorful rooms, each decorated in different colors of damask, velvet, and silk, some in royal crimson and others in shades of lavender. Keep an eye out for a few curiosities, such as the large bear on the floor of Emperor Franz Joseph's study, the colorful ceramic stove featuring fruit and pastoral scenes in his reception rooms next door, and the pink marble-clad room where Empress Maria Theresia stayed in 1751.

The palace grounds can be visited without a ticket.

Emperor Franz Joseph's study in the Gödöllő Royal Palace

Make sure you wander through the gardens, where you'll find an arboretum, statues, and acres of protected parkland. You could easily spend an afternoon relaxing in the gardens alone.

✪ Baroque Theater

Grassalkovich-kastély 5852, Ady Endre sétány, tel. 06/28-410-124, www.kiralyikastely.hu, guided tours only on Sat and Sun 10:30am, 11:30am, 2:30pm, 3:30pm, HUF 1,600 (HUF 1,200 with palace admission)

The old Baroque Theater is tucked inside the southern wing of the palace. Count Grassalkovich II built the theater, which is one of the oldest stone theaters in Hungary, in the 1700s. It measures 25 meters (82 feet) long, 8 meters (26 feet) wide, and 9.5 meters (31 feet) high, and it wasn't purpose built: the former three-story wing was reconstructed to accommodate the theater. Although it wasn't used when the Habsburgs were in residence, it was reconstructed in 2003 and sometimes holds performances today.

You can only visit the theater with a guide. Tours (30 minutes) run on the weekends at designated times. The tour takes you up on the stage, which still uses the same system of painted sets as it did when it was built, and below stage where you can see the complex pulley system that runs all that theatrical magic.

✪ Horthy's Bunker

Grassalkovich-kastély 5852, Ady Endre sétány, tel. 06/28-410-124, www.kiralyikastely.hu, guided tours only on Sat and Sun 10:30am, 11:30am, 2:30pm, 3:30pm, HUF 1,400

Hidden under the southern side of the palace, below Queen Elizabeth's Garden, you'll find the bunker once belonging to Miklós Horthy, an admiral who served as Hungary's Regent from 1920 to 1944. This bunker located some 10 meters (33 feet) underground was built in 1944 and can fit 20 people in its 55-square-meter (600-square-foot) space. Horthy's plan for the bunker was it would operate as a military headquarters. You enter the bunker from inside the palace, descending a narrow staircase that takes you into the two rooms and a narrow corridor. One of the rooms has been reconstructed with furniture from the period, giving you a glimpse at how the bunker looked and the equipment

Descend below ground to this 1940s bunker that once belonged to Admiral Horthy.

they planned to use down there. There is also an exhibition about the bunker's history and its renovation. And if you can smell a hint of gasoline, that's because the Soviet troops filled the bunker with gasoline in the 1950s—and no one's been able to get rid of the odor.

Food

Gödöllő is a compact town, so most places will take 10 minutes or less to reach on foot from the palace. You could grab an early lunch in Budapest, or bring a picnic with you to one of the many parks surrounding the palace. However, I highly recommend heading to the Caravalla Café, even if it feels a little out of the way (although just a 10-minute walk). It's a small oasis where you could relax for the day.

CAFÉ AND RESTAURANT
Solier

Dózsa György út 13, tel. 06/20-350-4011, www.solier.hu, Sun-Mon 11:30am-9pm, Tue-Sat 11:30am-10pm, HUF 2,490-4,890

Solier provides day-trippers a chance to taste gourmet dishes in its chic two-story café and restaurant. The ground-floor café offers tempting and delicious cakes baked on site, whereas the upstairs restaurant with views over the downtown area is elegant and simple in hues of peach and gray, punctuated by fairy lights and contemporary art. The food, however, is anything but minimalist, with each dish presented artfully. Try the chef's recommendation, a seasonal menu that changes regularly. There is also a budget-friendly daily menu on weekdays.

CAKES
✪ Caravella Café

Szilhát utca 40, tel. 06/28-746-297, www.caravellagastro.hu, Wed-Sun 10am-6pm, cakes HUF 450-600

Caravella specializes in homemade cakes and good coffee, and it also hosts literary events, baking workshops, and whiskey tasting nights. The café resides in a farm house with a charming vintage interior decked out with quirky retro objects like scales dangling from a lantern and an old ship's rudder. In the summer, take a seat in the magical little garden. Try the gluten-free *Mandulás piskóta*, a delicious almond-flour cake, or the tasty egg- and dairy-free caramelized cinnamon, apple, and walnut cake. Feline lovers will love the little tabby who comes and goes.

Grab a coffee and homemade cake in this little oasis in Gödöllő.

Transportation

GETTING THERE

The easiest way to get to Gödöllő is to take the local suburban train, which puts you down right next to the Royal Palace. The bus is also a good alternative, but it may be confusing for a non-Hungarian speaker to navigate as there are many stops inside the town. I would only recommend this option for the more adventurous traveler.

TRAIN

Trains operated by MAV run three times an hour from Keleti train station and take between 25 and 40 minutes to reach Gödöllő, depending on which train you catch. Faster trains are HUF 896, whereas the slower services cost HUF 745. You can also take the local suburban train (HÉV H8, but check that it goes to Gödöllő—some lines go only as far as Kerepes), which leaves from Örs Vezér tere (take metro 2 to the end of the line). This line runs four times an hour and will drop you right next to the Royal Palace if you get off at Gödöllő Szabadság tér, but it does take 45 minutes to get there. If you have a metro pass, you only need to pay for the extension ticket, which is HUF 370.

For those walking from the train station, follow Ady Endre sétany to reach the palace (about 15 minutes). You can get a taxi if you prefer not to walk; try Szabad Taxi (06/28-410-410).

BUS

Direct buses operated by Volánbusz run two or three times an hour from the Stadion Bus Station (take metro 2 to Puskás Ferenc Stadion) and take 30-40 minutes (HUF 465 one-way). Get off at the stop called Gödöllő Szökőkút, and walk south down the main road for 5 minutes to reach the palace.

CAR

From Budapest, drive 30 kilometers (19 miles) northeast on the M3 to reach Gödöllő. The drive takes around 35 minutes. Parking in the town costs around HUF 250 per hour.

LEAVING GÖDÖLLŐ

Trains and buses back to Budapest leave as late as 10pm; however, since most of the main sites close around 6pm, you shouldn't have a problem getting transport back to the capital.

SZENTENDRE

Itinerary Idea 144
Sights 146
Shopping 148
Food 150
Accommodations 151
Transportation 151

For a low-maintenance day trip

from Budapest, hop a train or boat to Szentendre (pop. 25,000). In the 18th century, the town had a thriving Serbian community, but it's also known for being an artists' colony since the 1920s and still sports the bohemian atmosphere, with hidden art and ceramic workshops tucked away in the town's courtyards and galleries. Shortly after getting off the train, or even off the boat, you'll find yourself wandering cobbled streets lined with stalls selling antiques and artists painting canvases set up on the sidewalk. Colorful houses

HIGHLIGHTS

✪ **BLAGOVEŠTENSKA ORTHODOX CHURCH:** This Baroque Orthodox church captures the village's Serbian heritage with its Eastern icons around the altar area (page 147).

✪ **ART MILL:** Located in in a converted saw mill, the Art Mill is one of the best temporary art exhibition halls in the country (page 147).

✪ **HUNGARIAN OPEN AIR MUSEUM:** Explore rural Hungarian life in this open-air museum that's divided up into sections representing different regions in the country (page 147).

✪ **SHOPPING ON BOGDÁNYI STREET AND DUMTSA JENŐ ROAD:** Pick up some handicrafts, artwork, or locally designed items from one of the many shops on these vibrant streets (page 148).

undulate under white church towers in warm tones from honeydew to claret red. It can get a little crowded in the summer months when visitors look for an easy way to escape the heat in the city, but in the spring and fall it's a lovely day trip. Since it's so close, you can also just visit for half a day if you fancy a change in scenery.

ORIENTATION

Szentendre is easy to navigate on foot, but most of the public transport will put you on the edge of the town. From there it takes 15 minutes to walk to the center, to Blagoveštenska Church and Fő tér, the main public square. Most of the sites are located around Fő tér or within 10 minutes' walk; however, the Hungarian Open Air Museum is a little out of town, and you will need a bus or a taxi to get there.

PLANNING YOUR TIME

It takes 40 minutes on the suburban train to reach Szentendre from Battyányi tér, and you only need a day or half a day to visit the town. However, since Szentendre is on the Danube Bend, you could combine it with a trip to one of the other nearby towns, like Visegrád (there is a direct bus from the bus station, which takes 45 minutes). Note that no luggage storage is available at the transit stations in town.

Fő tér is the colorful heart of this former artist's colony.

Itinerary Idea

You won't need more than a day in Szentendre. It's best to stroll along the cobbled streets or along the Danube Banks and just soak in the atmosphere of this former art colony. However, you could easily spend a whole day at the Hungarian Open Air Museum, so if you want to include it, start early.

ESSENTIAL SZENTENDRE

1 From the train station, grab the 878 bus to the stop marked Szentendre Skanzen. (Alternatively, you could get a taxi.) Your first stop, the **Hungarian Open Air Museum**, is just across the road from the bus stop. Expect to spend a couple of hours here. If you get here before the hour (the train goes on the hour), get the vintage Skanzen train to the end of the vast complex and work your way back to the entrance.

2 Get the bus back to the train station and head into town along the cobbled Kossuth Lajos street. Keep heading north until you get to Fő tér. Grab lunch at **Mjam.**

3 After lunch pay a visit to the **Blagoveštenska Orthodox Church** and explore the Eastern icons within.

4 Hike up the hill leading up to Templom tér and **St. John the Baptist Catholic Church** for views over the village.

5 Come down the hill and explore the shops along Bogdányi út, like the **Palmetta Design Gallery & Shop.**

6 **Return to Budapest by boat** in the summer if you can: the downstream journey is quicker than the one to reach Szentendre and takes only 50 minutes. The boat departs at 5pm. Otherwise, walk back to the suburban railway station.

Szentendre

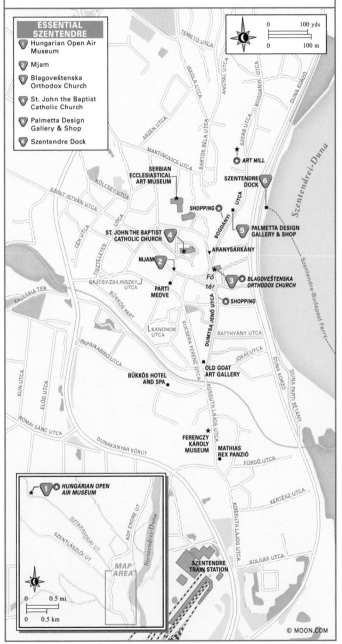

ESSENTIAL SZENTENDRE

1. Hungarian Open Air Museum
2. Mjam
3. Blagoveštenska Orthodox Church
4. St. John the Baptist Catholic Church
5. Palmetta Design Gallery & Shop
6. Szentendre Dock

| 0 | 100 yds |
| 0 | 100 m |

TEMETŐ UTCA

ISKOLA UTCA

ANGYAL UTCA

BOGDÁNYI UTCA

DUNA KORZÓ

Szentendrei-Duna

ARZÉN UTCA

BARTÓK BÉLA UTCA

SZERB UTCA

MARTINOVICS UTCA

★ ART MILL

KÖLCSEY UTCA

SERBIAN ECCLESIASTICAL ART MUSEUM ★

SZENTENDRE DOCK ⑥

SZENT ISTVÁN UTCA

UTCA

SHOPPING ✪

BOGDÁNYI UTCA

PALMETTA DESIGN GALLERY & SHOP ⑤

CÉH UTCA

ST. JOHN THE BAPTIST CATHOLIC CHURCH ④ ★

TISZTELETES

MJAM ②

ARANYSÁRKÁNY

Fő tér

BLAGOVEŠTENSKA ③ ✪ ORTHODOX CHURCH

Szentendrei-Budapest Ferry

KALVÁRIA TÉR

BAJCSY-ZSILINSZKY UTCA

BÜKKÖS PART

PARTI MEDVE

DUMTSA JENŐ UTCA

SHOPPING ✪

PAPRIKABÍRÓ UTCA

KANONOK UTCA

KUCSERA FERENC UTCA

BATTHYÁNY UTCA

DUNA KORZÓ

DUNA PARTI SÉTÁNY

JÓKAI UTCA

KUN UTCA

ELŐD UTCA

OLD GOAT ART GALLERY ✪

BÜKKÖS HOTEL AND SPA ●

KOSSUTH LAJOS UTCA

RÓMAI SÁNC UTCA

DUNAKANYAR KÖRÚT

FERENCZY KÁROLY MUSEUM ★

MATHIAS REX PANZIÓ ●

FÜRDŐ UTCA

KERTÉSZ UTCA

SZENTENDRE
ITINERARY IDEA

① ★ HUNGARIAN OPEN AIR MUSEUM

SZTARAVODAI ÚT

SZENTLÁSZLÓI ÚT

ADY ENDRE ÚT

Szentendrei-Duna

MAP AREA

| 0 | 0.5 mi |
| 0 | 0.5 km |

KOSSUTH LAJOS UTCA

BOLGÁR UTCA

SZENTENDRE TRAIN STATION

© MOON.COM

145

Sights

Although Szentendre is a city you can appreciate simply by getting lost in the narrow, steep, back streets around **St. John the Baptist Catholic Church** (Templom tér, Vár Domb, Tue-Sun 10am-5pm) or by taking a stroll along the Danube, there is plenty to keep you busy for the day.

FERENCZY MUSEUM

Kossuth Lajos utca 5, tel. 06/26-779-6657,
www.muzeumicentrum.hu,
Tue-Sun 10am-6pm, HUF 1,400

When arriving by the local suburban train or by bus, the Ferenczy Museum is the first museum you'll reach on your way into town. This 18th-century mansion with canary-yellow walls once belonged to the Hungarian Impressionist artist Károly Ferenczy and his family. The museum spreads over three floors and hones in on the local art history, with works from Ferenczy and other Szentendre-based artists. Head to the second floor to see work by the founders of the 1920s artists' settlement known as "The Eight," along with interesting temporary exhibitions.

This museum is part of the Ferenczy Museum Center, a network of 10 museums scattered around Szentendre, but being on the way into the town, it's a good place to get your bearings and figure out your own art itinerary.

Blagoveštenska Church

✪ BLAGOVEŠTENSKA ORTHODOX CHURCH

Fő tér, tel. 06/26-310-554,
Tue-Sun 10am-5pm, HUF 400

You know you've reached the heart of Szentendre when you see the Blagoveštenska Church. This Baroque building looks like your average 18th-century Hungarian church on the outside, but you'll find an ornate Serbian Orthodox heart within. The church served the Serbian community residing in Szentendre between the 14th and 19th centuries, and its heritage shows through the wooden paneling varnished in black with accents of gold and the traditional Eastern icons around the altar.

SERBIAN ECCLESIASTICAL ART MUSEUM

Pátriárka utca 5, tel. 06/26-312-399,
Tue-Sun 10am-6pm, HUF 700

Explore Szentendre's Serbian heritage through the collection of sacred objects and icons on display at the Serbian Ecclesiastical Art Museum. It's a small private museum, made up of only two large rooms on two floors with an interesting display of iconography, including a 14th-century glass painting depicting the crucifixion. Most of the collection dates back to the 18th and 19th centuries. Make sure you stop to look at the defaced portrait of Christ hanging on the wall on the upstairs floor—legend has it that an anti-Habsburg mercenary slashed it in a drunken rage, and when told of his deplorable action once sobered up, he threw himself in the Danube and drowned.

✪ ART MILL

Bogdányi utca 32, tel. 06/20-779-6657,
www.muzeumicentrum.hu, Tue-Sun
10am-6pm, HUF 1,400

Don't let its remote location deceive you: the Art Mill, which occupies three floors of a converted 19th-century red-brick saw mill, is one of Hungary's most important modern art centers, with temporary exhibitions from both local and international artists. You'll find it on the far northern side of town, but worth the scenic 1.4-kilometer (about 1 mile) walk to see its diverse displays of light and sound installations, cutting-edge photography, and multimedia art as well as more traditional art forms like painting and sculpture. You can catch a glimpse of local art here, as it's the central exhibition place for artists living and working in the town.

The Art Mill hosts modern art exhibitions.

✪ HUNGARIAN OPEN AIR MUSEUM

Skanzen, Sztaravodai út, tel. 06/26-502-537,
www.skanzen.hu Tue-Sun 10am-5pm
Apr-Nov, HUF 2,000

If you want to get a taste for village life in rural Hungary, then make the trek up to the Hungarian Open Air Museum. The museum spreads out over 46 hectares (114 acres) divided into areas representing different regions within Hungary, so you can take a trip from the Great Plains to a village in Transdanubia in just one afternoon.

whitewashed village replica inspired by the countryside of north Balaton

Wander by whitewashed farmhouses topped with thatched roofs and sweeping windmills, peppered with a few churches and bell towers. Slip inside the houses for a glimpse of rural life, with rooms decked out with hand-painted ceramics, wooden furniture, and colorful embroidered fabrics. Some of the buildings feature actors in period dress, recreating roles like the blacksmith, store clerk, or school teacher to give you an immersive experience in old Hungarian life. You can also take a train ride through "Hungary"—and through time—on the Skanzen Train (www.skanzen.

hu/en/plan-your-visit/good-to-know/ skanzen-train, HUF 500, departures from the Railway Station Building 10am-4pm on the hour), which dates back to 1927 (but is fully renovated). If you're lucky to make it for one of the days when a fair takes place, usually on the weekends and around festivals, you may catch local artisans and craftspeople around selling unique souvenirs such as embroidered fabrics or decorated gingerbread hearts.

To get to the Hungarian Open Air Museum, grab the bus operated by Volánbusz 878 (on weekdays) and 879 (on weekends) next to the local train station, usually going from bay 7. The bus takes around 20 minutes and costs HUF 230. A taxi will set you back around HUF 3,000. The museum is only open from spring to fall.

Skanzen, an open-air ethnographic museum

Shopping

SHOPPING DISTRICTS
✪ BOGDÁNYI STREET AND DUMTSA JENŐ ROAD

Szentendre's arts and crafts shopping scene buzzes through the streets clustered around Fő tér and the Orthodox Church, particularly on **Bogdányi Street** and **Dumtsa Jenő Road.** Shops selling folk crafts, contemporary design, and fine art gather along these cobbled streets, and painters usually sit on the sidewalk putting

Szentendre is a great spot to do a bit of shopping.

their brush to the easel with stacks of their paintings propped against the yellow- or ochre-colored walls, ready for you to buy one.

GALLERIES

Palmetta Design Gallery & Shop

Bogdányi út 14, tel. 06/26-313-649, www.palmettadesign.hu, daily 10am-6pm

Couple István and Anna Regős established the Palmetta Design Gallery back in 1998 in a 200-year-old wine cellar under their house at the heart of Szentendre. Twenty years later their mission to create a space dedicated to Hungarian and international design lives on—locals and tourists flock through the doorway of their Baroque house and down the stone steps to visit their showroom. Pick up one of Anna Regős's hand-woven handbags or peruse curiosities from other designers, such as FruFru's matchboxes that double as fridge magnets featuring Hungarian landscapes,

or notepads with updated motifs of Hungarian folk art.

Parti Medve

Városház tér 4, tel. 06/20-254-3729, Mon-Fri 7:45am-6:45pm

Parti Medve is the multitasking sanctuary in the Szentendre shopping scene, occupying a two-story Baroque townhouse opposite the City Hall, where you'll find a café, gallery, and bookshop on site. A great place to take the kids, it has toys and books for adults and kids—in English, too—as well as art for sale. Grab a table on the terrace or wander up the spiral staircase to the indoor café for a cup of tea or coffee, before taking home a book, mug, bag, plushy toy, or a local piece of art.

Old Goat Art Gallery

Dumtsa Jenő utca 15, tel. 06/30-523-9184, daily 11am-6pm

This charming gallery run by an artist husband-and-wife pair, Hungarian

Eszter Györy and American Osiris O'Connor, has a new-age vibe with colorful surreal paintings and "Soul Angels," angel-shaped statuettes made from alabaster sometimes decorated with paint, Swarovski stones, Bohemian crystals, and Murano glass. Each angel comes with a birth certificate and a number—their "adopter" gets to name them. You can also pick up handcrafted metal pendants and rings. Most of the art work and sculptures are created by the couple, who are happy to chat about their art when you visit the shop.

souvenir shop in Szentendre

Food

HUNGARIAN
Aranysárkány

Alkotmány utca 1/a, tel. 06/26-301-479, www.aranysarkany.hu, daily noon-10pm, HUF 2,500-5,900

The name Aranysárkány, meaning Golden Dragon, may evoke Chinese food but actually carries usual Hungarian favorites from goulash soup to wild boar ragout, plus a few non-Hungarian wildcards such as Serbian dishes. They have a fun variation of a personal Hungarian favorite, fried cheese, that uses breaded port salut, smoked and non-smoked brie, cranberry jam, and tartar sauce. Forgot your reading glasses and struggling with the menu? No worries—they have a selection of prescription glasses in an old tea box you can borrow! The atmosphere here is intimate and cozy, with rusty carpet weaves and vintage brass pots and pans decorating the walls.

INTERNATIONAL
Mjam

Városház tér 2, tel. 06/70-440-3700, daily 11am-10pm, entrées HUF 2,500-4,750

You will find an abundance of paprika-laden restaurants scattered around Szentendre, but if you want something a little different that gets away from the violin music and goulash, then try Mjam. From the outside,

Mjam restaurant

it looks like your typical Baroque townhouse, but inside this breezy, minimalist restaurant you can tuck into a bold Caribbean fusion menu, with items such as duck breast smoked with tea leaves.

Accommodations

Bükkös Hotel & Spa

Bükkös Part 16, tel. 06/26-501-360, www.bukkoshotel.hu, HUF 25,000-35,000 d including breakfast

Just off the Danube Promenade, the Bükkös Hotel and Spa offers a wellness retreat and an atmospheric spa with relaxing mood lighting where you'll find a hot tub, saunas, steam bath, and even an ice room. There are 22 cozy rooms with views over the town or the Bükkös stream. The décor is modern and clean, mostly white with a pop of neutral colors. A full buffet breakfast—with sparkling wine—is included in the price, plus the option to go half board, meaning breakfast and dinner is included.

Mathias Rex

Kossuth Lajos utca 16, tel. 06/26-505-572, www.mathiasrexhotel.hu, HUF 16,500 d including breakfast

This boutique hotel is housed in a historic building in the heart of Szentendre's old town. The aesthetic is minimalism meets rustic living, where each room is decorated with elegant wood furniture, colorful woven rugs, and large windows letting in lots of light. A delicious breakfast is included in the price, with cold cuts, cheese, rolls, and sliced pepper and cucumber.

Mathias Rex hotel

Transportation

GETTING THERE

Szentendre is a popular day trip from Budapest since it's so easy to get to from the city center. The journey by train is the most comfortable. The boat is the slowest way to get there but allows you to take in the scenery along the Danube, including Budapest's landmarks and the tree-covered Danube islands. Also, you can cut out all the walking from the train and bus station as the boat will put you down in the center.

CYCLING UP THE DANUBE

Ride down the EuroVelo 6 route, one of Europe's most famous and longest cycling routes, at least for part of the way. This over-4,000-km (2,500-mi) route following many of Europe's famous rivers runs along most of the Danube, but you don't have to ride the entire route to enjoy the riverside views from the bike path. Rent a bike, get out of the city, and follow the famous river.

BIKE RENTAL IN BUDAPEST
YELLOW ZEBRA
Lázár utca 16, www.yellowzebratours.com/yellow-zebra-szentendre-bike-tour. php, rates begin at HUF 1,000 per hour
Rent a bike from a company like Yellow Zebra, which also does private bike tours to Szentendre, if you prefer to have someone guide you.

BIKE BASE BUDAPEST
Podmaniczky utca 19, www.bikebase.hu, rates begin at HUF 2,200 for 5 hours, Apr-Sep
Bike Base Budapest is another option that's centrally located for rentals.

BUDAPEST TO SZENTENDRE (27 KILOMETERS/17 MILES)
Budapest's most popular cycling trail is the route on the Buda side of the river to Szentendre. This dedicated paved bike path skirts the banks of the Danube with amazing views and plenty of stopover opportunities on the way. The route is mostly flat, so you won't need to worry about cycling up any hills; focus on the tree-clad riverside landscape all the way to Szentendre. You can take the bikes on the HÉV, the local suburban rail network, back to Budapest.

Once the route gets you out of the center, you'll pass a few of the city's lesser-known curiosities, like the **Óbuda Gasworks**, a disused gas factory that looks more like something out of a fairy tale with its turreted water

TRAIN

From Budapest, you can grab the **H5** local suburban train (at the time of writing there were plans to turn this into a metro line) operated by BKK (www.bkk.hu) from either Batthyány tér or under Margaret Bridge—just make sure you catch the one going all the way to Szentendre and buy a Suburban Railway Extension ticket that covers the region outside Budapest. (Note that this is sold by how many kilometers you go outside the city boundary—from the city to Szetendendre is a 15 km ticket.) You can buy these from the ticket office in the metro station or from the purple ticket machines across town. If you only have a local ticket, the inspector who gets on at Békásmegyer can sell you an extension, usually for around HUF 370 extra.

The train journey takes around 40 minutes. Tickets cost HUF 760, and trains run every 20 minutes (every 10 minutes in peak times) from 4am to 11:30pm. When you arrive in Szentendre, take the underpass just north of the station and then continue north along Kossuth Lajos utca. It will take 10-15 minutes to reach the town center on foot.

BUS

You can take a bus 880, 889, 890 with **Volánbusz** (www.volanbusz.hu) from Újpest-Városkapu in Budapest, which is accessible with metro line 3. The bus towers. The trail then turns down to **Római Part,** popular for its Danube beaches. You can stop off here for a few *fröccs* (a white or rosé wine spritzer) at one of the many riverside bars, like the bike-friendly and stripy-deck-chair-clad **Fellini Római Kultúrbisztró** (Kossuth Lajos üdülőpart 5, www. felliniromai.hu, Mon-Thu 2pm-11pm, Fri noon-midnight, Sun-Sat 10am-midnight). You can either end your route here and cycle back to the city, or continue onward toward Szentendre.

Once you get beyond the city limits, 1 kilometer (about half a mile) north of Budapest, keep an eye out for **Lupa Island** to your right, a small island only accessible by bike, and **Lupa Tó (Lupa Lake)** to your left. The lake has a popular local beach complete with sand and palm trees. (Pay HUF 1,000-3,500 to enter the beach.) **Ebihal Büfe** (Budakalász, Lupa-szigeti révátkelő, daily in summer 8am-11pm), a bar and café set on a moored boat on the river opposite the island, is a good place to stop for lunch before continuing the remaining 10 kilometers (6 miles) on to Szentendre.

BUDAPEST TO VÁC (40 KILOMETERS/25 MILES)
An alternate route on the Pest side of the river leads to the Danube Bend town of Vác. This route is a mix of regular roads and a paved bike path. The good news is that it is relatively flat all the way, and this route is less crowded than the one to Szentendre (on the other side of the river), which is very popular in summer.

Just like from Szentendre, you can usually take your bike back with you on the train (most have a compartment for bikes). If you want something different on the way, take a detour to off-beat **Népsziget** (which is still in Budapest, just in the northern suburbs, approximately 8 km/5 mi from the center), an islet that's home to old ship-building factories and quirky fried-fish stands and art collectives. If you decide to bike over here, check out **Kabin** (Népsziget út 727, in the summer season daily noon-midnight), a colorful bar on the north end of Népsziget that backs up to the river and looks across to Római Beach on the Buda side.

ride is only 25 minutes and costs HUF 310, but considering you need to take a metro all the way out of the city, it's not the most convenient way to get to Szentendre; it's a good alternative if you have issues getting the H5. Or if you miss the H5 coming back, the **bus station** is right next to the train station, so you have an alternative. Buses run every 20 minutes during the day (fewer services after 8pm) from 5:30am to 10:55pm.

BOAT
In the summer, **Mahart Passnave** (www.mahartpassnave.hu) runs boat services to Szentendre from downtown Budapest, at either the Vigadó tér dock or the Batthyány tér. It departs Budapest at 10:30am, getting to Szentendre around noon. There is also an afternoon line going at 2pm, getting there at 3:30pm. The journey back (leaving at 7pm) is much quicker, only 50 minutes, as you're going downstream. One-way tickets cost HUF 2,540, round-trips HUF 3,820.

CAR
Szentendre is only a 30-minute drive from Budapest city center. Take the road along the embankment on the Buda side (the west side of the river) and drive north on **Route 11.** The town is signposted, and you won't need a motorway vignette (a toll pass you need on all the country's highways) on this route. **Parking** is strictly regulated

153

boat docked on the Danube in Szentendre

in Szentendre and costs between HUF 280 and 360 per hour, depending on where you park. The highest parking rates are usually around the Danube promenade.

GETTING AROUND

The best way to get around Szentendre is to walk, and apart from the Hungarian Open Air Museum, you won't need to get public transport around town. While the walk to the center follows a straight line, it will take around 15 minutes to get there from the bus and the train station (which are located in the same place), so budget some extra time to walk back and forth.

If you want to get a taxi, you can call a couple of local companies: Szentendre Taxi (tel. 06/20-266-6662) or Szentendre Taxi 8 Nagy István (tel. 06/26-314-314).

LEAVING SZENTENDRE

The last suburban railway train back to Budapest leaves around 11:30pm, or 11:50pm on Friday nights and weekends. The last boat back to Budapest departs at 7pm. You can also take the boat from Szentendre up the Danube Bend to Esztergom (2 hours) at 10:30am (if you want to make your trip very early or you're spending the night). There is also a direct bus from the bus station to Visegrád (45 minutes).

DANUBE BEND

If you're into scenery coupled with history and dramatic views, then the Danube Bend is the day trip for you. North of Budapest, the Danube River threads through hills and valleys, passing medieval castles, Baroque towns, and wild hillsides. The entire Danube Bend follows the snaking river from Esztergom down to Szentendre, and it gets its name from the twists it makes through the valley.

Highlights of the region include the grand basilica at Esztergom, the medieval citadel at Visegrád (which has one of the best views of the

Itinerary Ideas 157
Vác 160
Visegrád 163
Esztergom 167

HIGHLIGHTS

✪ **TRAGOR IGNÁC MUSEUM, MEMENTO MORI EXHIBITION:**
See 18th-century mummies excavated in the Baroque town of Vác at this exhibit in a cellar under the Tragor Ignác Museum (page 160).

✪ **VISEGRÁD CITADEL:** Hike up to this medieval citadel to see the Danube Bend from above and immerse yourself in the region's history (page 163).

✪ **ESZTERGOM BASILICA:** Climb the dome of the largest church in Hungary for 360-degree views over the river and across to Slovakia (page 167).

✪ **BOATING FROM ESZTERGOM TO BUDAPEST:** See the Danube Bend at its most beautiful—from the water—as you sail from Esztergom back to Budapest on a four-hour cruise (page 169).

river from above), and the charming cobbled streets and colorful Baroque houses of Vác. However, the real magic of this region is the rolling landscape embracing it. Even from the car, bus, or train window, you can take in the forest-covered hills and the low-lying islands where crooked trees bend down to graze the water. However, in my opinion, the best way to appreciate the scenery hugging the river is to grab a boat or a hydrofoil from Budapest or from one of the towns on the Danube Bend in the spring and summer. This journey is particularly magical in the spring when the acacia blossoms carpet the water in the narrow channel between Visegrád and Szentendre, releasing a gorgeous perfume.

ORIENTATION

The towns of the Danube Bend are relatively close to each other, but the absence of bridges means it can be a little complicated to get between them. Visegrád and Esztergom lie to the southwest of the river as it bends,

with Vác on the northeastern bank. There is a ferry between Visegrád and Nagymaros, a small town just across the river that is connected to Budapest by train. You can take a hydrofoil from Vác to reach cities on the west side of the river, but there is only a hydrofoil around 10am going northward, and one at 5:30pm from Visegrád arriving 5:50pm in Vác, so you're better off taking the train to Nagymaros and then the ferry.

With the exception of Esztergom, most of the towns are small and you can easily walk to the sites.

PLANNING YOUR TIME

The Danube Bend covers a vast area. You can either explore parts with a rental car, sail down the river and enjoy the scenery from the boat going to or from Budapest, or simply pick one or two of the destinations to visit.

It only takes an hour to an hour and a half to reach the towns on the Danube Bend, but there is so much to see in each location that you can easily

Danube Bend

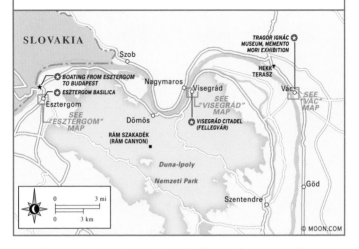

spend a day exploring the area. If you have one day and would rather not rush, I recommend taking the train to Esztergom and then the 4pm ferry back down the river. This will get you back to Budapest around 8pm, and you get to experience the nature of the Danube Bend in a leisurely way. If you're in a hurry, maybe just go to Visegrád for a day trip.

Itinerary Ideas

To explore the Danube Bend thoroughly, spend a couple of days here with an overnight stay in Visegrád. Leave most of your luggage in Budapest at your hotel or a luggage storage facility (www.budapestluggagestorage.com, €10 for 24 hours per piece), bringing only what you need in a light backpack, as there is nowhere to store luggage.

DAY 1: VÁC AND VISEGRÁD

1 Take the train to Vác and make **Vác Cathedral** your first stop.

2 Visit the nearby **Tragor Ignác Museum's Memento Mori Exhibition** for a peek at 18th-century mummies.

3 Spend some time walking around the Baroque town, ending with a pastry or a delicious cake at **Mihályi Patisserie.** Then take the train onward to Nagymaros. (If you didn't make it to the patisserie, stop at one of the kiosks by the dock for a snack, like *lángos*, a deep-fried dough topped with cheese.)

157

Itinerary Ideas

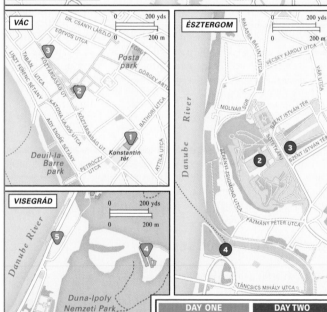

DAY ONE	DAY TWO
1 Vác Cathedral	1 Royal Palace
2 Tragor Ignác Museum's Memento Mori Exhibition	2 Esztergom Basilica
3 Mihályi Patisserie	3 Prímás Pince
4 Visegrád Citadel	4 4pm boat back to Budapest
5 Renaissence Restaurant	

© MOON.COM

Once you get to Nagymaros, board the hourly (leaving on the hour) ferry across the river—there are some great photo ops for the citadel here.

4 Fifteen minutes later, step off the ferry in Visegrád and hike up **Visegrád Citadel** (or get a taxi—the ticket office at the dock will call one for you) for amazing views over the Danube Bend.

5 Hike down the hill and have dinner at the theatrical **Renaissance Restaurant** before heading to your hotel.

DAY 2: VISEGRÁD AND ESZTERGOM

1 Start the day at the **Royal Palace** for beautiful Renaissance architecture and lovely close-up views of the river.

2 Take the bus to Esztergom (45 minutes) and head up to **Esztergom Basilica.** Make sure you climb up to the dome to appreciate the grandeur and scale of the cathedral.

3 Try some Hungarian food and wine in **Prímás Pince** in the cellars under the basilica.

4 When you're done exploring the town, take the **4pm boat back to Budapest.** Relax and watch the scenery of the Danube Bend float by on this four-hour cruise.

Vác's quirky museum

Vác

To Hekk Terasz

KABÓCA VENDÉGHÁZ

Rákóczi tér

NYUGATI TRAIN STATION

Posta park

VÁCZ HOTEL

MIHÁLYI PATISSERIE

TRAGOR IGNÁC MUSEUM, MEMENTO MORI EXHIBITION

Vác - Esztergom Ferry

Vác - Budapest ferry

Danube River

VÁC CATHEDRAL

Konstantin tér

Deuil-la-Barre park

Vác - Tahitótfalu ferry

VÁCI RÉV

Rózsakert

© MOON.COM

Vác

Vác (pop. 33,000) lies just 30 kilometers (19 miles) north of Budapest on the east bank of the Danube. It's the perfect alternative to the more crowded Szentendre, as you can explore its historic cobbled streets with churches and Baroque townhouses, or stroll along the Danube side promenade, away from the crowds that flock to the other side of the river. If you love history, you'll find plenty of it in Vác, one Hungary's oldest towns and once the local seat for the Catholic church.

It takes 10 minutes to walk from the train or bus stations (which are next to each other) in Vác to the town center and the Danube, so the best way to explore this Baroque town is on foot. Just head south in the direction of the river. If you arrive by boat, this will put you down near the town center, only minutes away on foot.

SIGHTS

✪ TRAGOR IGNÁC MUSEUM, MEMENTO MORI EXHIBITION

Marcius 15 tér 19, tel. 06/30-555-3349, www.muzeumvac.hu, Tue-Sun 10am-6pm, HUF 1,200

For something truly offbeat, head to the cellar under Március 15 tér 19 to discover the 18th-century mummies and painted coffins found in a secret crypt that was walled up for 200 years. You can see some of the coffins as well as rosaries, crucifixes, icons, and coins excavated in the crypt at the permanent Memento Mori Exhibition in this cool cellar under the Tragor Ignác Museum. The museum also has other exhibitions, including the Ars Memorandi exhibition (included in the price), focusing on the history of the town from the liberation of Ottoman rule to the "Golden Age of Vác" at the end of the 18th century.

Vác's cathedral

VÁC CATHEDRAL

Schuszter Konstantin tér 11, tel.
06/27-814-184, www.vaciegyhazmegye.hu,
Mon-Sat 10am-noon and 2pm-5pm,
Sun 7:30am-7pm Mar-Nov, free

The impressive Vác Cathedral is just a five-minute walk southeast from the Tragor Ignác Museum. This neoclassical cathedral—in an awkwardly epic scale compared to its more humble surroundings—was built in the 18th century. Its grand entrance is marked

by a gate of Corinthian columns leading into a surprisingly breezy interior with cream-colored walls and a vibrant fresco painted by Franz Anton Maulbertsch on the vaulted dome.

FOOD
Hekk Terasz

Sánc dűlő, tel. 06/70-252-7295, Sun-Thu
11am-9pm, Fri-Sat 11am-10pm, entrées
HUF 1,490-3,500

Enjoy some freshly caught and cooked fish at Hekk Terasz. This restaurant on the Danube is a little out of town on the bicycle route but worth the 50-minute walk along the river for its fish dishes and riverside views. Book in advance if you plan to go, as it's very popular with locals and day-trippers from Budapest. The fish is priced by weight, so prices will vary depending on the size and type of fish. If you're not sure what to order, go for the namesake *hekk* (freshwater hake) that comes deep-fried, and have some fries with their homemade herb- or mayonnaise-based dips.

Mihályi Patisserie

Köztársaság út 21, tel. 06/20-390-3367,
www.mihalyipatisserie.com, Tue-Sun
10am-6pm, cakes HUF 990-1,600

Mihályi Patisserie may have only three tables, but its cakes are a work of art. Whether you want to sit with a coffee

Mihályi Patisserie

Adrenaline junkies may want to venture deep into the **Pillis Hills** on the western side of the Danube Bend. Ten kilometers (6 miles) west of Visegrád, Rám Canyon (**Rám Szakadék** in Hungarian) is a 1.2-kilometer-long (0.75-mile-long) canyon that is more like an adventure course than a hike. The canyon is linked with ladders scaling the walls beside waterfalls, with handrails set into the rock to help you maneuver up the rock face. Wear good hiking shoes, and expect to get wet (the river runs alongside the course, and you will find yourself scaling waterfalls at parts). Although you don't need to be an experienced climber—I climbed the canyon as a 9-year-old when the river froze—it can be dangerous, and you should proceed with care. Heavy rain can cause flash floods, and in winter the ice makes it difficult to scale.

Even though the canyon is just 10 kilometers (6 miles) from Visegrád, there is no public transport to reach it, so you could either take a **taxi** (10 minutes) or take a **local bus** to Dömös. From downtown Dömös, take Szent István utca to Királykúti utca and follow the road up into the hills. The canyon is well signposted (Rám Szakadék). It's a 3-kilometer (2-mile) hike from Dömös to the entrance of the canyon.

and a cake or get a few macarons to go to savor by the riverside, you'll be glad you popped in for something sweet.

ACCOMMODATIONS
Vácz Hotel

Honvéd utca 14, tel. 06/30-388-7746, www.vachotel.hu, HUF 21,900-25,000 d including breakfast

This boutique three-star hotel with 14 rooms blends retro details like patterned wallpaper and wood paneling with modern lighting and design. Rooms are spacious with an en suite bathroom, flat-screen TV, and a fridge, and the price includes a lavish buffet breakfast. The location is central—a 10-minute walk to the cathedral.

Kabóca Vendégház

Dózsa György út 28, tel. 06/30-493-2559, www.kabocavac.hu, HUF 17,000 d, apartment only

This charming little guesthouse owned by a French couple is just five minutes from the historic center of Vác. The guesthouse is essentially a self-catering home that can accommodate up to five people on its two floors with a large kitchen, a terrace, and a garden. There is a vaulted wine cellar

(which you can use with the owners' permission) and even a small homemade chapel with frescoes by the owners' friend.

GETTING THERE

From Budapest, the easiest way to get to Vác is by train from Nyugati train station (25-40 minutes, HUF 650). Trains run every half an hour from 4:45am to 9:50pm.

In the summer, there is a hydrofoil with Mahart Passnave (www. mahartpassnave.hu) from the Vigadó dock in Budapest at 10am (40 minutes, HUF 3,300).

If you're athletic, you can cycle the path up the Danube. The 40-kilometer (25-mile) route is a mix of regular roads and a paved bike path along the Pest side of the Danube. It's relatively flat, and less crowded than the path to Szentendre (on the Buda side of the river), which is very popular in summer. Most trains running to Budapest have dedicated sections where you can store your bike.

You can reach Vác by car by driving up Váci út in Pest until you reach Route 2. The journey by car will take an hour, and parking in Vác costs HUF 300-400 per hour.

Visegrád

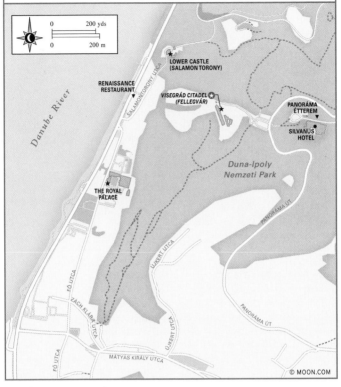

LOWER CASTLE
(SALAMON TORONY)

RENAISSANCE
RESTAURANT

VISEGRÁD CITADEL
(FELLEGVÁR)

PANORÁMA
ÉTTEREM

SILVANUS
HOTEL

Danube River

SALAMONTORONY UTCA

Duna-Ipoly
Nemzeti Park

THE ROYAL
PALACE

ÚJKERT UTCA

FŐ UTCA

ZACH KLÁRA UTCA

ÚJKERT UTCA

PANORÁMA ÚT

PANORÁMA ÚT

FŐ UTCA

MÁTYÁS KIRÁLY UTCA

0   200 yds
0   200 m

© MOON.COM

Visegrád

To really appreciate the beauty of the
Danube Bend, head to Visegrád (pop.
1,800), a small town on the west bank
of the river at the tightest point of the
bend, and the only point where the
Danube flows north. Most people
pick Visegrád for its medieval castle
perched on the top of the hill, which
you can reach either by car or by hiking the foot-trodden paths through the
woodland past the Calvary, an open-
air representation of the crucifixion
of Christ.

SIGHTS
✪ VISEGRÁD CITADEL
(Fellegvár)

Várhegy, tel. 06/26-598-080, daily
9am-5pm Mar and Oct, 9am-6pm Apr-Sep,
9am-4pm Nov-Dec, 10am-4pm Jan-Feb
HUF 1,700

Towering over the valley, the Visegrád
Citadel can be seen from miles away,
whether you arrive by train or boat.
It dates back to the 13th century and
its ruined ramparts give it a romantic
edge. From the top, get ready for some

Hike up to the top of the hill to visit the medieval Visegád Citadel.

of the best views in Hungary, overlooking the most dramatic curve of the Danube Bend. The citadel itself is also a fascinating slice of history, and although it looks ruined from afar, part of it is still intact. You can still patrol the old walls, visit the armory, and even see a mini-waxwork museum inside the citadel.

You can drive or take a taxi, which takes around 10 minutes from the center of town and costs around HUF 1,000, or, if you're feeling athletic, hike up to the top, which takes around an hour. From the dock of the Nagymaros-Visegrád ferry, take the road going west up the hill, turn left up Magasköz utca, and then take the path through the woods up to the Calvary. Just follow the trail up the hill (it's very steep and rocky, so wear good shoes) and you will reach the Citadel in another 20-40 minutes.

LOWER CASTLE (Salamon Torony)

Salamontorony utca,
www.visegradmuzeum.hu,
Wed-Sun 9am-5pm Apr-Sep, HUF 700

The Lower Castle, located halfway up the hill to the south of town, is accessible by taking the stairs leading up from the boat jetty for the Budapest boat line. It was a fortification system built in the 13th century that used to connect the Citadel with the Danube and once protected the vulnerable southern entrance. The highlight here is the Solomon Tower, a hexagonal tower that now houses a museum about the town. It gets its name from a local legend that Solomon (an 11th-century Hungarian king) was guarded in the tower after losing against King László and Géza in battle.

THE ROYAL PALACE

Fő utca 29, tel. 06/26-597-010,
www.visegradmuzeum.hu, Tue-Sun 9am-5pm
HUF 1,300

Before you leave, make sure you head over to the partly reconstructed Renaissance palace used by King Matthias set on the riverbank. This beautiful palace is easy to reach—no climbing required, just a 10-minute walk from the Nagymaros ferry—and is also accessible for people with disabilities, with ramps and elevators installed in the complex. The palace ruins are very beautiful, with the reconstructed buildings bringing the ruins to life, like the arched-lion Matthias Fountain made out of pink marble and the colonnaded 15th-century courtyard surrounding the fountain.

the Royal Palace by the river

FOOD
Renaissance Restaurant

Fő utca 11, tel. 06/26-398-081,
www.renvisegrad.hu, Sun-Fri noon-10pm,
Sat noon-11pm, entrées HUF 2,900-5,500

This family-owned restaurant taps into Visegrád's historical spirit with a medieval feast served up in homemade crockery and locally supplied dishes. It's theatrical, but the food (Hungarian Renaissance meals given a modern upgrade) is actually good—try the venison goulash or freshly grilled trout, all washed down with some Hungarian wine, of course. In the summer you can sit out on their terrace with full views of the river. You can even dress up for the part if you want, or just take a look at the period costumes hanging by the entrance, waiting to be tried on.

Renaissance Restaurant

Panoráma Étterem

Fekete-hegy Hotel Silvanus,
tel. 06/26-398-311, www.hotelsilvanus.hu/
en/hotel/gastronomy/panorama-restaurant,
daily 7am-10pm, HUF 2,390-5,790

Panoráma Étterem at the Hotel Silvanus has the most amazing terrace overlooking the bend in the Danube. The menu oscillates between Hungarian dishes mostly focused on game, like their goulash served in a mini cauldron, and more international flavors, like their gourmet venison burger. It's 3.5 kilometers outside the town, very close to the citadel, so you may want to either take a taxi or visit after your hike to the castle.

ACCOMMODATIONS
Silvanus Hotel

Feketehegy, tel. 06/26-398-311,
www.hotelsilvanus.hu, €112-260 d

It's worth staying at the Silvanus just for the view. From the top of the hill, just 300 meters (330 yards) from the Visegrád Citadel, the view over the Danube Bend is spectacular. The Silvanus also boasts a spa and wellness facility, with an outdoor pool with a view over the valley, plus an indoor pool, saunas, and an aroma and salt chamber. Spa treatments on offer include Ayurvedic treatments. The hotel has a retro hunting lodge feel with dark wood-paneled walls and autumnal colors. Most price packages include breakfast and dinner.

GETTING THERE

Bus is the most direct way to get to Visegrád, but in summer, boat is of course the best option.

Bus

The most direct way to get to Visegrád is to take the 880 bus from Újpest-Városkapu in Budapest (accessible on metro line 3), which takes 1 hour 15 minutes (around HUF 750). Buses run once or twice an hour depending on the time of day (more frequent around 1pm to 4pm) from 5:35am till 10:55pm.

You can also take local bus 880 or 882 from the Szentendre train station (around HUF 465).

Train and Ferry

You can grab a train run by MÁV (www.mavcsoport.hu) to Nagymaros, a town just across the river from Visegrád, from Nyugati train station in Budapest (40 minutes, HUF 1,120) and take the hourly ferry across the river. Trains go twice an hour from 4:45am until 9:50pm. Once you get to Nagymaros, you need to walk 5 minutes westward down Magyar utca to the ferry.

From Nagymaros, the first ferry leaves at 6:30am, then goes on the hour from 8am to 8pm. The journey across the river takes around 15 minutes and costs HUF 450. You can also bring a car across for HUF 1,550.

Ferries leave Visegrád 45 minutes past each hour from 7:45am till 7:45pm.

Boat

In the summer the best way to get there is by hydrofoil run by Mahart Pasnave (www.mahartpassnave.hu) from Vigadó at 10am daily in the summer (returning from Visegrád at 6pm), which takes an hour to get to Visegrád (HUF 4,300 one-way, HUF 6,500 round-trip).

There is also a slower boat route run by the same company that takes three and a half hours from Budapest, leaving Vigadó at 9am, with the return journey taking two and a half hours (faster as you're sailing downstream), leaving Visegrád at 5:40pm. Tickets cost HUF 3,180 one-way, HUF 4,760 round-trip. The dock for the Budapest boat is not in the same place as the ferry coming over from Nagymaros, but is toward the north next to the Lower Castle.

Car

It takes around 30 minutes to drive to Visegrád from Szentendre. There is one route that will take you through the Pilis Hills but this is complicated, so it's easier to follow Route 11 along the Danube banks to the town. This will also offer striking views along the river. From Vác things get a little more complicated as there are no bridges across the Danube in the area, so you will need to take a ferry in Vác to Tahitófalú (going once an hour,

HUF 1,500 per car and HUF 430 per person) and then continue on Route 11. This journey will take around an hour. Alternately, you can drive back to Budapest and take the Megyeri Bridge across the Danube and join Route 11. Another variation is to drive northward 20 minutes to Nagymaros and take the ferry across, which also runs on the hour at the same rates. In Visegrád, parking costs around HUF 300 per hour.

GETTING AROUND

The town itself is compact and takes minutes to get around on foot; however, getting up to the castle is a strenuous uphill hike. There's not too much in terms of public transportation. If you need a taxi while you're in town, call Visegrád Taxi (tel. 06/20-266-6662). You can also ask for a taxi at the Nagymaros-Visegrád ferry ticket office when you arrive in Visegrád, as they also manage the taxi service.

Esztergom

The Danube Bend ends, or rather begins, at the Hungarian-Slovak border by the town of Esztergom (pop. 28,000). Many come to Esztergom for the photogenic view from Hungary's largest basilica, which looms over the river. Vác may have been once the center of Catholicism in Hungary, but that torch has been passed upstream to Esztergom, the hometown of Hungary's first king St. Stephen. In fact, Esztergom was the royal seat of the country from the 10th century to the mid-13th century, so you'll find plenty of history around the old castle walls and historic city streets to keep you busy once you've visited the main site.

SIGHTS

✪ ESZTERGOM BASILICA

Szent István tér 1, tel. 06/33-402-354, www.bazilika-esztergom.hu, Mon-Sat 9am-7pm, Sun 9am-6pm May-Sep, daily 9am-6pm Sep-Oct and Apr, daily 9am-5pm Mar, daily 9am-4pm Nov-Jan, free entry for the church, HUF 700 dome, HUF 1,500 combined ticket to the crypt, dome, and treasury

If you thought St. Stephen's Basilica in Budapest was impressive, wait till you visit the Esztergom Basilica, which is the largest church in Hungary, rising 72 meters (236 feet) high to its dome! Entry is free for this impressive cathedral, and it's open to visitors all year round, but if the weather is good (and you're not scared of heights) it's worth the climb up the numerous stairs to the dome. This will take you up to the panorama terrace first—a large hall with a window overlooking the river and a café halfway up the church—then even more stairs up to the colonnaded corridor on the outside under the dome. You'll already be treated to wonderful views over the town, but wait in line to get right up to the top of the dome (numbers are restricted). You can walk all the way around for 360 degrees of the whole region overlooking the Danube, Slovakia (just on the other side of the river), and the hills leading further south down the Danube Bend. You can also see the treasury and the crypt on your visit to this classical-style cathedral.

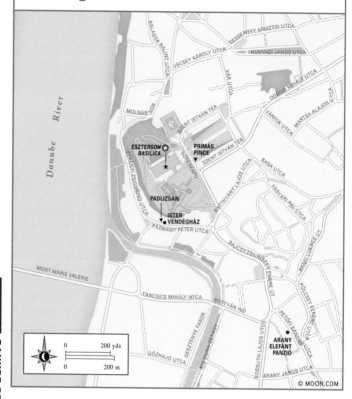

Esztergom

FOOD

Padlizsán

Pázmány Péter utca 21, tel. 06/33-311-212, daily noon-10pm, entrées HUF 2,000-2,500

Padlizsán ("eggplant" in English) lies at the base of the castle walls, looking up toward the Basilica in a small baroque townhouse. The food lives up to the view, with modern, seasonal Hungarian dishes from grilled pike perch from the Danube to autumnal chicken in wild mushroom sauce to vegetarian fried cheese served with cranberry sauce and apple compote.

Prímás Pince

Szent István tér 4, tel. 06/33-541-965, www.primaspince.hu, Mon-Thu 10am-9pm, Fri 10am-10pm, Sun 10am-5pm, HUF 1290-6990

Prímás Pince in the cellars below the basilica feels more like a museum than a restaurant, with high-vaulted ceilings and stone blocks. But if you're looking for great wine and food, Prímás delivers, as it carries 100 Hungarian wines—including rare varieties—and you'll find plenty of creative takes on Hungarian dishes on the menu. Try the aged wild boar tenderloin served with a sauce made from the famous Eger "Bull's Blood" red wine

WALKING TO SLOVAKIA

If you want to get amazing views of Esztergom and sneak another country in, walk across the **Mária Valéria bridge** (a 10-15-minute walk) over to Štúrovo, Slovakia, for wonderful vistas of the basilica and the city. In truth, there's not much to see in Štúrovo, but for some it's worth the journey for the views alone (not to mention the novelty of adding another country to your trip). Although there are no passport checks (Slovakia and Hungary are in the Schengen Zone), it's a good idea to bring it with you just in case. There are a couple of cafés and restaurants on the riverside, like **BAT** (Námestie slobody 17/17, Štúrovo), which has a nice view but is rather average. Bring Euros if you plan to spend this side of the river.

and plums. You can also pay a visit to the exhibition about wine, showing the history of the Hungarian church and winemaking in Hungary.

TOP EXPERIENCE

⭐ BOATING FROM ESZTERGOM TO BUDAPEST

The best way to spend a day in Esztergom is to take the train up from Budapest and spend a couple of hours exploring the Basilica and the area surrounding it before having lunch. Then take the 4pm slow boat back to Budapest for a leisurely four-hour Danube cruise—you will also get the best views of the Basilica from the water. Just sit back, relax, and watch the landscape slip by as you pass the hills around Visegrád and then the marshy island around Szentendre dotted with storks and other wildlife at the golden hour—in the late spring the water here is filled with fallen acacia petals and smells divine! Unlike the faster hydrofoil, there is also a bar on this boat.

Climb up the top of the famous Esztergom Basilica for incredible views.

the view of the basilica from the river

ACCOMMODATIONS

Ister Vendégház

Pázmány Péter utca 17, tel.
06/20-823-0540, www.istervendeghaz.hu,
HUF 19,500-22,000 d, apartment only

Just 300 meters (330 yards) from the Basilica, this guesthouse with two apartments is a rustic, vintage home-away-from-home with cozy décor like painted wood paneling on the door, ceramic stove heaters, and ship steering wheels, along with other quirky details. The larger apartment also has a game room with a foosball table. A wine cellar is open for guests, and there is a patio with a BBQ.

Arany Elefánt Panzió

Petőfi Sándor utca 15, tel. 06/30-993-7472,
www.esztergomszallas.hu, HUF
11,000-13,970 d

The best features of this small guesthouse are its private courtyard garden and its central location. There are five rooms with two to three beds; each comes with a TV, Internet, bathroom, and wardrobe. You can get a good breakfast with cold cuts, eggs, bread, and vegetables for HUF 1,500.

GETTING THERE

Train

There are regular trains from Nyugati train station in Budapest that take a little over an hour (HUF 1,120) to get to Esztergom, but these will still leave you about a 40-minute walk from the center. Trains run every half an hour from 4am until 11:15pm. You can either take a taxi to town (around HUF 1,000), or hop on local bus 1 or 11 (HUF 150) and get off at Bazilika.

Boat

In the summer, the best way to reach Esztergom is by hydrofoil, operated by Mahart Passnave (www.mahartpassnave.hu), which departs at 10am from Vígadó, and takes 1 hour 30 minutes (HUF 5,300 one-way,

HUF 8,000 round-trip). The return ferry leaves at 5:30pm, getting back to Budapest at 7pm.

The slow ferry by the same company leaves Budapest at 9am (taking 5 hours 20 minutes) and leaves Esztergom at 4pm (taking 4 hours). A one-way ticket is HUF 3,820, a round-trip HUF 5,720. I highly recommend taking the slow boat back in the summer for a scenic leisurely cruise.

Both the boat and the hydrofoil also stop at Visegrád, if you want to break your journey there.

Bus

There are buses run by Volánbusz (www.volanbusz.hu) running between Esztergom and Visegrád. These take 45 minutes and run hourly at 40 minutes past from Esztergom. If you're coming from Visegrád, services go at 50 past the hour from the bus stop next to the jetty. Tickets cost around HUF 465. You can also take a Volánbusz bus to Esztergom from Árpád Híd bus station in Budapest, which takes 1 hour 15 minutes and costs around HUF 930. However, I recommend the train over the bus because it's more comfortable, and finding the Árpád Híd bus station in Budapest is difficult if you don't know the city.

Car

It takes an hour to drive to Esztergom from Budapest. Take Route 10 on the Buda side of the river from Flórián tér in northern Buda and follow the signs till Esztergom. Parking costs around HUF 300 per hour.

GETTING AROUND

If you need a taxi in Esztergom, try Esztergom Taxi (tel. 06/30-634-0403) or Taxi 1000 (tel. 06/20-622-1000).

LAKE BALATON

Itinerary Ideas 176
Balatonfüred 178
Tihany 181
Badacsony 185
Siófok 188

Lake Balaton, with its stretches of turquoise water dotted with yachts and sailboats, is perhaps the most memorable escape from Budapest. The largest lake in Central Europe, it's just a couple of hours from the capital. When the temperatures rise, it seems most of Budapest flees the city to find refuge along the beaches of the "Hungarian Sea."

You can think of Balaton as being split into north and south. The northern shore is more beautiful, with volcanic hills lined with

HIGHLIGHTS

✪ **KOSSUTH LAJOS SPRING:** Drink healing water straight from this colonnaded spring in Balatonfüred (page 179).

✪ **THE BENEDICTINE ABBEY OF TIHANY:** Visit the lake's most iconic monument not just for the history but for the view over the lake just next to the Abbey (page 182).

✪ **WINERIES IN BADACSONY:** Try the local wine on a volcanic hill overlooking vineyards and the lake (page 186).

✪ **THE FERRIS WHEEL:** See Balaton from above on this 50-meter-tall (165-foot-tall) Ferris wheel in Siófok (page 190).

✪ **BEACHES IN SIÓFOK:** Relax on the beach of your choice: Siófiok Main Beach for a resort-like feel, or Golden Coast Public Beach for a quieter experience and wonderful sunset views (page 190).

vineyards and elegant resorts, while the south gets the golden beaches and lakeside party spots like Siófok. There is something for everyone, whether you want to hike up into the hills, take a plunge in the lake, just relax along the water on a summer's day sipping a glass of *Kéknyelű*, a white wine made from a local grape from Badacsony, or hit the bars in Siófok.

ORIENTATION

Balaton is split into the north and south region. Siófok is located on the southern shore, while Balatonfüred, Tihany, and Badacsony are located on the northern shore. Balatonfüred and Badacsony are connected by a direct train line, while a regular bus service runs between Balatonfüred and Tihany. To get between the north and south shore, you can take the ferry from Balatonfüred or Tihany to Siófok.

If you take the **train** from Siófok to Szántód (only a 15-minute ride),

you can ride across to Tihany-rév on the local **ferry** (8 minutes, HUF 700), which runs every 40 minutes. But you will need to **hike** up to the town or take a local **bus** (which goes from the dock). You can also take a **pleasure boat** from Siófok to Balatonfüred, which goes every hour and a half from 10am to 7pm (1 hour, HUF 1,800). This boat will also take you to Tihany afterward, docking just below the town (1.5 hours, HUF 2,000).

taking the ferry on Lake Balaton

Most of the towns are quite compact, but you may need to walk 15-20

Lake Balaton

Map showing the area around Lake Balaton including towns: Ajka, Devecser, Sümeg, Zalaszentgrót, Tapolca, Balaton-felvidék Nemzeti Park, Hévíz, Keszthely, Badacsony, Wineries in Badacsony, Balatonboglár, Fonyód, Lengyeltóti, Balaton-felvidéki Nemzeti Park, Marcali, Zalakaros. Roads marked 84, 77, 71, 76, 760, 75, 7, 68, M7. Scale bars: 5 mi / 5 km. See Detail box near Badacsony.

minutes from the **train station** in Balatonfüred.

PLANNING YOUR TIME

Travel time to Balaton ranges from 1.5 hours to 2.5 hours from Budapest, depending on the destination.

The area around Lake Balaton is vast, and realistically you won't be able to hit all the listed towns in a day. If you have only one day, choose the town or area that interests you the most and focus your trip there. It is also possible to combine Siófok with Balatonfüred or Tihany, but you could also just

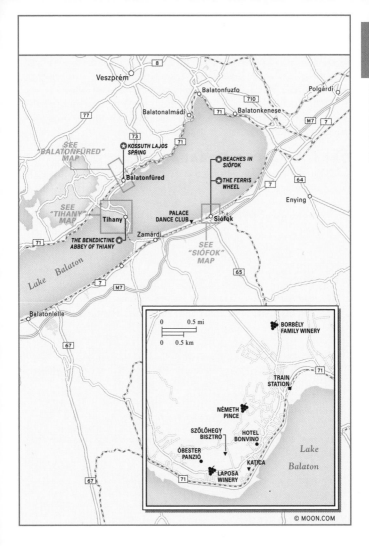

focus on Balatonfüred and Tihany in the same day, or Balatonfüred and Badacsony, if you want to do two destinations. Balaton is a place locals come to escape the heat of the summer, so expect a relaxed holiday vibe—the last thing you'll want to do is rush around from town to town. Take the train down and spend a relaxed day by the lake like a local.

Itinerary Ideas

You could easily spend a couple of days exploring the towns and the countryside around this beautiful lake. If you want to see as much as you can, spend the night in Balatonfüred and explore the northern part with Tihany, and then take the boat over to Siófok for the beaches. (If you're more into nightlife, you may want to reverse the itinerary and stay in Siófok for the night.)

DAY 1: TIHANY AND BALATONFÜRED

Take the train to Balatonfüred, then grab the bus to Tihany outside the train station. Don't bring too much luggage, as there are no lockers in the train station.

1 When you arrive in Tihany, stop for lunch at **Régi Idők Udvara És Skanzen.**

2 After lunch, head over to **the Benedictine Abbey of Tihany** for a dose of abbey history.

3 For the best views in town, go to **Rege Cúkrászda.** Admire the lake and the sailboats below over a coffee and a lavender cake at this magical little café.

4 Buy a few lavender gifts at one of the many shops, such as **Tihanyi Levendula Galéria,** and get the bus back to Balatonfüred (20 minutes).

5 Back in Balatonfüred, take a pleasant stroll along the **Tagore Promenade** at sundown.

6 Stop at the **Kossuth Lajos Spring** for some fresh-from-the-source healing mineral water.

7 Enjoy dinner with some good local wine at the **Horváth House Wine Gallery** before retiring to your hotel.

DAY 2: SIÓFOK

Get the 10am boat over to Siófok, which takes 50 minutes.

1 Head up the famous **Siófok Water Tower** for views over the town, and maybe grab a coffee at the rooftop café.

2 Wander down the **Petőfi Promenade,** a 1.6 km (1 mi) stretch lined with restaurants and bars that runs parallel to the beach.

3 Pop into **Mala Garden Restaurant** for beachside views and fusion food.

Itinerary Ideas

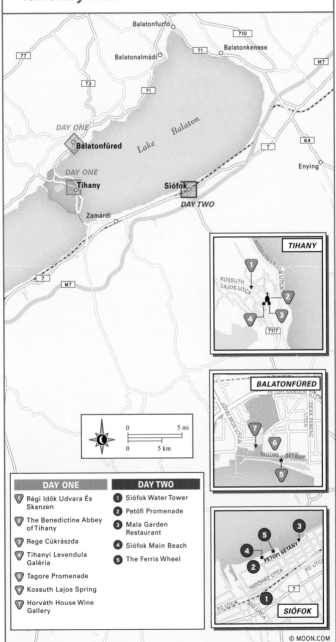

DAY ONE

1. Régi Idők Udvara És Skanzen
2. The Benedictine Abbey of Tihany
3. Rege Cúkrászda
4. Tihanyi Levendula Galéria
5. Tagore Promenade
6. Kossuth Lajos Spring
7. Horváth House Wine Gallery

DAY TWO

1. Siófok Water Tower
2. Petőfi Promenade
3. Mala Garden Restaurant
4. Siófok Main Beach
5. The Ferris Wheel

© MOON.COM

4 Relax for the afternoon, soaking up some sun on Siófok Main Beach.

5 When you're done sunbathing, board the Ferris wheel for a ride overlooking the lake before grabbing the train back to Budapest.

Balatonfüred

Balatonfüred (pop. 13,000) is a historic resort on the northern shore of Balaton, where you'll find palatial hotels and villas once frequented by the artistic elite from Budapest overlooking the water. It's a couple of hours by train from Budapest, making it the perfect gateway.

Balatonfüred has an old-world appeal as a historic resort and is a great choice for a quiet, yet elegant, day by the lake. It's more than just lakeside town; artists and writers were drawn to the scenic northern shore of Lake Balaton for their health as well as

the views. (The town sits on carbonated mineral springs, which you can drink straight from the Kossuth Lajos Spring tucked under the colonnaded pavilion.) The town is populated with 18th- and 19th-century villas, a wooded park, and a scenic promenade with a marina and riverside cafés and restaurants.

SIGHTS
TAGORE PROMENADE
This tree-lined promenade running along the northern shore makes for wonderful strolls along Lake Balaton.

Balatonfüred is an elegant resort on the northern shore of the lake.

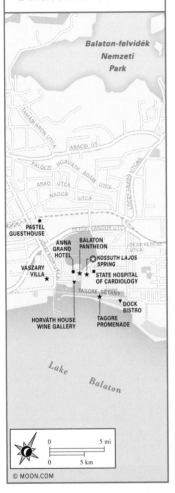

Balatonfüred

Balaton-felvidék
Nemzeti
Park

PASTEL
GUESTHOUSE

ANNA
GRAND
HOTEL

BALATON
PANTHEON

KOSSUTH LAJOS
SPRING

VASZARY
VILLA

STATE HOSPITAL
OF CARDIOLOGY

TAGORE SÉTÁNY

DOCK
BISTRO

HORVÁTH HOUSE
WINE GALLERY

TAGORE
PROMENADE

Lake
Balaton

0   5 mi
0   5 km

© MOON.COM

BALATON PANTHEON
Gyógy tér, free

Tucked under the arches of the building on the northeastern side of Gyógy tér is an interesting pantheon featuring placards to the famous figures who came to Balatonfüred to take their cures, a kind of who's who of the town, that then stretches out into a woody parkland gently crawling up the hill.

VASZARY VILLA
Honvéd utca 2-4, tel. 06/87-950-876,
http://kultura.balatonfured.hu,
Tue-Sun 10am-6pm, HUF 1,800

Step inside this beautiful late-19th-century villa, the former home of the once prominent Vaszary family. The most famous of the family is Hungarian Impressionist painter János Vaszary, whose paintings are exhibited in the villa. The museum also has a delightful collection of art and artifacts from the 18th century.

✪ STATE HOSPITAL OF CARDIOLOGY AND THE KOSSUTH LAJOS SPRING
Gyógy tér 2, free

I personally love Gyógy tér around the whitewashed walls of the State Hospital of Cardiology—the largest in Hungary—which has drawn in a list of artistic celebrities, including Nobel Prize-winning Indian poet Rabindranath Tagore. Next to the famous hospital, you can get some shade under the trees or under the colonnade surrounding the 19th-century Kossuth Lajos mineral spring, which as far as mineral springs go actually tastes good. The spring spouts out of a four-sided stone fountain lying under a neoclassical pavilion. Bring your own cup or bottle, and just press the

It runs from the marina to the lakeside Eszterházy Beach and Waterpark (Aranyhíd sétány, tel. 06/87-343-817, www.balatonfuredistrandok.hu/eszterhazy.html, daily 8:30am-7pm June-Aug, HUF 1,250). The promenade is split into a pedestrian path and a bicycle path, with prominent views over the lake.

Kossuth Lajos Spring is said to have healing properties.

button next to the tap on the spring to fill it. The water is said to be high in iron and has been used to treat cardiovascular, digestive, and diabetes-related diseases, but it is also a good, free thirst quencher in the hot summer months.

FOOD
Horváth House Wine Gallery
Gyógy tér 3, tel. 06/30-458-7778,
www.horvath-haz.hu, Sun-Thu noon-8pm,
Fri-Sat noon-9pm, entrées HUF 3,690-5,690
Horváth House Wine Gallery lies in the cellar of a prestigious 19th-century villa, but despite external appearances, it has a modern interior that couples well with the old winemaking apparatuses you'll find on-site. Although the beat is local wine from Balaton, make sure you try their *pálinka* or, if you prefer to stay dry, their artisanal syrups. They have an excellent selection of game dishes like wild boar and venison, but you can also pick from some fish dishes.

Dock Bistro
Tagore sétány 9, tel. 06/70-636-6707,
daily 10am-10pm, entrées HUF 1,990-3,490
For something laid-back close to the water, this trendy bistro decked out in wood and flooded with light (thanks to its large glass panels) captures the breezy-easygoing attitude of Balaton on a summer's day. You can get your usual holiday comfort foods, like gourmet burgers, steaks, ribs, pizzas, and more. If you want something international, familiar, and good quality, this downtown bistro can get you into the summer-beach mood.

ACCOMMODATIONS
Anna Grand Hotel
Gyógy tér 1, tel. 06/87-581-200,
www.annagrandhotel.hu, €126-220 d
including breakfast and dinner
More than 200 years old, this grand hotel captures the elegant spirit of Balatonfüred. Set right next to the Balaton Pantheon and the Kossuth Lajos spring, and only 100 meters (330 feet) from the lake, it has one of the best addresses in the city. There are more than 100 rooms and a 1,200-square-meter (13,000-square-foot) modern wellness department fully equipped with a pool, sauna, hot tub, and steam bath; there is also a bowling alley in the hotel. Foodies

the Anna Grand Hotel at night

will love the homemade cakes based on 19th-century recipes made on the premises at the hotel café. Try to peek into the grand ballroom, which since 1824 has been hosting the famous Anna Ball, held once a year on a Saturday around the end of July.

Pastel Guesthouse

Eötvös Károly Köz 2, tel. 06/70-209-7521, www.pastelguesthouse.com, €45-55 d

Pastel is an elegant guesthouse decked out with a chic, vintage aesthetic in natural pastel shades of gray and light brown, with green and rustic chandeliers and vases filled with fresh flowers. There is a communal kitchen in the guesthouse, and the owners live upstairs ready to help should you need anything. This is a good choice for adults looking for a peaceful getaway, as the hosts ask that guests do not bring children under 16. Free parking included at the property, and it's only 10 minutes from the lake.

GETTING THERE AND AROUND

TRAIN

From Budapest, the easiest way to get to Balatonfüred is by train (2 hours, HUF 2,725), serviced by MÁV (www. mavcsoport.hu) from Budapest Déli station. Direct trains run four times a day between 8am and 3:55pm, and the last train leaving Balatonfüred goes at 6pm. In Budapest you can also take metro line 4, operated by the Budapest public transport system, BKK, in Budapest to the Kelenföld train station in the western suburbs and take the train to Balatonfüred from there.

The center of Balatonfüred is a good 15-20 minute walk southeast from the train station. Call Taxi Balatonfüred (tel. 06/30-751-7518) if you prefer not to walk, or take the local bus lines 1 (every two hours, even-numbered hours), 1B (10 past the hour, every one to two hours), or 2 (every two hours, 30 past the hour for odd-numbered hours); buy a ticket (HUF 310) from the driver.

CAR

The drive from Budapest to Balatonfüred takes around an hour and a half. Take the M7 southwest of the city. Parking in Balatonfüred ranges from HUF 140 to 500 per hour depending on the zone and the season.

Tihany

Tihany (pop. 1,400) is a peninsula that sticks out into the middle of Lake Balaton. In my opinion, it is one of the most beautiful spots on the lake. The town rises high above the water, crowned with the Baroque bell towers of Benedictine Abbey. Although the main town lies perched on the hillside, you can hike to the shore down winding steps and paths slinking in and out of the woods past flaking villas to the jetty—or you can even follow marked trails that guide you to secret beaches you can't get to by car. If you come in June, the lavender fields are in full bloom, and you can pick your own bunches of lavender, but even off-season you can still buy all kind of lavender products at the vintage-style shops scattered around Tihany.

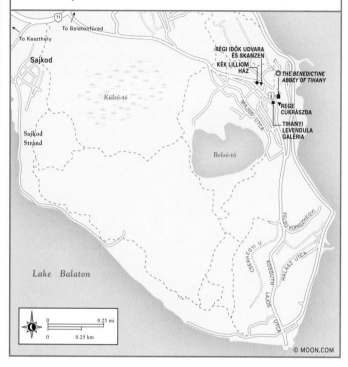

Tihany

SIGHTS

⭐ THE BENEDICTINE ABBEY OF TIHANY

András tér 1, tel. 06/87-538-200,
www.tihanyiapatsag.hu, daily 9am-6pm
Apr-Sep, 10am-5pm Oct, 10am-4pm
Nov-Mar, HUF 1,000

The ochre-colored Benedictine Abbey of Tihany with its twin bell towers rises above the town and the lake from the top of the volcanic hill. Entrance to the abbey includes the museum, which is accessed from the crypt of the church. The museum displays artifacts from the old abbey, manuscripts, and even contemporary art. Make sure you stop in the abbey shop on the way out and buy some of the craft beers brewed by the abbey monks.

Once you're done immersing yourself in history, head out to the rampart next to the abbey for the viewing platform. The views stretch out over the turquoise-colored lake dotted with little sailboats all the way to the hills of the northern shore and the high-rise hotels on the southern side of the lake.

HIKING

There are two lakes on Tihany itself, the Inner Lake (Belső tó) and Outer Lake (Külső tó), both of which formed from the craters of two volcanoes that make up the peninsula. You get spectacular views on the walks around them.

The Inner Lake lies next to the town. Take the streets down the hill from the abbey due west—keep an eye out for Major utca, which will bring you down to the lakeside, or, instead, head northwest from the abbey to Kiserdőtelep út and walk till you see the trails marked.

Another popular route is the wood-dense trail up to the Calvary, an open-air representation of the crucifixion of Jesus, with statues and crosses marking the trail up the hill. The trail winds through a forested valley to the medieval hermitage carved into the rocks by Greek Orthodox hermits in the 11th century. Begin the hike at the Calvary, just north of the monastery on Árpád utca, and walk up to the top. Make sure you turn around for amazing views of the abbey and Lake Balaton from the top of the hill. From here, you'll see signs marked to the hermitage (Barátlakások) and just follow the woodland trail. The hike will take around 40 minutes.

The **tourist information center** on Tihany (Kossuth Lajos utca 20, tel. 06/87-448-804, www.tourinform. hu, Mon-Fri 10am-4pm Jan-Apr, Sat 10am-3pm from mid-April-end-Apr, Mon-Fri 9am-5pm, Sat-Sun 10am-4pm May-June, Mon-Fri 9am-6pm, Sat-Sun 10am-6pm June-Aug, Mon-Fri 9am-5pm, Sat-Sun 10am-4pm Sep) can provide detailed information on hiking trails.

BEACHES
Sajkodi Strand

Sajkodi Sor 22, tel. 06/70-380-0328, www.sajkodistrand.hu, daily 8am-8pm May-Sep, HUF 400

The Sajkodi Beach lies on the western end of the peninsula, far away from the more popular and busier Tihany. It's a 50-minute walk or a 10-minute ride in a car (or a taxi). Compared to other beaches in Balaton, this one is quiet and hidden—perfect if you want to escape the crowds. The grassy banks

Tihany Abbey is one of the most famous landmarks of Lake Balaton.

leading down to the lake, with steps leading into the water, give this beach a green and romantic look. The views from here are incredible—overlooking the western side of the lake, you can see the volcanic mountains of the northern shore in the distance. You can rent a sunbed for HUF 500, and parking costs HUF 1,200 for the day. You can also rent water bicycles (HUF 2,000 per hour, from the ticket office) or kayaks (HUF 600-2,000 per hour).

SHOPPING
Tihanyi Levendula Galéria
Kossuth utca 41, tel. 07/366-3367, www. levendulamanufaktura.hu, daily 10am-6pm

This little boutique in the heart of Tihany specializes in all things lavender. Whether you want to buy bundles of dried flowers artfully wrapped up, artisanal soaps, lavender-based cosmetics, or even cute pastel floral pouches filled with the aromatic flower, you can find a charming gift here. The shop feels inspired by rustic, vintage Provence, with faded white furniture, vintage ceramics, and stone walls. There is another shop in the village on Batthyány út.

Tihany is famous for lavender.

FOOD
Régi Idők Udvara És Skanzen
Batthyányi út 3, tel. 06/70-284-6705, Tue-Sun noon-9pm, entrées HUF 3,150-5,200

This unique restaurant does more than just serve up local specials like Hungarian-style fattened goose liver with a ratatouille of local vegetables and egg barley or cold smoked trout served simply with bread and gherkins. The establishment doubles as an amateur ethnographic museum with old farm equipment hanging in the bar-terrace. It's worth walking around this peaceful garden and inside the whitewashed interior of this traditional Tihany farmhouse. Try the beer—which is brewed on-site.

Rege Cúkrászda

✪ Rege Cúkrászda
Kossuth Lajos utca 22, tel. 06/30-289-3647, www.apatsagicukraszda.hu, daily 9am-6pm May-Oct, cakes HUF 850-1,200

Rege Cúkrászda is a magical little café and confectionary set just beside the abbey. It merits a visit for its incredible terrace with perfect views and extensive panoramas from 150 meters (500 feet) above Lake Balaton. They serve all kinds of local delicacies such as craft beer made in the abbey next door and lavender lemonade, but a must-try is their *lavendula krémes*, a

Kék Lilliom is a traditional guesthouse.

layered custard cake with lavender-infused cream.

ACCOMMODATIONS
Kék Lilliom Ház

Visszhang 1, tel. 06/30-243-9369,
www.booking-tihany.com, €74-102 d
apartment including breakfast

Kék Lilliom Ház is a magical farmhouse complex at the heart of Tihany. From the street it's hidden, but enter through the wooden gate, climb the stone steps, and rise up into an enchanted garden. Swallows nest under the arches of the whitewashed porch in the summer and kids splash about in the small garden pool. The old thatched-roof farmhouse has been split up into apartments catering to two and also parties of four and five. Breakfast is an elaborate spread of seasonal and local specials, like fresh vegetables and local cheeses, and if the weather is good enough you can take it on the terrace; if not just sit in the beamed dining room by the fire.

GETTING THERE
TRAIN AND BUS

To get to Tihany from Budapest, first take the train to Balatonfüred. Just next to the train station you'll find a bus depot where you can get the bus to Tihany (it's written on the front of the bus). It will take about 30 minutes from the train station, and you get a really scenic ride thrown in. Buses are operated by Volánbusz (www.volanbusz.hu) and go two to three times an hour, up to 15 times a day, and take 20-30 minutes to reach Tihany (tickets HUF 310).

If you take the bus from Balatonfüred, this will put you down at the heart of the small town at the heart of the peninsula. From here most sites, like the famous abbey, are a 5- to 10-minute walk.

CAR

The drive from Balatonfüred takes around 10 minutes. Just follow Route 71 and the signs to Tihany. Parking prices around the town range from HUF 120 to 250 per hour, depending on the location.

Badacsony

Badacsony (pop. 2,300), a famous wine region on Balaton's northern shore, is known for its volcanic terroir and scenic vineyards. Badacsony lies around a volcanic hill of the same name that kind of looks like a plug—or more appropriately a cork—and you may need to trek up the hill to reach the best vineyards, but it'll be worth it for the view and the wine. The downtown part of Badacsony is a little touristy, with a jetty, souvenir shops, a beach, and restaurants, kind of like what you'll find in Balatonfüred and not

Badacsony is famous for its wines and vineyards.

really worth the extra minutes on the train. Your best bet is to hit the wineries—try some wine made from the local Kéknyelű grape—on the slopes of the hill to get the best out of Badacsony.

TOP EXPERIENCE

✪ WINERIES

The Badacsony wine region is spread out around Badacsony Hill and is away from the bustle of the port-side town, usually a 20-30-minute walk northward up the hill. To reach the wineries, it's best to walk or take a taxi (or drive if you have someone willing to be a designated driver).

Borbély Family Winery

Káptalantóti út 19, tel. 06/30-927-1414,
www.borbelypince.hu, open on demand,
tasting appointments by phone or online

Explore this beautiful winery—and drink wine—in the middle of a vineyard. It's worth coming in the summer to taste their wines on the terrace overlooking the surrounding countryside, but if the weather is off there is a cozy cellar, too. You need to call or reserve on their website in advance to register for tastings—you can choose whether you want to try 6, 8, or 10 wines (HUF 3,000-6,000 per person). Try their Tomaj Badacsonyi Rózsakő–Olaszrizling-Kéknyelű blend for a classic Badacsony white with mineral hints.

To reach this family-run vineyard, get off the train at the Badacsonytomaj train station instead of Badacsony. Take Kert utca and continue north up the hill. The walk is around 20 minutes and the winery is signposted.

Németh Pince

Római út 127, tel. 06/70-772-1102,
www.nemethpince.hu, daily 11am-6pm
May-Oct, appointment only Nov-Apr

This is one of Badacsony's smallest wineries, but its central location (a 10-minute walk from the Badacsony train station) and familial atmosphere make it worth a visit. The vineyard has been passed down through the Németh family over the generations, and it specializes in late-harvested grapes, which makes their wines a little sweeter than the others in the region as the grapes retain more sugar. Another delightful detail is that their wines come in hand-painted bottles—and can be painted to order, so make the perfect gift. Try the Kéknyelű (HUF 1,000 for a glass) or the sweet ice wine—a dessert wine made from grapes that have been frozen on the vine (HUF 1,000).

Laposa Winery

Római út 197, tel. 06/20-777-7133, www.bazaltbor.hu, daily 11am-7pm

The Laposa Estate perches itself on the southern banks of Badacsony Hill overlooking Lake Balaton. Sip through a tasting selection of their quality wines on their terrace with amazing views. Wine tastings come with cold savory bites from local producers—but if you call in advance you can request a meal prepared from family recipes with local produce to go with the wines you want to try. You can choose to taste wines by the glass or try a guided wine tasting of six to nine wines (HUF 3,000-4,000 per person). You can reach Laposa on foot, a 15-minute walk northeast from the train station, or take a taxi.

FOOD

Szőlőhegy Bisztró

Kisfaludy Sándor utca 5, tel. 06/87-431-382, www.szolohegybisztro.hu, daily noon-9pm, entrées HUF 3,250-7,490

Szőlőhegy Bisztró wins when it comes to location, being high up on the hill overlooking Lake Balaton through the vines. Dine on local dishes and sip the wine from the surrounding vineyards

under their vine-covered colonnade above the lake. The menu changes on a seasonal basis, but if you can, try the catfish paprikás with homemade pasta served with cottage cheese, lardons, and sour cream, or the grilled zander fish served with a Kéknyelű wine sauce with sautéed vegetables and polenta.

Katica

Egry sétány 8, www.katicagast.hu, Wed-Mon noon-10pm May-Sep, entrées HUF 1,790-5,400

Katica is a family-owned restaurant in a wooden house between the vineyards and the town, great for families and hungry tummies. You can't go wrong with goulash, fish soup, or any of the local fish dishes with fresh catch from the lake, and you can be sure you won't leave hungry. But note that the wines served are only table wines, so if you want to taste something fancy, this is not the place for you.

ACCOMMODATIONS

Óbester Panzió

Római út 203, tel. 06/30-213-0225, www.obester.hu, €60-77 d including breakfast

This family-owned B&B resides in a 200-year-old building on the western side of the hill. It's a quiet sanctuary enveloped with walnut trees and vines, and it has amazing views across to the lake. The center of Badacsony is a short walk away. The B&B has eight rooms and two apartments, and all come with private bathrooms, refrigerator, and air-conditioning. The look of the hotel blends the old with the new—heavy, dark wood beams and pillars add character to the old farmhouse, whereas the décor is white, brightened up with colorful accents from the pillows and rugs, along with modern abstract art hanging on the walls.

Hotel Bonvino

*Park utca 22, tel. 06/87-532-210, www.
hotelbonvino.hu, €230-260 d including
breakfast and dinner*

Hotel Bonvino brings you the two
pleasures and pastimes on Lake
Balaton: wine and wellness. Just 300
meters (330 yards) from the shores of
the lake, this modern luxurious hotel
has 48 uniquely designed rooms drawing inspirations from the surrounding
wine region. There is a state-of-the-art
wellness area, with a stunning pool
with an artificial waterfall, a whirlpool
tub, Finnish and infrared saunas, and
a steam room. The hotel restaurant
serves up local dishes and snacks; try
the locally sourced mangalica ham or
goat cheese, and there are more than
100 wines on the wine list.

GETTING THERE
TRAIN

The easiest way to get to Badacsony is
by train operated by MÁV from Déli
train station in Budapest, in the direction of Tapolca. It's farther than
Balatonfüred, taking at least 2 hours
40 minutes from Budapest, but can be
over 3 hours if you take a slower train.
One-way tickets cost HUF 3,395, and
there are four trains per day, the first
leaving Budapest at 8am, the last at
3:55pm.

The last direct train leaves
Badacsony at 5:15pm, but you can
also come back later if you choose
an indirect train, such as the 8:30pm
train going to Székesfehérvár, where
you change for trains to Budapest.
Badacsony could be combined with
Balatonfüred as there are direct train
connections between the two (easier
if you do this with a rental car), but
unless you're spending the night, it's
best to choose either Balatonfüred or
Badacsony as you won't fit everything
into one day.

CAR

From Balatonfüred the drive takes
around 45 minutes on Route 71,
which is a scenic drive along the lake.
Most wineries have their own parking,
but public parking in the center of the
town close to the lakeside costs around
HUF 280 an hour.

GETTING AROUND

You can explore the area on foot
or get a taxi, like Badacsony Taxi
(06/20-544-4234).

Siófok

Set on the southern shore of the lake,
what Siófok (pop. 25,000) lacks in scenic hills of the north it makes up with
atmosphere, earning its title as the
"Capital of Lake Balaton." Budapest
flocks to its golden lakeside beaches
with its shallow water and its vibrant
nightlife in the summer. Siófok has
that "seaside" feel, with endless neon
signs, cocktail happy hours, and a
50-meter-high (165-foot-high) Ferris
wheel around the Petőfi Promenade.
Scale the water tower built in 1912,
where you'll find viewing platforms
and chic bars with incredible views
over the lake.

Because Siófok lies on the southern shore of the lake, it's difficult to

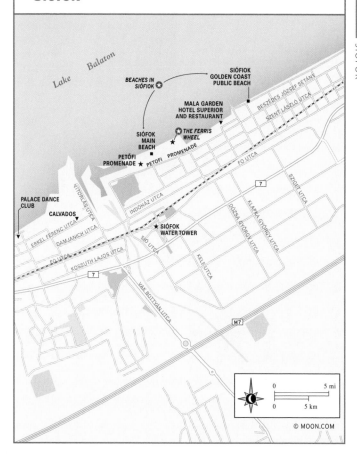

Siófok

© MOON.COM

combine with the resorts of the northern shore unless you're planning to spend the night.

SIGHTS

PETŐFI PROMENADE

Running parallel to Siófok Main Beach, the Petőfi Promenade is packed in summer with people in shorts, slapping the sidewalk with flip-flops as they walk along the mile-long stretch. Tall trees, umbrella-covered beach bars, restaurants, street food vendors, and pop-up shops in wooden huts line this road just south of the beach. After 7pm, it becomes a pedestrian-only zone, and by night it becomes a happening spot clad in neon lighting and party-goers staggering to and from the clubs and pubs. Most of the hotels in the area are immediately surrounding it.

✪ THE FERRIS WHEEL

Petőfi sétány, www.siofokoriaskerek.hu,
Sun-Thu 4pm-midnight, Fri-Sat 4pm-1am
June-Sep, HUF 2,000

Towering more 50 meters (165 feet) tall, the Ferris wheel in Siófok is the very first Hungarian-made wheel. Not only that, during the 10-minute ride you can enjoy views over Central Europe's most famous lake from open-air pods that can fit five to six people. You can see all the way over to Tihany and even spot the twin towers of its famous abbey, as well as the volcanic hills on the northern shore of the lake.

the Art Nouveau water tower in Siófok

the Ferris wheel on Siófok's main beach

Note that you can only access the Ferris wheel inside the Siófok Main Beach, so you will need to get a ticket for this, too, but if you go between 4 and 6pm, the beach entrance is included (get this ticket at the Kinizsi Pál utca entrance).

SIÓFOK WATER TOWER

Fő tér 11, tel. 06/30-244-8888, www.
viztorony.com, daily 9am-midnight June-Sep,
Tue-Thu and Sun 10am-5pm, Fri 10am-9pm,
Sat 10am-10pm Oct-May, HUF 850

Since it was built in 1912, the Siófok Water Tower has become a symbol of the town. It rises up 45 meters (150

feet), made out of reinforced concrete. This historic tower is now a huge tourist draw following its renovation in 2012. Now it has an open-air viewing platform with 360-degree views; the Water Tower Café & Oxygen Bar (same opening hours as above) and the Samsung Experience Center (same opening hours as above) are set inside the old tower. The Samsung Experience Center occupies the top floor on a rotating platform, with panoramic views and interactive touchscreen games.

TOP EXPERIENCE

✪ BEACHES
Siófok Main Beach

Petőfi sétány 3, tel. 06/84-310-327,
daily 8am-6pm May-Sep, HUF 1,000

Siófok's Main Beach is Balaton's largest beach, covering an area that's over 8 hectares (20 acres), with a capacity for 13,500 people. This is not the beach for you if you want peace and quiet, but with its Bluewave Flag (indicating the water quality here is excellent) and its high services, you can still get that resort feel in Hungary, even though it's a landlocked country. Although most of the beach area is covered with grass, the eastern part is sandy, popular for families with kids. Trendy young people head over to Plázs (www.plazssiofok.hu, entrance fee HUF 1,500), a beach club with a huge sundeck, pool, terrace, and sun loungers.

Siófok Golden Coast Public Beach

Szent István sétány, tel. 06/84-696-236, daily 8am-9pm, HUF 200 8am-4pm, HUF 100 4pm-6pm, free after 6pm

If you want an alternative to the Main Beach, head east to Siófok's Golden Coast Public Beach, which offers bathing on a budget. Tickets are cheap, and free after 6pm, and you have plenty of places to set a towel down on the 4-kilometer-long (2.5-mile-long) grassy stretch. The views are wonderful at sunset, so it's worth staying here till the sun goes down, after which you can saunter back to the Petőfi Prominade for the evening.

NIGHTLIFE

Being Hungary's "summer capital," Siófok is quite the party hub. The area surrounding the Main Beach pumps out techno music all day long, and crowds spill in an out of the bars surrounding Petőfi sétány, even while the sun beats down. But if you're still in the mood to party once night hits, you won't struggle to find happening nightlife. Stick around the Petőfi sétány area for its bars and clubs that will go on late into the night. Some bars have well-known Hungarian or international DJs when the season is swinging.

Palace Dance Club

Deák Ferenc utca 2, tel. 06/30-200-8888, www.palace.hu, daily 10am-5am July-Aug, HUF 2,000-2,500 cover charge

The Palace Dance Club may only operate through July and August, but it's still one of the hottest party spots on Lake Balaton—and most enduring, having been partying each summer since 1990. The club is split into indoor and outdoor sections, perfect for those hot summer nights, and there is even a pool (sometimes there are pool parties organized, but good luck fitting in there as the club is always packed). The Palace Dance Club has a legendary reputation, with big international DJs such as Carl Cox and DJ Tiësto having spun here. Expect big parties with foam or confetti.

The Renegade Pub is a ruin bar on the shores of Lake Balaton.

Renegade Pub

Petőfi sétány 3, tel. 06/20-317-3304, www. renegadepub.hu, Mon-Sat 7pm-7am, Sun 7pm-midnight June-Sep, no cover charge

The party goes on till late in this wooden-beamed pub on the busy Petőfi sétány. Things can get a little out of hand when the live music or the DJ kicks off the party and the dance floor gets so cramped that party-going hedonists will get on top of the tables to dance.

FOOD
Calvados

Erkel Ferenc utca 11, tel. 06/84-314-579,
www.calvados.hu, daily noon-10pm,
HUF 2,500-5,000 entrées

Calvados serves up a selection of Hungarian dishes with international inspirations. It's perched right next to the marina, about a 10-minute walk from the main beach area. Ask the server for recommendations, but you can fall back on the goose liver cooked in Tokaj wine sauce or any of their fish dishes from the local catch. Sit out on the terrace if you can get a table, but since there is a large indoor section, the restaurant is also open off-season.

Mala Garden Restaurant

Petőfi sétány 15/a, tel. 06/84-506-688,
http://en.malagarden.hu/restaurant,
daily 11am-10:30pm off-season,
11am-midnight peak season, HUF
2,790-6,990 entrées

Grab a table on the terrace at Mala Garden Restaurant overlooking the beach along the lake. The menu is eclectic, with modern takes on Hungarian favorites like paprika chicken and roasted pork cutlets, as well as some Mediterranean specials and Southeast Asian noodle dishes. You can try a range of Hungarian wines from their extensive wine menu, but if you're feeling adventurous, make sure you have a shot of the celery *pálinka!*

ACCOMMODATIONS
Mala Garden Hotel Superior

Petőfi sétány 15/a, tel. 06/84-506-688,
http://en.malagarden.hu, €82-125 d
including breakfast

Balaton may buzz with crowds on the beach by day and with its hedonistic nightlife by night, but Mala Garden offers an oasis of tranquility when you want some rest. The hotel backs onto the grassy banks of the Danube shore, with the deluxe rooms overlooking the lake (although all rooms have their own balcony). The rooms are a globetrotter's fantasy decorated with warm red walls, vintage kilims (hand-knotted Persian carpets), and handcrafted items from Bali. A luxurious champagne breakfast is included in the price, as is the use of the wellness center.

GETTING THERE
TRAIN

Siófok takes 1 hour 20 minutes from Déli station in the direction of Nagykanizsa. Tickets cost HUF 2,375, and trains run up to nine times a day, 6:30 am until 7:30pm. Siófok's main train station puts you right in the heart of the town, just a five-minute walk from the lake and the main sites like the water tower.

CAR

The drive from Budapest takes just over an hour; take the M7 southwest and follow the signs to Siófok. Parking costs between HUF 160 and 320 per hour depending on the location and the season.

EGER

Eger (pop. 53,000) has gone down in Hungarian legend as a bastion that resisted the Ottoman occupation in the 16th century. The city paints a vibrant picture, with Baroque houses adorned with intricate iron-work, in addition to the northernmost Ottoman minaret; its impressive medieval castle famed for its siege is still a draw today. All of this makes a perfect day trip for anyone who loves history. You can also come just for the wine. Eger is known for its spicy Bikavér (Bull's Blood)

Itinerary Ideas 195
Sights 196
Wine Cellars 200
Food 201
Accommodations 203
Transportation........204

HIGHLIGHTS

✪ **EGER CASTLE:** Explore the interior of this fortress-like castle along with the complex labyrinth of tunnels that snakes beneath it (page 196).

✪ **EGER MINARET:** Climb to the top of the northernmost Ottoman minaret, a relic left behind from the Turkish occupation (page 199).

✪ **WINE TASTING IN THE VALLEY OF BEAUTIFUL WOMEN:** This atmospheric valley outside Eger holds wine cellars ranging from simple to stunning, some of which are carved into the hillside. The cellars are conveniently next to one another (page 202).

wine—named partly for its deep red color, but also believed by the Turks to have given the Hungarians superhuman power during battle. Taste it in the wineries around the city, or head to the cellars embedded in the caves at the Valley of Beautiful Women.

ORIENTATION

Eger is a compact city that's easy to get around on foot, as most of the sites are clustered around Eszterházy tér and Dobó István tér. The only part that is a little further afield is the Valley of Beautiful Women, which you can reach via a 20-minute walk or a 5-minute taxi ride from the center. You can also take in the sights around the town on the little trackless train (**Eger Városnéző Kisvonat,** begins on Egészségház utca, www.kisvonatok.hu/eger, daily 10am-6pm, HUF 1,000) that will take you out to the Valley of Beautiful Women.

PLANNING YOUR TIME

It takes only two hours to reach Eger, and although you could see the main sites in a day, I recommend also spending half a day in the Valley of Beautiful Women and soaking up the atmosphere with a few glasses of wine. For this reason I would spend the night to get the most out of this beautiful Baroque city. A good option is to make a beeline to the castle and then explore some of Eger's other sites before ending up at the Valley of Beautiful Women for some wine.

If you need a little help getting oriented, head to the **Eger Tourinform** (Bajcsy-Zsilinszky utca 9, tel. 06/517-715, Mon-Fri 8am-6pm, Sat 10am-4pm). For **luggage storage,** Eger bus station has facilities where you can store any baggage (HUF 200 for the first hour, HUF 50 any additional hours, 6am-noon and 1pm-6pm weekdays, 8am-noon and 1pm-4pm weekends).

Itinerary Ideas

You can do Eger in a day, but if you spend the night then you can really enjoy the city at your own pace. If you're only going for the day, perhaps leave out the Valley of Beautiful Women and the Lyceum.

DAY 1

It's worth taking a tour (40 minutes) of the casemates at Eger Castle. Times vary, so call in advance; they usually leave every hour on the hour from the cash desk. You may need to ask for an English-language guide in advance, and pay an extra fee.

1 Start at Dobó István tér and admire the view of the castle from below, then cross the river and head north toward the **Eger Minaret.** If you fancy a climb, then go inside to the top of the minaret for an amazing panorama over the city. However, you'll be treated to more views soon, so if you want to save your energy just admire the impressive minaret from below.

2 Take the short walk up to **Eger Castle** and enjoy the vista on the road leading up by the castle walls. Enter the castle from the north entrance at the top (you will have to buy a ticket). Grab lunch at 1552 (located in the castle), then visit a few of the castle museums. If you were lucky enough to get on an English-language tour of the casemates, enjoy it!

the Dobó István tér

3 Stroll down from the castle, exiting on the southeastern side, and walk over to Egészségház utca and take the little sightseeing train to the **Valley of Beautiful Women.** Spend the evening exploring the wine cellars that take your fancy, accompanied by a snack of bread with pork or duck fat, or indulge in a cheese plate or cold cuts. When you're done, get a taxi back to the hotel.

4 If you're still hungry after all that snacking at the cellars, head back to the base of the castle at the south entrance, and get dinner at **Macok Bistro and Wine Bar,** which attracts Hungarians as well as an international crowd.

DAY 2

1 Start at **the Lyceum** to visit the Baroque library, the astronomical museum, and the camera obscura.

2 Once you're done at the Lyceum, head over to the **Eger Basilica.** Try to make it for one of the morning organ concerts (Mon-Sat 11:30am-noon, Sun 12:45pm-1:15pm May-Oct, HUF 800).

3 Wander over the cobbled streets to Dobó István tér for lunch at **Depresso Kávéház és Étterem.** If the weather is good, sit on the terrace with amazing views of the square and the castle.

4 Once you're ready to leave, head back to Budapest by bus. The **bus station** is within walking distance and there are frequent services in the afternoon.

Sights

✪ EGER CASTLE

Vár 1, tel. 06/36-312-744, www.egrivar.hu, Castle gate open 8am-6pm Nov-March, 8am-10pm Apr-Oct, exhibitions 10pm-4pm Nov-March, 10am-6pm Apr-Oct, HUF 1,700 for the museums, HUF 850 grounds (after 5:30pm high season, 3:30pm low season)

Eger Castle resides on 500 square meters (5,400 square feet) of land at the top of a hill and is built more like a fortress than a fairy-tale castle. It was built up over several centuries—you'll even find foundations of a 12th century cathedral on site—but most of what you see dates to the 15th and 16th centuries, including the Gothic Bishop's Palace (mostly a 20th-century reconstruction but still contains elements from the original 15th-century palace) and the wood-turret-topped stone walls of the Bornemissza Bastion (1554) at the main gate.

It's worth walking along the path running parallel to the battlements just for views over the terracotta-hued rooftops, the minaret, and the towers

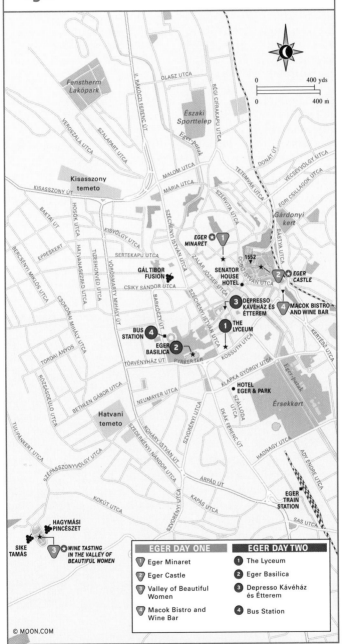

Eger

Eger

Fenstherm
Lakópark

Északi
Sporttelep

Kisasszony
temeto

EGER
MINARET ⓵

SENATOR
HOUSE
HOTEL

1552

EGER ⓶ EGER
CASTLE

GÁL TIBOR
FUSION

DEPRESSO ⓷
KÁVÉHÁZ ÉS
ÉTTEREM

MACOK BISTRO ⓸
AND WINE BAR

THE ① LYCEUM

BUS ⓸
STATION

EGER ⓶
BASILICA

HOTEL
EGER & PARK

Érsekkert

Hatvani
temeto

EGER
TRAIN
STATION

HAGYMÁSI
PINCÉSZET

SIKE
TAMÁS

⓷ WINE TASTING
IN THE VALLEY OF
BEAUTIFUL WOMEN

EGER DAY ONE

1. Eger Minaret
2. Eger Castle
3. Valley of Beautiful Women
4. Macok Bistro and Wine Bar

EGER DAY TWO

1. The Lyceum
2. Eger Basilica
3. Depresso Kávéház és Étterem
4. Bus Station

0 400 yds
0 400 m

© MOON.COM

of Baroque churches. High stone walls enclose the grounds housing a cluster of buildings, like the aforementioned the Bishop's Palace (including a museum of the castle on the second floor) and modern buildings containing the Eger Art Gallery.

There is a complex labyrinth of tunnels and casemates carved into solid rock running underneath the castle, some going as far as 24 kilometers (15 miles) from the town. Although you can only visit about 300 meters (330 yards) with a guide, it's fascinating to catch a glimpse of Eger's intricate castle engineering—part of the secret why Eger held out against the Turks for such a long time. The price for the museums includes admission to the casemates, whose entrance lies at the Dark Gate in the eastern part of the castle complex. When buying your ticket for the castle, ask about tours to the casemates (times vary, so call in advance; they usually leave every hour on the hour from the cash desk). Most tours are in Hungarian, but for an extra HUF 800 you can get an English-language guide, but you may need to ask in advance. Tours last around 40 minutes.

The best way to reach Eger Castle is to walk up the path from Tinódi Sebestyén tér at the foot of the castle, which will bring you up to the castle gate. The gentle 300-meter (330-yard) stroll up to the castle walls is worth it for the view alone. You'll see a panorama over the terracotta rooftops, church spires, and even the minaret.

THE LYCEUM

Essterházy tér 1, tel. 06/36-520-400, www. uni-eszterhazy.hu, Tower and Astronomical Museum www.varazstorony.hu, Tue-Sun 9:30am-5:30pm May-Aug, 9:30am-3:30pm

Eger Castle as seen from the top of the minaret

If you ever get lost, just look up to see the Eger Lyceum's tower.

Mar-Apr and Sep-Oct, 9:30am-1pm
Fri-Sun Nov-Dec and Feb-Mar, HUF 1,300;
Library Tue-Sun 9:30am-1:30pm Mar-Apr,
9:30am-3:30pm May-Sep, HUF 1,000

If you like beautiful old libraries, vintage observatories, and historic university buildings, then pay a visit to Eger's Lyceum, an 18th-century college building that is a particularly fascinating landmark. The Lyceum towers above the city center, even taller than the church and basilica. Climb to the top of the tower to see one of the three camera obscuras in the world that's still operational today. On the way up, you can break your journey with an astronomical museum set in an old observatory with 18th-century telescopes and curiosities, and there is also the "Magic Tower," an interactive physics laboratory that's fun for kids as well as adults. The highlight of the Lyceum, which began as a theological college in the 1700s, is the Baroque, wood-clad library with beautiful frescoes on the first floor.

✪ EGER MINARET

Knézich Károly utca, tel. 06/70-202-43-53,
www.minareteger.hu, daily 10am-6pm
Apr-Sep, 10am-5pm Oct-Mar, HUF 400

Eger may symbolize the Hungarian resistance against the Turks, but you'll find plenty of traces of the Ottomans embedded into the cityscape. Eger's minaret—the northernmost building from the Ottoman era in Europe—is quite the sight, rising 40 meters (130 feet) with 97 spiral steps to the top. The Turks built the minaret in 1596 following their victory. When the Habsburg army recaptured the town 91 years later, they tried to pull it down with 400 oxen, but the tower held out. The balcony at the top of the tower is worth it for the view, but it is rather narrow and you may feel dizzy or claustrophobic, since the stairway up is also pretty tight.

EGER BASILICA

Pyrker János tér 1, tel. 06/36-420-970,
www.eger-bazilika.plebania.hu,
Mon-Sat 7am-7pm, Sun 1pm-7pm

Eger Basilica is the third largest in Hungary, after Esztergom and Budapest. You'll find this neoclassical basilica facing the Lyceum, looking like an overwrought Roman temple with imposing Corinthian columns.

Eger Minaret is one of the few relics left behind from the city's Turkish siege.

Eger's Basilica is one of the largest in the country.

It merits a look inside (especially if you appreciate frescoes), and the murals that adorn the three huge domes in bright bold colors will impress any art lover. Music lovers should pay a visit to one of the daily half-hour organ concerts (Mon-Sat 11:30am-noon, Sun 12:45pm-1:15pm May-Oct, HUF 800).

Wine Cellars

Wine has got its tendrils into Eger like the vines climbing the terraces surrounding the town. Thanks to Eger's mild microclimate, you can find both excellent whites and reds in the region. Although you can get single-varietal wines, particularly from the quality cellars, Eger is most famous for its cuvées. The spicy, blood-red Egri Bikavér—the Bull's Blood of Eger—blends three to five grape types. If you're partial to whites, try the Egri Csillag—the Star of Eger—a dry, crisp white blend made from local grape types with floral and fruity notes.

There are good wine producers in Eger. Keep an eye out for St. Andrea, Bolyki, or Orsolya. However, these wineries are located far out of town and require a car to get you there. If you want to taste local wine, sample some Eger specials at the following cellar.

Gál Tibor Fusion

Csiki Sándor utca 10, tel. 06/20-852-5002, www.galtibor.hu, Tue-Thu 10am-7pm, Fri-Sat 10am-11pm, Sun 10am-1pm
Winemaker Gál Tibor has 40 hectares (100 acres) of vineyards around Eger, but the good news is you don't need to

go far out of town to try these fantastic wines. In downtown Eger, Gál Tibor Fusion occupies a 1,400-square-meter (15,000-square-foot) complex, home to a 500-year-old wine cellar in addition to a bar and a wine tasting room that can seat 120 people. The building is worth the visit for its blend of modern design, with features like wireframe lampshades and chalkboard art, and its history. There is also a free museum dedicated to the history of Bull's Blood wine on the first floor. Try the zingy and floral Egri Csillag or the pinot noir rosé with hints of strawberry.

Food

Macok Bistro and Wine Bar

Tinódi Sebestyén tér 4, tel. 06/36-516-180, www.imolaudvarhaz.hu/en/the-macok-bisztro-wine-bar.html Sun-Thu noon-10pm, Fri-Sat noon-11pm, entrés HUF 2,950-7,900

Just because Macok Bistro and Wine Bar lies by the entrance of the castle doesn't make it a tourist trap. You'll find Hungarians and an international crowd at this eccentric restaurant that blends industrial chic with its own quirky style. But what's even better is its modern, adventurous kitchen, offering gourmet degustation menus at excellent prices. Creative dishes, such as duck liver brûlée served with homemade milk loaf and plum jam, or coconut and pumpkin soup with pumpkin seed mousse, are beautifully presented and use locally sourced ingredients. The wine list features Eger's best local wineries—try some spicy reds from St. Andrea, Gál Tibor, or Attila Pince.

Depresso Kávéház és Étterem

Érsek utca 14/Dobó tér, tel. 06/30-886-6742, www.depresso.hu, Mon-Thu 9am-8pm, Fri-Sat 9am-9pm, Sun 9am-6pm, entrées HUF 2,100-3,150

This third-wave café wins the best terrace view in the city with front row seats overlooking Dobó Square and the castle. Pick up light bites like sandwiches and salads, plus excellent breakfast foods like bagels and eggs till 11:30am. There also are more substantial meals on offer, like pulled water buffalo burgers and seasonal dishes, along with local wine, Hungarian craft beer, and mixed drinks. Make sure you end your meal with one of their excellent specialty coffees. I am partial to their Depresso Tonic (a shot of espresso served with iced tonic and lemon) in the summer.

Macok is a great spot for lunch.

✪ WINE TASTING IN THE VALLEY OF BEAUTIFUL WOMEN

A must visit in Eger is wine cellars around the Valley of Beautiful Women.

For quality wine, you may be better off going to a wine bar in Eger or a winery in the surrounding countryside, but if it's atmosphere you're looking for, the Valley of Beautiful Women (Szépasszony-völgy) has it in spades.

There are close to 200 cellars embedded in a crescent-shaped valley in the suburbs of Eger. Some of the cellars are stunning: completely carved into the hillside and looking more like a church than a wine cellar. Others are more modest with just a few plastic chairs propped up against the bare cave walls. I love going from musty cellar to cellar, tasting wine straight from the barrel. The experience is best shared with friends and with a slice of *zsíros kenyér*—bread spread with goose or pork fat, raw onions, and paprika (and, yes, it is more delicious than it sounds)—or a *pince lepény*, a kind of baked savory pancake with cheese and ham (these are usually extra and will set you back around HUF 500).

There are dozens of legends behind the region's seductive name, by the way. One recounts the story about a beautiful Hungarian girl who escaped marriage to a Turk by giving him some Bull's Blood wine (he wasn't used to drinking wine), and another says the beautiful women were prehistoric goddesses who received sacrifices in the valley.

1552

Eger Castle, tel. 06/30-869-6219,
www.1552.hu, daily 11am-10pm,
entrées HUF 2,790-6,890

1552 is the only restaurant in Eger Castle, but it has done something quite original, combining Hungarian cuisine, Turkish dishes (a nod to its Ottoman past), and cutting-edge culinary techniques. Daunted by the menu? Go for the game, as chef Mátyás Hegyi's specialty is wild boar. The décor inside is bold, with claret leatherette seating, exposed brick set against patterned peach wallpaper, Turkish-style tiles, and bulbs hanging inside birdcages. This is not a place to come when you're in a hurry, though, as the service can be a bit slow.

WINES

The wines vary depending on the harvest and the winery, but you can find the famous red cuvée, **Bull's Blood,** and other wines like those from indigenous grapes including **Egri leányka** (a dry white wine), **olaszrizling** (a white wine that can be sweet or dry), and **hárslevelű** (an aromatic sweet white). Should you like any of the wine, you can take some back in a plastic bottle— directly from the barrel, one liter will cost around HUF 1,000— which is only a good idea if you plan to drink it before your flight home.

WINE CELLARS

Wine cellars in this area are informal, and most people come for the experience rather than to visit a specific cellar. However, the two following are worth seeking out:

HAGYMÁSI PINCÉSZET

Szépasszony-völgy 19, tel. 06/20-326-4364,
www.bormester.hu, daily 9am-11pm
Stepping inside this cellar feels more like you've entered a temple dedicated to wine. Set on two levels, this wine cellar fortified with bricks can fit up to 100 guests. Old winemaking equipment hangs on the stone walls, and a stone statue resides in the niche in the brick arch above the bar. You can try 18 wines here, as well as two types of *pálinka*. If you're hungry you must try their *pince lepény*!

SIKE TAMÁS

Disznófősor 43, tel. 06/742-9024, www.sikeboraszat.hu,
Mon-Thu 10:30am-9pm, Fri-Sat 10:30am-11pm, Sun 9am-7pm
This 100-meter-long (330-foot-long) cellar carved into the rock in the hillside fits 120 people inside and 60 on the terrace. Wines are matured in oak barrels and bottles in the inner part of the cellar, and the great thing about this traditional cellar is the staff who are happy to teach you about the wines you're drinking. Individuals and small groups can drop in for tastings, but do contact the cellar in advance if you're coming in a big group. Taste their merlot or syrah, or their blend of Egri Csillag if you prefer a white.

GETTING THERE

The cellars are a 20-minute **walk** from Eger's city center. You can also take the little **trackless train** to Szépasszony-völgy or take a **taxi** (you can ask for Valley of Beautiful Women if you can't pronounce the Hungarian). The valley is compact and all the cellars lie right next to each other, so just explore the area on foot.

Accommodations

Hotel Eger & Park

Szálloda utca 3, tel. 06/522-222,
www.hotelegerpark.hu, €90-170 d
including breakfast

The Hotel Eger & Park is actually two hotels: the Park Hotel was Eger's first hotel, which opened in the 1929, and is built in a neo-Baroque style, whereas the Hotel Eger was built at the end of the 20th century. Today the two hotels are joined by a connecting corridor, and guests from both hotels can use the state-of-the-art wellness facility and spa, with thermal water pools, swimming pools, infrared sauna, aroma cabin, and salt chamber. The Park Hotel is much smaller, with only 35 rooms, whereas the Hotel Eger has over 170 rooms. You can find the filling buffet breakfast in the elegant dining rooms in the Park Hotel.

Senator House Hotel

Dobó tér 11, tel. 06/36-320-466, www.
senatorhaz.hu, €64-81 d including breakfast
Senator House Hotel lies right at the heart of Eger in an 18th-century inn. There are 11 cozy rooms on the upper floors decorated all in white with accents coming from brightly colored oil paintings, pillows, and flowers. The reception area, filled with curiosities and antiques, shares

the Park Hotel

the ground floor with a restaurant. The best thing is really the location, as rooms look out to either Dobó square or one of the narrow side streets.

Transportation

GETTING THERE

You can catch the train operated by MÁV to Eger from Keleti train station in Budapest (2 hours, HUF 2,725). You can also get a direct bus with Volánbusz from the Stadion bus station in Budapest (2 hours, HUF 2,725). There are nine trains a day from 5am until 7pm, and buses run every half hour 8:15am-10:45pm. When you get arrive in Eger by bus, you will be in the city center (the bus station is a 3-minute walk from Eger Basilica). The train, on the other hand, puts you a 20-minute walk away in the south of the town. Local bus services are sporadic, so you may be better off taking a taxi (which will set you back around HUF 1,000). Try

City Taxi Eger (tel. 06/36-555-555) if you need a cab.

The drive by car takes around 1 hour 40 minutes from Budapest. Take the M3 northeast and keep an eye out for signposts to Eger. Parking costs in Eger range between HUF 200 and 360 per hour.

LEAVING EGER

The last bus back to Budapest leaves Eger at 8:15pm. The last train to Budapest leaves at 7pm.

From Eger, it's possible to continue on to Gödöllő by train, changing at Havtan (the journey takes 1 hour 45 minutes). If you're traveling by car you could make a detour back via Hollókő (1.5 hours driving).

HOLLÓKŐ

An hour's drive northeast of

Budapest, Hollókő (pop. 380) is a living museum for Hungarian village life and a UNESCO World Heritage site. As you wander down its cobbled streets and dip in and out of its numerous tiny museums, shops, and workshops in the historic houses, you'll catch a glimpse into the local culture.

Hollókő is a Palóc settlement. This ethnic subgroup of Hungarians from the northern part of Hungary and southern Slovakia are renowned for their colorful clothes, rich traditions, and hearty

Itinerary Idea 207
Sights 208
Food 211
Shopping.............. 212
Accommodations 214
Transportation........ 215

HIGHLIGHTS

✪ **HOLLÓKŐ CASTLE:** Hike up to a 13th-century castle for amazing views and a step back into medieval times (page 208).

✪ **VILLAGE MUSEUM OF HOLLÓKŐ:** This museum is a charming little time capsule that shows you how people lived in the village back in the 1920s (page 210).

✪ **SHOPPING FOR FOLK ART AND GIFTS:** If you're looking for unique and handcrafted Hungarian folk art—from ceramics, wood carvings, and leatherwork to hand-stitched embroidery you can buy on the roadside from old ladies—Hollókő is the place to do it (page 212).

food. Apart from the picture-postcard village with its pristine white houses and ethnographic curiosities, Hollókő also has an impressive medieval castle whose romantic ruined battlements overlook rolling hills carpeted with miles of unspoiled woodland.

ORIENTATION

Hollókő is a small village and it's easy to get around on foot. The Old Village is mostly car-free—and is also mostly cobblestone, so make sure to wear good shoes. The bus from Budapest drops you off near the Old Village, which is a five-minute walk away (just follow the signs), and around 15-20 minutes from the castle (take the road up the hill and follow the signs). It's very difficult to get lost as there are signposts in most places, even from the castle back into the village.

If you're looking for tourist information, start at the Hollóköves Kávézo–Infocafe (Kossuth út 50, tel. 06/20-626-2844, www.holloko. hu, daily 8am-4pm), where you can grab a cup of coffee and get oriented before you hit the main sights in the village.

Hollókő is a compact town that's easy to get around on foot.

PLANNING YOUR TIME

Hollókő is a great day trip for anyone interested in learning about Hungarian rural life and traditions. The town is easily visited in less than a day. It's an hour's drive from Budapest to Hollókő, or two hours if you take the bus (which follows a not-so-direct route to the village). If you're traveling by car, you could combine a stop in Hollókő with the journey back from Eger.

Itinerary Idea

You don't really need more than a day in Hollókő as the village is quite compact. Taking the direct bus gives you the perfect amount of time to see everything; it arrives in the village at 10:30am and departs at 4pm. That's more than enough to visit the castle, most of the museums, grab lunch, and do some shopping.

ESSENTIAL HOLLÓKŐ

1 Get off the bus and walk uphill, following the signs for Hollókő Castle. You'll reach the medieval castle after a 15-20 minute walk. Spend an hour wandering the various rooms and the battlements.

2 Follow the signs down to the village, along paths taking you past the woods. The path brings you out by the Palóc Doll Museum, which is like an ethnographic costume museum but in miniature. Step inside to see the colorful costumes.

3 Taste some local wines at Borpatika next door and tuck a bottle into your bag to take home.

4 Try a few slices of cheese at the Gazduram Sajtboltja as a pre-lunch aperitif.

5 Head into the Village Museum for a quick glimpse into the way locals used to live, then visit the Handicraft Printer's Museum next door.

6 Once you've got an appetite, head to Muskátli Vendéglő for a lunch of local Palóc dishes.

7 Take as stroll around the village to Szent Márton Church, one of the town's main landmarks (and a great spot for a photo op).

8 Time to shop! Explore folk art at a few of the craft shops, such as Fazekas Ház, before boarding the 4pm bus back to Budapest.

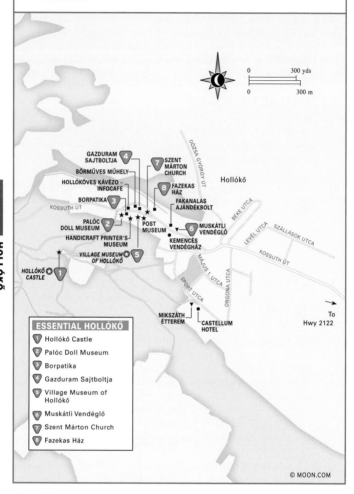

Hollókő

ESSENTIAL HOLLÓKŐ

1. Hollókő Castle
2. Palóc Doll Museum
3. Borpatika
4. Gazduram Sajtboltja
5. Village Museum of Hollókő
6. Muskátli Vendéglő
7. Szent Márton Church
8. Fazekas Ház

© MOON.COM

Sights

✪ HOLLÓKŐ CASTLE

Szállások út 30, tel. 06/30-508-2454,
www.hollokoivar.hu, daily 10am-5:30pm
mid-Mar-Oct; HUF 900

It's only a 15- to 20-minute walk from the bus stop at the edge of the village, but once you've reached this medieval castle you'll feel like you're in the middle of the countryside. From the ruined castle walls, the views spread out below you over the tree-clad Cserhat Hills.

Although the view alone makes the visit worthwhile, you should head into the main tower and get a glimpse back into the castle's life. The 13th-century castle has quite a history. First it served as a fort in the Middle Ages before it got captured by the Turks in the 17th century and then liberated by a Polish king in the 18th century. It mostly fell into ruin until renovations began in the 1960s. Today it's a mix between romantic ruins and a renovated immersive experience into its history. Inside the tower, various chambers are decked out in reproduction furniture with the occasional wax figure. You can wander into a 13th-century banquet hall, kitchen, bedroom (check out the wooden toilet just hanging over the edge), and the tiny bed in the guard's watchtower. There is also a small room with an interactive game allowing you to walk through the old castle, plus a documentary (in Hungarian only). Expect to spend over an hour at the castle.

SZENT MÁRTON CHURCH

Kossuth utca, tel. 06/32-388-528,
no opening hours, free

Szent Márton Church resides at the heart of the old village. It was built in 1889, on the site of a 16th-century granary. There are no official opening hours, but you can usually peek inside this tiny wooden church behind the bars just inside the entrance (you normally can't go in), and if you come at 8am on a Sunday you can join in the mass. The interior is very simple: a few benches covered with red cushions and embroidered tablecloths on the altar. However, the church exterior is one of the main landmarks of the town with its whitewashed walls and wooden tower. The church stands

Hollókő Castle

Szent Márton Church lies at the heart of the historic village.

on the crossroads between Kossuth utca and Petőfi Sándor utca, and it presents the perfect photo op of the village landscape—especially in the spring when the flower bed in front of the church is in full bloom.

MUSEUMS

Hollókő has a handful of interesting museums. Most are small and can be seen in about 20 minutes, so you can visit a good number on even a one-day trip.

✪ Village Museum of Hollókő

Kossuth utca 82, www.holloko.hu, daily 10am-6pm Apr-Oct, 10am-4pm Nov-Mar, HUF 400

See what village life was like in the early 20th century in this small, three-room museum in an old house in the heart of the village. You enter the kitchen, which despite appearances doubled as a bedroom because its chimney and stove served as the house's only source of heating. To the right, you'll see a room filled with farm equipment; the most interesting curiosity is a mobile crib that looks like a baby swing, which was used in the fields so the mother

could keep an eye on her child while she worked. The room to the left of the kitchen is known as the "Clean Room," with a large bed piled high with hand-embroidered bedding. This bed was only really used for births and deaths—or special occasions and hosting guests. The look of the house dates to the 1920s, after it was renovated following a fire in 1909 that destroyed most of the straw rooftops in the village. You only need 20 minutes here, but take some time to appreciate the little details, such as the turquoise wooden beams to keep the flies out, the embroidery, and painted crockery, and oddities like the smoking chamber where meat was smoked for preservation.

Palóc Doll Museum

Kossuth utca 96, tel. 06/30-394-4424, daily 10am-5pm Mar-Oct, HUF 400

This one-room museum (which is more like a long hall) is home to some 200 porcelain dolls decked out in realistic folk costumes. Most of the dolls are from the region, but there are a few dolls from Slovakia and Transylvania in the collection. The costumes, not the dolls, are the main feature here; some have traditional embroidery or intricate bead work, while others are adorned with ribbons, headdresses, and head scarves. It's like an ethnographic costume museum but in miniature. Although the museum is tiny, there's plenty of details and color to keep you interested for a good 20 minutes.

Handicraft Printer's Museum

Kossuth utca 84, tel. 06/70-774-8060, daily 10am-5pm Mar-Oct, HUF 200

This one-room museum is one of the village's quirkiest sites. It is home to a 1900s printer's shop with tools invented by Johannes Gutenberg, a 200-year-old printing press, hand-set type, and various prints. You can get hands-on: create your own poster or a Hollókő postcard. The museum staff give live demonstrations of the equipment and provide a little context into the history of the items. This museum stands out from the others in the village because it offers an insight beyond rural folk life. For any bookworm, it's fascinating to see these vintage printing presses in action. Other highlights include antique leather-bound books that are more than 100 years old, like a Bible whose last owner died in 1909. And if you're looking for a unique gift, you can pick up hand-bound notebooks, mini books with the phrase for "I love you" in every language, art prints, posters, and diaries.

Post Museum

Kossuth utca 80; tel. 06/30-435-3893; www.postamuzeum.hu/en/muzeumok/7/ postamuzeum-holloko; 10am-6pm Tue-Sun, Apr-Oct; HUF 600

The Post Museum takes you back in time to the village and the region's postal history. There are two rooms in this museum, and like the others in the village it takes up an entire house. A charming garden—which you can spot thanks to the red letter box—leads into the museum. Inside, the exhibition is a mix between old stamps and letters, a vintage postal uniform, and a few curiosities such as an old telephone switchboard. I personally love the few paintings on display showing the life of postal workers in the county. Many of the descriptions and historical contexts are in Hungarian, but it's worth a 20-minute visit if you love old stamps, letters, and local history.

Food

Hollókő is part of the Palóc ethnographic region. Although Palóc food overlaps with classic Hungarian cuisine, there are a few little nuances that make it different from dishes you'd find in the rest of the country. Soups play an important role in the regional cuisine and are usually hearty, thickened with milk, flour, or sour cream. Potatoes are also a core ingredient in Palóc cooking, and dishes are often spiced with fried onions, crumbled pork scratchings, buttermilk, cottage cheese, sour cream, and cabbage.

PALÓC
Muskátli Vendéglő

Kossuth utca 61, tel. 06/32-379-262, www. muskatlivendeglo.hu, Wed-Sat 11am-6pm, Sun 11am-5pm, entrées HUF 1,550-3,100

This centrally located restaurant feels like you've stepped into a magic garden and barn, where hand-painted plates and old farm tools adorn the walls. Although you can still find the Hungarian favorites, the best thing about this traditional restaurant is its focus on local Palóc dishes. Try the Palóc soup, a sour soup made with chunks of meat, vegetables, and sour cream, or the Nográd pork chop, a hearty dish named after the local county and served with garlic and mustard sauce and *sztrapacska,* a north-Hungarian potato pasta mixed with tangy ewe's cheese.

HUNGARIAN
Mikszáth Étterem

Sport út 14, tel. 06/21-300-0500, http://hotelholloku.hu/en/hotel/gastronomy/ mikszath-restaurant, daily 7:30am-10pm, entrés HUF 2,100-7,500

The Mikszáth Restaurant is part of the Castellum Hotel and serves fine dining and new-wave versions of local specials. Dishes are inspired by local cuisine with a gourmet twist. Try the sous-vide Mangalica pork cutlets—made with a local Hungarian breed of pig famous for its furry coat and delicious fatty meat—with a crispy parmesan crust

Muskátli Vendéglő serves Palóc specials in the center of Hollókő.

and served with tomato jam and mashed potatoes. The restaurant can fit 120 people and is more like a hotel banquet room (guests with half board also have a buffet). In nice weather you can sit out on the terrace with views over the surrounding hills.

Shopping

✪ FOLK ART AND GIFTS

Hollókő is famous for its folk arts and crafts. Most of the shops are set inside the whitewashed, historic village houses on **Petőfi Sándor utca** or **Kossuth utca**—although you may find old ladies camped out by Szent Márton Church selling lace and embroidery as well. Most shops feel like craftspeople's homes and function as workshops as well as showrooms. You could easily spend an afternoon browsing, but bring plenty of cash as most shops won't take credit cards—you can be pretty sure you won't leave empty-handed.

Fazekas Ház

Petőfi Sándor utca 4, tel. 06/30-924-5052, www.holloko-fazekashaz.hu, daily 9am-8pm

It's hard to miss this pottery house—just follow the little ceramic mushrooms in the flower bed and you'll find the house covered in ceramic plates. Inside is a diverse range of local pottery from potters in the village. Designs are a mix of bright and modern to more traditional motifs. Pieces cost between HUF 2,000 and 10,000 depending on the style.

Fakanalas Ajándékbolt

Kossuth utca 65, tel. 06/30-335-5202, daily 9am-5pm

For unique handmade souvenirs, try this woodworkers' shop, whose name translates as "Wooden spoon gift shop." Take home a little wooden toy, colorful hand-painted wooden spoons, or salt and pepper shakers in the shape of a mini hussar, a uniformed Hungarian-soldier from the 19th century, from this cute wood-clad shop in the heart of the village.

Bőrműves Műhely

Petőfi Sándor utca 9, tel. 06/20-928-0714, daily 9am-5pm

This leatherworks is the place to go if you're looking for quality leather products. Tibor Princz has been in the leather industry for 10 years, but after starting out making equestrian equipment, he moved into creating other leather items such as bags, jewelry, wallets, belts, dog leashes, and more. Many of this craftsman's designs are based on ancient Hungarian nomadic styles, with items decorated with puncturing, sewed motifs, and riveting. Some are even accented with gold from a local goldsmith. Everything here is handmade and utterly unique.

Buy some ceramics at one of the many local craftshops like Fazekas Ház.

FOOD ITEMS
Gazduram Sajtboltja

Kossuth utca 85, tel. 06/20-326-2894, daily 10am-5:45pm

The best thing about this cheese shop is that you can try the different local cheeses on offer. Ask for a sliver to taste before buying. Most cheeses cost around HUF 3,000-5,000 per kilogram depending on the type, or you can get a cheese board to eat in the tasting room or the garden for around HUF 1,000. Take home a young gomolya cheese, which is traditionally made with sheep's milk accented with paprika or thyme, or an aged gomolya with a stronger taste. A few local specials change day to day, such as blue cheese or brie, and are worth trying.

Try the local specials, like the cheeses from the local cheese shop.

Borpatika

Kossuth utca 94, tel. 06/20-213-7147, daily 10am-4pm

If the barrel out front and the vines painted around the wooden door inside didn't give it away, the musty-cellar smell tells you this is a wine shop. But it's more than just a place to pick up a bottle. The kind owners let you taste these wonderful local wines free of charge, but prepare yourself to come away with a bottle (most sell for HUF 1,500-3,000). All the wines are local and unique—you won't find many of these elsewhere. Try the one made from the Nero grape, a dry red with the aroma of roses.

HOLLÓKŐ EASTER FESTIVAL

Hollókő Old Village, tel. 06/32-579-010, www.husvetfesztival.com, HUF 3,500-4,000

Hollókő comes to life on Easter weekend. Normally the village is like a museum, but when it's Easter weekend and Easter Monday, the whole village shows up in brilliantly embroidered costumes, lining the cobbled streets with Palóc dishes and local crafts. The highlight of the event is the **water pouring,** when local girls are doused with buckets of water on Easter Monday as part of a Hungarian tradition. There is also a **medieval fair** happening in the castle. Note that you can only visit the village with a **ticket,** which you can get at the entrance to the events, and it includes entry to all the museums.

One of the most important events of the year in Hollókő is Easter.

Accommodations

Castellum Hotel

Sport út 14, tel. 06/21-3000-500, http://hotelholloko.hu, HUF 35,000-45,000 d including breakfast

Perched on a hill above the village, with views over the surrounding hills, the four-star Castellum Hotel is a great retreat from urban life. This hotel, a modern contrast to the historic village, resembles a glass cube from the outside but spoils you with amazing views from each room. There are 68 modern rooms accented with wood details. Most come with balconies. There is a wellness area with a swimming pool, whirlpool tub, and saunas. A lavish buffet breakfast is included in the price, and there is an option for half board.

Kemencés Vendégház

Kossuth utca 58, tel. 06/20-411-1233, www.kemenceshaz.hu, HUF 10,000-20,000 d

Experience rural life in one of the traditional houses in the heart of the old village. The apartments are clad in wood and feature authentic details like glazed ceramic stoves or embroidered curtains. Apartments come with a terrace or a garden, and you're treated to a stunning view! If you want to use the barbecue or the metal cauldron to cook, they're provided free of charge. Breakfast is extra (around HUF 3,000), as is the sauna (HUF 3,000).

the Castellum Hotel

Transportation

GETTING THERE

BUS

On weekends, the direct bus from Budapest to Hollókő (two hours, HUF 2,200) leaves the Stadion bus station (take metro line 2 to Puskás Ferenc Stadion) at 8:30am and 3:15pm, and it returns from the village at 4pm and 7:30am. This is the easiest way to make a day of it. Alternatively, you can take a bus from Újpest Városkapú to Széchény and transfer, which takes 2.5 hours (HUF 2,200). This indirect bus goes every two hours. All buses arrive next to the edge of the Old Village, which is a 5-minute walk away, or you can follow the signs to the castle, a 15-20 minute walk.

CAR

From Budapest

From Budapest, drive 95 kilometers (60 miles) northeast on the M3 and then turn north on Route 21 at Hatvan to reach Hollókő. Take the exit at Pasztó to the west. This will take you on a bumpy country road; follow the signs from here to the village. The drive takes around 1 to 1.5 hours, depending on traffic.

Once you get into the village, parking areas are signposted. If you follow József Attila út and take the second road to the left, this will lead you to the main parking lot. Parking costs HUF 400 per hour or HUF 1,200 for a day (more than 3 hours). This location will put you very close to the Old Village and right next to the trail leading to the castle.

From Eger

Drive northeast out of Eger on Route 24 until Egerbakta and then head north on Route 23 toward Bátonyterenye. Once you reach Bátonyterenye, turn southward on the Route 21, and after Pásztó exit the route and take the junction going right (northwestward) and follow the signs to Hollókő (it is well signposted the whole way). The 87-kilometer (54-mile) journey takes 1.5 hours.

LEAVING HOLLÓKŐ

The last direct bus for Budapest leaves Hollókő at 4pm, but you can get the last bus back to Budapest at 6pm by transferring at Széchény.

SOPRON

Itinerary Idea 219
Sights 222
Nightlife 226
Performing Arts 227
Food 228
Accommodations 230
Transportation 232

Perched on the Austrian border,

the picturesque city of Sopron (pop. 60,000) is clustered around an old town enclosed by the stones of the former city wall. It's famous for its 13th-century fire tower—58 meters (190 feet) tall—which you can climb for views over the rusty-red rooftop tiles and church spires across to the misty hills in the distance. The city is just as fascinating on the ground, where clues into Sopron's history lie scattered around the cobbled streets, from the subterranean Roman forum and

HIGHLIGHTS

✪ **OLD TOWN:** The city's main attraction is its Old Town as a whole, which lies behind a cluster of the stone city walls. Wander the pristine cobbled streets and take in the little details of its eclectic, historic houses (page 222).

✪ **THE FIRE TOWER:** This 13th-century tower is a symbol of the city, and from the top you'll get the best views in town (page 222).

✪ **THE OLD SYNAGOGUE:** Catch a glimpse into Sopron's Jewish history (page 223).

its medieval city walls to Renaissance buildings and Baroque churches.

The town feels more Austrian than Hungarian, and because it's only an hour away from Vienna, many people reside here and commute across the border. You'll hear Hungarian and German spoken in equal measure, not just because so many Austrians come over to get dental treatment, but also because most locals are bilingual. If you look on the map, you'll notice that Sopron juts into Austria's Burgenland region, yet it stayed firmly inside Hungary following a 1921 referendum—the city voted to remain a part of Hungary rather than get absorbed into Austria when the borders were redrawn after the collapse of the Austro-Hungarian Empire. This decision earned Sopron the title of Hungary's "most faithful city."

Life in Sopron is leisurely, and it's especially pleasurable when you drink some of the local wine. Try the reds made from the Kékfrankos grapes or the white gewürztraminer wines from the surrounding vineyards.

ORIENTATION

The center of Sopron is compact and easily navigated on foot. From the train station it's about a 15-minute walk north to the walls of the Old Town, but you can also get a taxi if you're worried you'll get lost or are short on time.

Most of the city's famous sites are around the historic Old Town. Várkerület marks the eastern border of the Old Town, which is where you'll find restaurants, cafés, and Sopron's own grand hotel, the Pannonia. To the

Most of the old town is located inside the old city walls.

Sopron's old town is full of history.

west of Várkerület, the city splits into cobbled lanes and historic plazas, but you won't get lost—just look up and follow the Fire Tower.

PLANNING YOUR TIME

A day is enough to catch the main highlights of Sopron, but you may want to spend the night if you'd like to explore the museums in-depth and take in the city at a more leisurely pace. It would be hard to combine Sopron with any other day trip destinations from Budapest, as it lies on the far west side of the country. It takes around 2.5 hours to reach Sopron by train, so it is a long day trip but easily manageable due to the city's small size. You could combine Sopron with Vienna if you're

heading there too: instead of taking a direct train back to Budapest, break the journey for a night here.

There are a couple of tourist information offices and info points in Sopron. The main Tourinform Sopron office (Szent György utca 2, tel. 06/99-951-975, www.turizmus. sopron.hu, daily 9am-5pm Oct-May, 10am-6pm Jun-Sep) lies inside the Old Town, but there are Infopoints at the Fire Tower (Előkapu 2-7, tel.06/99-505-006, daily 10am-6pm Oct-Apr, 10am-8pm May-Sep) and on the Várkerület (Várkerület 96, daily 9am-5pm Oct-May, 10am-6pm Jun-Sep).

You can store luggage in the lockers at Sopron train station. The price depends on the size (HUF 400-500), but make sure you have coins on you.

Itinerary Idea

The town of Sopron is compact (many sites reside on the same square, Fő tér), and you can explore the best of it in one day. That being said, it's more comfortable to spend the night—you can get started early in the morning and catch the train back in the evening, or travel in the morning and stay overnight. This itinerary covers the must-see highlights that will keep you busy for a day, and it also assumes you're arriving in Sopron in the morning and staying the night.

ESSENTIAL SOPRON

1 Kick-start the day with a coffee and a homemade pastry at Kultúrpresszó.

2 Wander down the Várkerület due north until you see a small cobbled street, Tűztorony utca, to your left. Head up it and look up to spot the most iconic building in the city: the Fire Tower. Go inside the entrance, cross the Roman ruins to the ticket office, and buy a ticket. Climb up to the top of the tower for the sweeping views over Sopron. It's a lot of steps, but worth it.

3 Descend the tower and make a beeline to Fő tér. Get to know Sopron's history at the museum in the Fabricius House. Expect to spend a couple of hours here.

4 Grab some lunch at the historic Gambrinus Ház. It merits a visit for the building alone, but don't miss out on the Bramboráky, a Czech potato with a sour cream.

5 Leave the square and pop into the Goat Church on Templom utca (just on the corner of the square) for a half hour to appreciate this historic church with a quirky story.

6 Head back to the main square, and turn down Új utca to the Old Synagogue to discover the city's Jewish history.

7 If you're heading back to Budapest, now might be a good time to leave. If you're spending the night, head over to the Varker Café & Wine to try some local wines.

8 Hungry? Head north a couple of streets to Balfi út for dinner at Erhardt.

Sopron

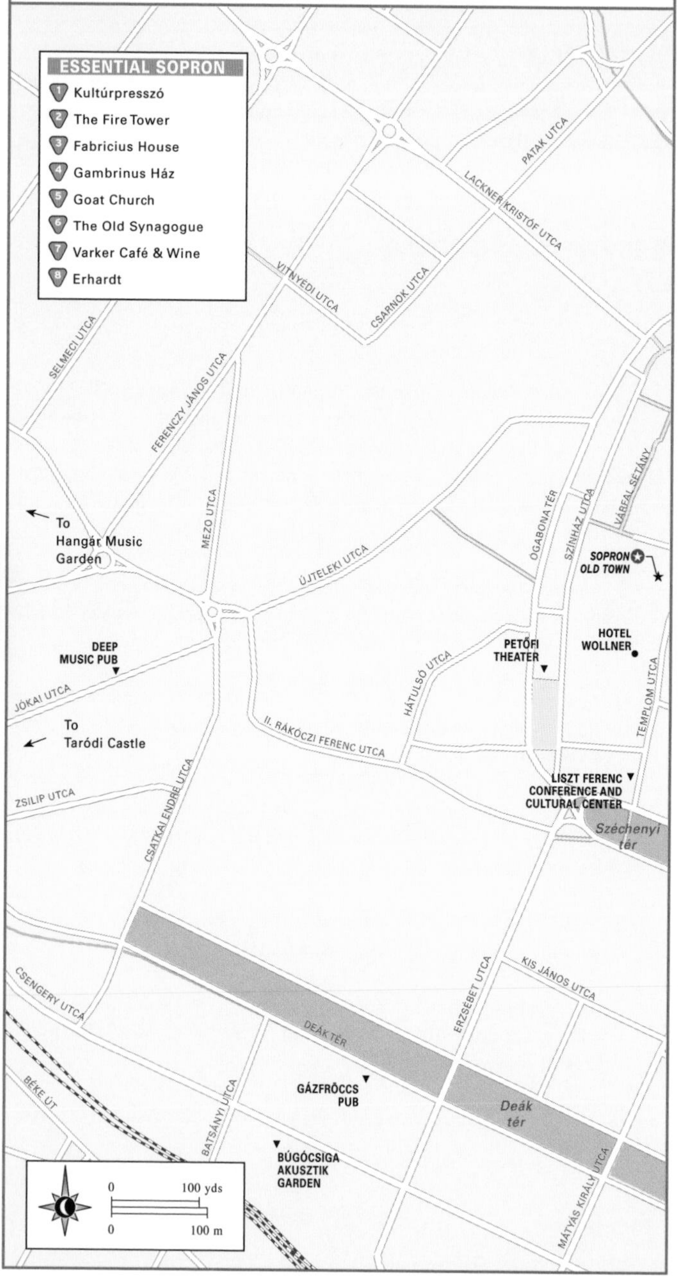

ESSENTIAL SOPRON

1. Kultúrpresszó
2. The Fire Tower
3. Fabricius House
4. Gambrinus Ház
5. Goat Church
6. The Old Synagogue
7. Varker Café & Wine
8. Erhardt

SOPRON

PATAK UTCA

LACKNER KRISTÓF UTCA

VITNYÉDI UTCA

CSARNOK UTCA

SELMECI UTCA

FERENCZY JÁNOS UTCA

MEZŐ UTCA

ÚJTELEKI UTCA

OGABONNA TÉR

SZÍNHÁZ UTCA

VÁREÁL SÉTÁNY

→ To
Hangár Music
Garden

SOPRON
OLD TOWN
★

HOTEL
WOLLNER
●

DEEP
MUSIC PUB
▼

PETŐFI
THEATER
▼

JÓKAI UTCA

→ To
Taródi Castle

HÁTULSÓ UTCA

TEMPLOM UTCA

II. RÁKÓCZI FERENC UTCA

CSATKAI ENDRE UTCA

ZSILIP UTCA

LISZT FERENC ▼
CONFERENCE AND
CULTURAL CENTER

*Széchenyi
tér*

CSENGERY UTCA

ERZSÉBET UTCA

KIS JÁNOS UTCA

BÉKE ÚT

DEÁK TÉR

BATSÁNYI UTCA

GÁZFRÖCCS
PUB
▼

*Deák
tér*

BÚGÓCSIGA
AKUSZTIK
GARDEN
▼

MÁTYÁS KIRÁLY UTCA

| 0 | 100 yds |
| 0 | 100 m |

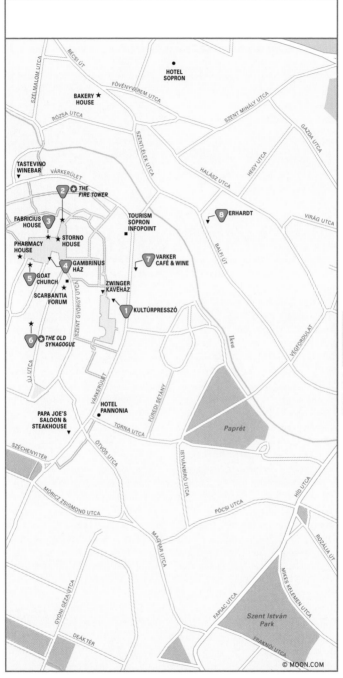

SOPRON

© MOON.COM

Sights

Most of the sites listed below (except the Baker's House and Táródi Castle) are located within the Old Town, and many reside on the same square, Fő tér.

❂ SOPRON OLD TOWN

Sopron's heart is its Old Town, much of which lies enclosed in the remnants of the former city wall. Although Sopron never had a castle, the wall served to protect its citizens, and parts of it still dominate the outline of the city today.

The Old Town is a beautiful patchwork quilt of buildings and styles. It's worth spending an hour just wandering through the cobbled streets, making sure you stop to look up and mind the details—the curved and carved wooden doorways, the occasional floral stucco, or the colorful walls. Once you've explored the city streets, hike up to the Castle Wall Promenade (take the Forum underpass from Várkerület and go behind the Zwinger Kávéház and follow the signs), etched with overgrown ivy and pathways that lead you behind hidden courtyards and residences. Other minor landmarks include the Cézár Pince (Hátsókapu 2), a Baroque building in hues of faded turquoise and white that was built over a Roman gate tower and two-story medieval buildings, the grand historicist Town Hall (Fő tér 1), and the pink Rococco Bezerédj House (Templom utca 6). Many of the buildings you'll see, whether Baroque, rococo, or from the 19th century, have sprung up over Roman or medieval foundations.

Sopron's most famous landmark is its historic Fire Tower.

❂ THE FIRE TOWER

Fő tér 5, tel. 06/99-311-327, www.tuztorony. sopron.hu, daily 10am-6pm, HUF 1,150

The Fire Tower is not just the city's symbol but one of Hungary's most famous landmarks. The tower rises some 58 meters (190 feet) above the Old Town and offers the best vantage point in the city—especially in the morning, when a touch of mist lingers over the town.

The entrance will take you past old Roman ruins excavated beneath the tower. This part is free and you don't need a ticket, but you'll have to cross the excavations to get to the ticket office. From here you can take the walkway over the ruins to the tower, and then it's a long climb up but worth every step. Just before the top, you'll come to the lookout balcony—a Baroque addition to the tower, with literal 360-degree views over the whole of Sopron. You can continue up the stairs to the very top of the tower, where an installation shows you the history of the fire that consumed the city in the Middle Ages. The 13th-century tower served as a lookout for any fires in the area, which could easily spread through the then-wooden city, and signal the danger to the whole of Sopron. If you're able to climb a lot of stairs, you shouldn't miss this famous landmark.

✪ THE OLD SYNAGOGUE

Új utca 3, tel. 06/99-311-327,
www.sopronimuzeum.hu,
Tue-Sun 10am-6pm Apr-Oct, HUF 800

The Old Synagogue is one of the city's earliest medieval monuments, and it's worth stopping in for a taste of Sopron's Jewish history.

Sopron's Jewish families settled around today's Új utca (New Street) in 1300. The street once bore the name Zsidó Street (Jew Street) after its Semitic residents. The Jews in this part of the city built the first residential houses on the street and this medieval synagogue that's easy to spot as it's set back from the street by a depth

Catch a glimpse into Sopron's medieval Jewish life at the synagogue.

of one house. It functioned as a prayer house, a school, and an assembly hall. The entrance leads you down a corridor to the main hall, where the focus is on the pulpit and the ark, which is adorned with motifs of vines and grapes. There are two rooms in the synagogue, for men and women; the women's section had its own exit—and could watch the events in the great hall through a narrow slot in the window. There was also a Mikve, a ritual bath used for purification purposes.

In 1354 Sopron's Jews were expelled from the city by King Louis I, and the synagogue fell into abandon until its renovation in 1967. Expect to spend about an hour here.

FABRICIUS HOUSE

Fő tér 6, tel. 06/99-311-327,
www.sopronimuzeum.hu, Tue-Sun 10am-6pm,
HUF 900 per exhibition

In the Fő tér, stop to take a closer look at this mansion that once belonged to the town magistrate. It may look like a typical Baroque townhouse, but it's one that's built upon layers of history. There are three exhibitions in the building, and the most interesting is the Roman lapidary in the cellar with a collection of sarcophagi and altar stones. On the two floors facing away from the main square, an archaeological exhibition covers the ancient history of the town, from the Illyrians, Celts, and Romans through to the 16th century. Delicate jewelry carved out of amber (Sopron was on the old Amber Road), Illyrian urns covered in a rune-like script, and a 1,200-year-old goblet are counted among the treasures. The first floor looking over the street covers the history of the house from the 17th and 18th centuries, giving you insight into life in the house through lavish furnishings such as carved oak wardrobes and canopy beds.

GOAT CHURCH

Templom utca 1, tel. 06/30-667-4101,
www.bencessopron.hu, daily 8am-6pm
Apr-Oct, 8am-4pm Nov-Mar, HUF 900

This church dates back to the 13th century and gets its curious name from a local story about a goatherd who uncovered buried treasure on this spot and used the loot to fund the church's construction. It was built by the Franciscan order but was repurposed in the 18th century by the Benedictine monks who resided in the adjoining 14th-century monastery.

Despite the church's medieval origins, you'll find a lot of Baroque ornamentation that was added much later, such as the elaborate altar flanked by columns of pink marble, a large dark-toned painting by Stephan Dorfmeister depicting the ascension of Christ, or the pulpit adorned with a cast of carved cherubs. See if you can spot the sculpture of an angel hugging a goat on one of the pillars!

Admission includes the Columbarium, the crypt below the church, which has had quite a modern makeover with machine-cut marble sarcophagi and cinerary urns. You can also visit the Chapter House, which is the prayer house in the old Benedictine monastery. You can see medieval frescoes, gothic pillars, and even gargoyles representing the seven deadly sins here. There is a small museum as well, and you won't want to miss the charming gift shop where you can pick up local products like homemade preserves or grab a cup of coffee before heading out.

SCARBANTIA FORUM

Új utca 1, tel. 06/20-364-2263,
www.scarbantia.com, daily 10am-6pm
(advance reservations necessary), free

The Scarbantia Forum is the only Roman forum in Hungary. The 2,000-year-old ruins from the Roman city of Scarbantia lie some 5 meters (16 feet) below today's city. You can see columns, sculptures, paving stones, and walls marking the layout of this old marketplace. Scarbantia was an important Roman city on the Amber Road, a trade route running from the Baltic Sea to Italy named for the amber it transported. Cities like Scarbantia prospered along the Amber Road in Roman times. If you're on the way to the Forum from Fő tér, keep an eye out for a placard on the square marking the position of the former road.

To reach the forum, head into the Tourinform office on the corner of Szent György street and Új street and go below street level. Admission is free, but you'll need to call Dr. János Gömöri at the listed number to make an appointment to visit (which is by guide only).

The Goat Church gets its name from a local legend.

PHARMACY HOUSE

Fő tér 2, tel. 06/99-311-327,
www.sopronimuzeum.hu/en/2017/08/25/

pharmacy-house, Tue-Sun 10am-2pm
Apr-Oct, HUF 500

In the 16th century, the city council wanted to destroy this gothic building to widen the square, but when King Lajos II intervened, it became the country's first protected monument. Today it's a museum dedicated to the 17th-century "Angel Pharmacy" that operated from the historic building. It was also the home to Adam Gensel, a physician and meteorologist who discovered the effects of the weather on the body; he lived here in the 17th and 18th centuries. The Gensel family extended the house in the mid-19th century, and it became the first pharmacy museum in the country in the 1960s.

The museum offers an immersive experience into the life of a traditional apothecary. There is a mix of valuable scientific tomes from the 16th and 17th centuries, as well as a fully recreated shop with the original counter used in the Angel Pharmacy, brass-handled drawers, and ceramic vials. The most interesting objects in this small museum are less scientific and more rooted in superstition. See if you can spot items inscribed with alchemical markings or amulets to ward off the gaze of the evil eye. There is even a special hat used to protect children against epilepsy.

STORNO HOUSE

Fő tér 8, tel. 06/99-311-327, www.
sopronimuzeum.hu/en/2017/08/25/storno-
collection, Tue-Sun 10am-6pm, HUF 1,000

What's not to love about a house belonging to a former chimney sweep who became one of the most significant restorers in the city? The Storno House gets its name from its ex-sweeping owner, Ferenc Storno, who acquired the Baroque corner house at the end of the 19th century. The

house dates back to the 15th century and even hosted King Matthias in the 1480s. It passed down over the centuries to different families, sticking with the Stornos before becoming a museum. (Another claim to fame is that Hungary's most famous composer, Franz Liszt, gave a few concerts here in the 19th century.)

The two-story house resembles a castle from the outside. Inside, the collection is adorned with lavish decorations and artwork. Ferenc Storno also became an artist, and his sons followed him on this path, using the apartments to exhibit their work. You can still see their collection on the second floor, along with their collection of antiques, weapons, glass, and the highlight, the stunning bay window adorned with stained glass. The first floor is home to a local history exhibition, which carries a separate entry fee of HUF 700.

BAKERY HOUSE

Bécsi utca 5, tel. 06/99-311-327,
www.sopronimuzeum.hu/en/2017/08/25/
bakery-house, Tue-Sun 2pm-6pm May-Sep;
HUF 500

Glimpse back into 17th-century life at this original baker's house, which dates to the 1600s. Records show the first owner was baker Joachim Huber, who lived here from 1686 to 1699. The house became a museum when the last baker died in 1972.

Enter the small museum on the right side of this one-story Baroque house, which is where the bakery was. You can see leavening cabinets, dough baskets, and the large furnace used to bake loaves of bread over the centuries. You can also see the residential part on the left side, two rooms and a kitchen, which gives you an idea of the life of a baker's family. The house was built for what was essentially a

24-hour job: the baker couldn't leave the bakery for long periods of time, so having a residence in the building was vital. The old flour-storage room functioned as a confectioner's shop in the 19th century.

TARÓDI CASTLE

Csalogány köz 36, tel. 06/70-572-2818,
daily 9am-6pm Apr-Oct, 10am-4pm
Nov-Mar, HUF 600

Although most of Sopron's sights are set in the Old Town, this curious one is a little further afield. At first glance, from the ivy-consumed stone walls and the turrets sticking up above the trees in the suburbs, you'd think this was a medieval original. However, Taródi Castle is a modern-day folly, a passion project by István Taródi, who for 50 years built this strange home. It had been his childhood dream to own a stone castle. He began the structure in 1959 after studying castles all over Hungary, and he worked on it until his death. The building resides on 4,300 square meters (about 1 acre) of land and belongs to Taródi's family, who still live in the castle but open part of it to visitors. Buy tickets at the gate. Inside, the complex weaves you through drafty passages, past stained-glass windows, and into stone chambers. You wouldn't know it's a new castle just by looking at it.

You can reach the Taródi Castle in 10 minutes by taxi; otherwise it's a 40-minute walk from the Fire Tower. If you're staying in Sopron for longer than a night, it's worth the visit up here. Expect to spend an hour or two.

Nightlife

Sopron is not a city famed for its nightlife, but it does have a university campus that's part of the University of West Hungary (until 2017 it was the University of Sopron) so the city has young blood who like to go out. Nightlife in Sopron is no frills: you'll mostly find pubs with a local live music scene, but if you come in the summer when the Volt Festival is on, the city buzzes with life—even late at night.

BARS AND PUBS
Deep Music Pub

Jókai utca 6, tel. 06/70-329-7268,
Sun-Thu 6pm-3am, Fri-Sat 6pm-4am

In a vaulted, brick-clad basement just outside the Old Town, the Deep Music Pub runs late into the night every night. The program is mostly house and drum and bass, but sometimes the music branches out into blues, metal, rock, and alternative. The vibe is lively but laid back, usually with a group of students battling over the foosball table and groups drinking beer in well-worn armchairs.

Gázfröccs Pub

Deák tér 28, tel. 06/99-787-783,
www.gazfroccs.com, Mon-Thu 5pm-1am,
Fri-Sat 5pm-2am

Gázfröccs resembles a Budapest ruin bar transposed into Sopron. The main draw is the gorgeous terrace garden, shaded by trees on the top and covered with gravel on the ground. It's a little outdoor oasis in the heart of the city. The pub's décor inside is funky, with furniture stuck to the ceiling. The venue is open late and brings DJs and music acts in, but many people come here for its street food like burgers, pizzas, soup, and fried chicken strips.

Búgócsiga Akusztik Garden

Csengery utca 30-32, tel. 06/20-347-2979, www.bugocsigagarden.hu, Tue-Thu 5pm-2am, Fri-Sat 7pm-3am

This alternative cultural space near the train station fills its schedule with a diverse program: exhibition openings, grunge concerts, disco parties, and even movie nights. Cover charge is in the range of HUF 500 to 2,000 depending on the event, and some are free. Part of the venue is outdoors in on a terrace, but inside it has a ruin pub vibe. The brick walls are usually adorned with local art, and the atmosphere is cozy, even when the crowds get big.

Hangár Music Garden

Vándor Sándor utca, tel. 06/20-912-4064, www.hangarmusicgarden.hu, Fri-Sat 9pm-3am

On the edge of town in an old industrial area, the Hangár Music Garden may look shady, in a graffiti-covered brick building surrounded by pipes and chimneys from the nearby beer factory and power station, but it's a big music hub on the weekend. Its remote location means things can get loud, and inside its no-frills industrial layout presents the perfect stage for rock gigs. Its program list includes some of Hungary's biggest bands, so you can expect a great atmosphere here. There is a cover charge, which varies depending on the event, usually between HUF 1,500 and 2,500. It's a half-hour walk from the city center, but you can also get a taxi (five minutes).

Performing Arts

Petőfi Theater

Petőfi tér, tel. 06/99-517-517, www.soproniszinhaz.hu

This gorgeous theater was originally built in 1840 but got its current look from the renovations in 1909. Make sure you stop to look up at the frescoes above the entrance before heading in for a show. The theater has a diverse program of operas, ballet, plays, and concerts. Programs are in Hungarian; catch a music or dance production to enjoy an evening of culture without the language barrier getting in the way. Tickets range from HUF 2,000 to 4,500 depending on the show.

Liszt Ferenc Conference and Cultural Center

Liszt Ferenc utca 1, tel. 06/99-517-500, www.procultura.hu

Despite the name, this concert hall and cultural center had nothing to do with the famous composer (it was merely named after him), but it does reside in a beautiful 19th-century building. It's a large building used for all kinds of conferences and cultural events, with eight event rooms, an exhibition hall, and an area that can fit 1,200 people. Shows are eclectic, from children's theater and puppet theater to modern dance and even quiz nights. Prices range from HUF 700 to 3,000 depending on the show.

Food

Sopron is in an interesting location: it's just across the border from the Austrian Burgenland and also close to Slovakia, and even the Czech Republic. Hungarian food dominates the regional cuisine, but you can find Czech and Slovak dishes in the local restaurants, and maybe even some Austrian influences, especially in the patisseries. The Hungarian side of Lake Fertő, a large lake mostly located in Austria (called Lake Neusiedl over the border), is just outside the town, so freshwater fish is a local specialty to watch for on the menus.

Another thing to try is the local wine. You can get dry whites, spicy reds, and late-harvest dessert wines. It's best to pair with local dishes, and with the variety of wines, you can find the right one to complement any dish.

HUNGARIAN
✪ Erhardt

Balfi út 10, tel. 06/99-506-711, www. erhardts.hu, Sun-Thu 11:30am-10pm, Fri-Sat 11:30am-11pm, entrées HUF 2,990-5,990

Tucked away inside a 16th-century building, Erhardt specializes in traditional Hungarian cooking and a few international dishes. The restaurant spreads out over this old townhouse with vaulted ceilings, brick-clad cellars, and the beautiful secluded garden under the shade of a chestnut tree. Try one of the dishes made with fresh fish caught in nearby Lake Fertő, like the catfish paprika with cottage cheese noodles, or pan-roasted pike-perch fillet with vegetables covered in lemon-spiced butter. They also serve a delicious

grilled goose liver with a Tokaj apple-balsamic vinegar sauce.

Erhardt carries quality local wines to accompany your dinner. If you want the perfect pairing with your food, request a three-course wine dinner, which serves a white Irsai Oliver with the starter, followed by a full-bodied Kékfrankos, and ending with a sweet late-harvest Zenit—all from Sopron vineyards. This costs around HUF 11,600, but email the restaurant in advance to request it. And if you try a wine you like, you can buy a bottle from their shop to take home.

Gambrinus Ház

Fő tér 3, tel. 06/99-784-452, www. gambrinushaz.hu, Sun-Thu 10am-11pm, Fri-Sat 10am-midnight, HUF 1,930-4,880

It's worth a visit to Gambrinus for the building alone, which served as the town hall until the 15th century. Today, the building is a curious mix of styles with Baroque, rococo, and even Art Nouveau influences, whereas on the inside there are still many medieval features. The food here is a mix of Czech and Hungarian dishes; try the bramboráky, a Czech potato with a sour cream, which comes in a variety of toppings.

CAFES AND COFFEE
Varker Café & Wine

Várkerület 49, tel. 06/70-770-0121, Mon-Thu 8:30am-10pm, Fri-Sat 8:30am-midnight, Sun 10am-6pm, entrés HUF 1,790-2,790

This café just outside the Old Town is a great place to grab breakfast in the morning—or one of the mouthwatering desserts on display in the

Zwinger Kavéház is a hidden Art Nouveau-style confectionary.

glass cabinet by the window. Rather than ordering a single dish, I would suggest either trying a few of their wines by the glass with a cheese plate, or going for their weekly menu that changes regularly. It's a relaxed place, and it's easy to while the hours away in one of the brown leatherette couches or on the terrace with a few glasses of wine.

Kultúrpresszó

Várkerület 96, tel. 06/30-299-6140,
www.kulturpresszo.hu, Mon-Fri 8am-7pm,
Sat 8:30am-8pm, Sun 9am-7pm, breakfast
and snacks HUF 880-2,850
Sopron's first specialty coffee shop is a great spot for breakfast or brunch. You can get all the new-wave coffee favorites like Chemex and Espresso Tonic, and if you're hungry there are homemade pastries, sandwiches, dip platters, and granola. It's a bright an airy café lined with books and an awesome mural depicting the Hungarian photographer Robert Capa. The crowd is young and arty, and the service is friendly.

Zwinger Kavéház

Várkerület 92, tel. 06/99-340-287,
www.domotoricukraszda.hu/zwinger.php,
Mon-Sat 8am-7pm, cakes HUF 425-620
This beautiful café resides in a conservatory-like building with large

Kultúrpresszó is a funky new wave café with great coffee and breakfast.

bay windows and stained glass that's hidden in a courtyard. Inside, the Zwinger Kavéház draws inspiration from Art Nouveau style and is a relaxing refuge in the city. They serve delicious cakes, ice cream, coffee, and tea. Try their jasmine tea that opens like a flower when you pour hot water on it.

ECLECTIC
Papa Joe's Saloon & Steakhouse
Várkerület 108, tel. 06/99-340-933,
www.papajoe.hu, daily 11am-midnight,
entrées HUF 2,800-24,090

Walk into the Wild West just outside Sopron's Old Town. This playful restaurant—complete with swinging doors, Jack Daniel's signs, and notes stuck to the wall—specializes in steaks grilled on wooden embers, which you can wash down with one of their 100 whiskeys. You can get all kinds of steak cuts, but if you are starving and you've got the money, then tackle the 1 kg (2 lb) grilled tenderloin! Or go for something more modest, like a smaller cut, BBQ ribs, or the house burger.

WINE BARS
Tastevino Winebar
Várkerület 5, tel. 06/30-519-8285,
www.tastevino.hu, Tue-Sat noon-midnight,
glass of wine HUF 400-2,000

This vaulted wine bar and shop on Várkerület is a good place to stop for a pre-dinner aperitif and some local wine. The selection includes wines from both Sopron and other parts of Hungary available by the glass. Since it's also a shop, get a bottle to go if you like what you've tried. They serve the customary cheese plates, cold cuts, olives, and the usual snacks to accompany the wine, and the on-site sommeliers can help you learn a bit more about what you're drinking.

Accommodations

✪ Hotel Pannonia
Várkerület 75, tel. 06/99-312-180,
www.pannoniahotel.com, HUF
11,000-97,000 d including breakfast

The Hotel Pannonia is Sopron's oldest hotel, whose history goes back to 1500. However, the building you see today is from the 19th century and evokes the spirit of Central Europe's old grand hotels. There are 79 rooms in a variety of styles; some are modern, others have Baroque furniture. A standard twin will come with simple décor and facilities. Prices vary depending on the room. The hotel also has a wonderful spa area with a pool, saunas, salt room, and a gym. A lavish buffet breakfast is served in a spectacular colonnaded hall.

The Hotel Pannonia is built on the site of one of Sopron's oldest hotels.

Volt is one of the largest music festivals in the country.

Harkai út 34, www.volt.hu, one-day pass HUF 12,990-15,990, four-day pass HUF 29,990-37,990

Sziget Festival may be Hungary's most famous, but Volt comes in close behind. This multi-genre festival held in Sopron's suburbs brings in some 100,000 visitors per year for a diverse program scattered across six or more stages. Beyond music headliners—both international acts and Hungarian ones—top DJs take the party late into the night. If you need to detox the next day, there are daily yoga sessions and art events. The festival lasts four days, with the option to camp (HUF 1,990-4,990 per person). The town gets pretty busy this time of year, so if you're planning to visit Sopron while Volt is on, book your hotel in advance. Although the festival crowds may not pile into any fine dining establishments, I'd still advise you book a table in advance.

Hotel Wollner

Templom utca 20, tel. 06/99-524-400, www.hotelwollner.com, HUF 22,900-27,900 d including breakfast

This four-star hotel located in the Old Town is family-owned and captures the charm of Sopron's history. Highlights of the hotel are the stone spiral staircase, its hanging garden built up on the old city wall, and a courtyard decked out with tables and chairs on the ground floor. The 18 rooms are a throwback to the past, decorated in hues of royal red, gold, and green with wooden furniture. There is a sauna and a fitness room on site, plus a wine bar in the cellar.

Hotel Sopron

Fővényverem 7, tel. 06/99-512-261, www.hotelsopron.hu, HUF 32,400-40,000 d including breakfast

The modern Hotel Sopron is the perfect place to relax after a day immersed in history. The highlight of this 100-room hotel is the wellness center on the third floor, where you're treated to panoramic views over the Old Town and the Fire Tower from the whirlpool tub. Some of the higher-tier rooms also come with a view. There is an outdoor pool and a garden the overlooks the city. The rooms here are contemporary, mostly white with splashes of color; some even come with a balcony.

Transportation

GETTING THERE

TRAIN

Direct trains run from Budapest Keleti Pályaudvar every 2 hours and take 2.5 hours to reach Sopron. Train tickets cost HUF 4,735 one-way.

You can easily **walk** to town from the **train station;** it'll take around 15 minutes northeast on Erzsébet utca or Mátyas Király utca. If you're traveling with luggage or you want to save time, you can grab a **cab** from the station, which should cost around HUF 1,000.

CAR

From Budapest, drive 215 kilometers (134 miles) northwest on the **M1** and take the exit 129 for **Route 85.** You'll go onto the M85 for a time before going back onto **Route 85** and then **Route 84** reach Sopron. The drive takes around 2 hours 20 minutes.

You can only drive into the Old Town with a permit, so you'll need to park in designated **parking areas.** Zone 1 of parking is located just outside the Old Town on Várkerület (street parking) and costs HUF 420 per hour.

GETTING AROUND

Lővér Taxi (tel. 06/99-333-333) is the city's main taxi company. You should be able to get a cab with them around the clock.

LEAVING SOPRON

The last direct train back to Budapest leaves at 6:20 pm. If you miss that one you can still take the 7:44 pm train to Győr and transfer to a train going to Budapest Déli. This journey will take longer, just under 4 hours, but at least you won't be stranded.

PÉCS

Set in the southeastern part of

Hungary near the Croatian border, historic Pécs (pop. 145,000) is Hungary's fifth-largest city and one of the most beautiful in the country. With its rich historical sites, from the 4th-century Roman necropolis to the mosques left behind by the Ottoman occupation, Pécs has plenty to keep your days packed. The city is also famous for its glazed ceramics and tiles produced by the Zsolnay factory, which sits in a former industrial area that's been converted into an exciting cultural hub packed with museums, parks, and

Itinerary Ideas 235
Sights 238
Nightlife..............245
Shopping.............246
Food 247
Accommodations 249
Transportation........251

HIGHLIGHTS

⭐ **MOSQUE OF PASHA QASIM:** Pécs's most famous landmark, the Mosque of Pasha Qasim, is the largest and most spectacular Turkish-built structure in Hungary (page 238).

⭐ **ZSOLNAY FOUNTAIN:** This glazed metallic-green fountain, which looks more like something from ancient Babylon, is a product of the Zsolnay factory. It makes for the city's best photo op (page 239).

⭐ **CSONTVÁRY MUSEUM:** Tivadar Csontváry's surreal paintings of romantic foreign landscapes from Sicily, the Middle East, and the Balkans are on display at this museum located in the heart of Pécs (page 241).

⭐ **SOPIANAE EARLY CHRISTIAN MAUSOLEUM:** This 4th-century collection of underground tombs dates to the Roman era. These early Christian burial chambers come decorated with rich frescoes (page 243).

⭐ **ZSOLNAY CULTURAL QUARTER:** Pécs thrived with the ceramics business in the 19th and early 20th centuries, and the beautiful tiled factory complex now functions as a cultural district with museums, theaters, shops, and cafés (page 244).

theaters. Art lovers can keep busy at the numerous galleries in the city center, like those dedicated to Tivadar Csontváry and Victor Vasarely. Pécs is a must-see for Art Nouveau lovers: the city is peppered with Secessionist details, like the eosin-glazed fountain on Széchenyi ter and the grand Palatinus Hotel. After you tire of all the cultural exploration, simply sit on a terrace, sip a glass of spicy red wine from the nearby Villány region, and watch the world go by. Blessed with a temperate climate and laid-back culture, Pécs is often described as being a Mediterranean-style city.

You can get oriented in the city by taking the little dotto train.

ORIENTATION

Much of the center of Pécs can be navigated on foot—most of the city's important sites are within walking distance. The Zsolnay Cultural Quarter is a little far from the city center, although it's still only a 20-minute walk west from the Mosque of Pasha Qasim. Public transportation is sparse and confusing to navigate for a non-local, so the best way to get around is to walk or take a taxi.

The focal point of the city is the main square, Széchenyi tér, the home of the Mosque of Pasha Qasim. Leading off from the square to the west is Király utca, a cobbled street lined with cafés, restaurants, shops, theaters, and hotels.

PLANNING YOUR TIME

Although you could do Pécs in a day from Budapest (it would be a very long day), you'd only get to see the most famous sites in the very center before having to board the train again. I recommend spending the night, or even two, in this historic town to get the most out of it. It takes just under three hours to reach Pécs from Budapest by train and just over two hours by car.

TOURIST INFORMATION

There is one tourist information office in Pécs. Pécs Pont (Széchenyi tér 1, tel. 06/72-511-232, www.iranypecs.hu, Mon-Fri 8am-6pm, Sat 10am-6pm) is a wheelchair-accessible multifunctional space that offers more than just leaflets and information; it also has a café, a souvenir shop, public toilets, and luggage storage. There are luggage storage facilities in the train and bus stations, too. Rates are usually HUF 200-500 for 24 hours.

If you're planning to hit the museums, it's worth investing in an Irány Pécs card (https://kartya.iranypecs. hu/en/index.html, HUF 2,000 for the first day, additional HUF 500 for each extra day), which offers free or discounted entry to 30 attractions. Get this card at the Pécs Pont.

Itinerary Ideas

Dedicate one day to the sites branching off Széchenyi tér, with a visit to the Mosque, the Early Christians Mausoleum, the surrounding museums, and the Cathedral. Another day could easily be spent exploring the various museums at the Zsolnay Quarter and the spectacular Zsolnay Mausoleum.

DAY 1

1 Explore the majestic Mosque of Pasha Qasim, the largest and most spectacular Turkish-built structure in Hungary.

2 Head over to the Csontváry Museum for a spot of art. Expect to spend an hour here.

3 Go back in time to the Sopianae Early Christian Mausoleum.

4 Once you've packed your morning with ecclesiastic history, art, and architecture, you'll have worked up an appetite! Good news: it's only a five-minute walk to the Balkán Bisztró.

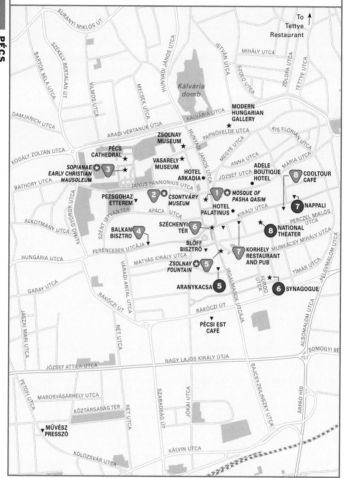

5 Once you've refueled, walk over to the **Zsolnay Fountain** for the best view of the city—you can snap a wonderful shot of the Mosque of Pasha Qasim from here.

6 Get some pre-dinner drinks at a spot on **Széchenyi tér** (Főtér is a good choice), sample a few glasses of local wine and watch the world go by on the square.

7 Wander down to Király utca for dinner at the **Korhely Restaurant and Pub**.

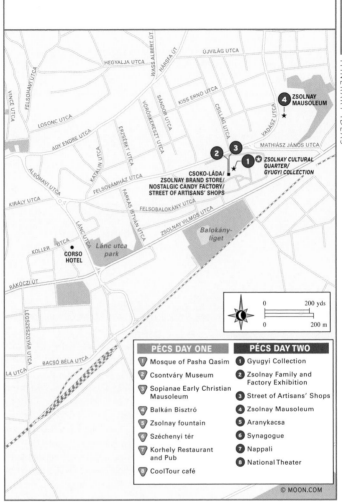

HEGYALJA UTCA

ÚJVILÁG UTCA

WASS ALBERT ÚT

HARSFA ÚT

4 ZSOLNAY MAUSOLEUM ★

VINCE UTCA

FELSŐHAVI UTCA

LOSONC UTCA

KISS ERNO UTCA

CSILLAG UTCA

VADÁSZ UTCA

SÁNDOR UTCA

VÖRÖSKERESZT UTCA

ADY ENDRE UTCA

ERZSÉBET UTCA

MATHIÁSZ JÁNOS UTCA

2 **3**

1 ★ ZSOLNAY CULTURAL QUARTER/ GYUGYI COLLECTION

KATALIN UTCA

ALSOHAVI UTCA

FELSŐVÁMHÁZ UTCA

CSOKO-LÁDA/ ZSOLNAY BRAND STORE/ NOSTALGIC CANDY FACTORY/ STREET OF ARTISANS' SHOPS ★

KIRÁLY UTCA

FARKAS ISTVÁN UTCA

FELSŐBALOKÁNY UTCA

LÁNC UTCA

ZSOLNAY VILMOS UTCA

Balokány-liget

KOLLER UTCA

● CORSO HOTEL

Lánc utca park

RÁKÓCZI ÚT

LÉGSZESZGYÁR UTCA

0   200 yds

0   200 m

BACSÓ BÉLA UTCA

LA UTCA

PÉCS DAY ONE	PÉCS DAY TWO
1 Mosque of Pasha Qasim	**1** Gyugyi Collection
2 Csontváry Museum	**2** Zsolnay Family and Factory Exhibition
3 Sopianae Early Christian Mausoleum	**3** Street of Artisans' Shops
4 Balkán Bisztró	**4** Zsolnay Mausoleum
5 Zsolnay fountain	**5** Aranykacsa
6 Széchenyi tér	**6** Synagogue
7 Korhely Restaurant and Pub	**7** Nappali
8 CoolTour café	**8** National Theater

© MOON.COM

8   After dinner, enjoy some drinks at **CoolTour Café.**

DAY 2

Fuel up with a good breakfast at your hotel, because you're heading to the **Zsolnay Cultural Quarter** for the day. Buy a ticket at the info point and spend the morning exploring the museums in the complex.

1   First head to the **Gyugyi Collection** to see some of the Zsolnay factory's most stunning creations.

2 Explore the **Zsolnay Family and Factory Exhibition** to learn more about the factory and the history of the family behind it.

3 If you want to do a spot of shopping, check out the **Street of Artisans' Shops,** especially the Nostalgic Candy Factory.

4 Head out of the complex and go up to the **Zsolnay Mausoleum** for some peace and quiet.

5 Grab a taxi down or walk 25 minutes to the **Aranykacsa** restaurant for a late lunch.

6 Visit the **Synagogue** nearby.

7 Head back up to Király utca to grab a few drinks at **Nappali.**

8 If you can, catch a performance at the **National Theater.** If there is nothing showing, it's still worth stopping by to see the building.

Sights

A little **sightseeing train** (www.pecsikisvonat.hu, HUF 1,600) runs on the hour from 10am to 5pm from the southeastern side of the Mosque of Pasha Qasim. It takes 50 minutes to circle the town's main sites and can help you get better oriented when you arrive.

✪ MOSQUE OF PASHA QASIM

Hunyadi út 4, tel. 06/30-373-8900,
www.pecsiegyhazmegye.hu/en/attractions/
mosque-of-pasha-gazi-kassim, Mon-Sat
9am-5pm, Sun 1pm-5pm, HUF 1,900

If you go to Pécs you cannot miss the former Mosque of Pasha Qasim, which has become a symbol of the city and its Turkish past. Although it now functions as the Parish Church of Gyertyaszentelő Boldogasszony (Candlemass Church of the Blessed Virgin Mary in English), it's the largest—rising 23 meters (75 feet) high—and most spectacular Turkish-built structure in Hungary.

For almost 150 years, Pécs belonged to the Ottoman Empire, and this 16th-century mosque built by Pasha Qasim testifies to the long-term Turkish plan to make Pécs a permanent home. In 1686 Pécs was liberated from Ottoman rule, and the mosque evolved with the city's Christian demographic, becoming a church in the early 18th century. Although its minaret was taken down (legend says it was struck by lightning before the Jesuits later demolished it) and the interior was adapted to cater to Catholic masses, you can still spot clues from its Islamic past. Inside the church is a decorated *mihrab* (an Islamic praying niche) that faces the holy city of Mecca, and there are spots on the walls where you can see Arabic script quoting lines from the Koran.

Mosque of Pasha Qasim

Today the church is decorated with colorful frescoes; make sure you look up into the dome, which has an indigo starry night sky, angels, and flowers. Even if you've seen your fair share of European churches, this unique mosque/church will be something different: it blends architectural elements from East and West, and Christian symbolism with Muslim ones, in its arched windows, oak pews, and holy-water containers that were once a bath for the Pasha Qasim.

SZÉCHENYI TÉR

It's a good idea to start your visit in Széchenyi tér, as this square marks the historical center of Pécs. It was the town's marketplace back in the Middle Ages and went through a variety of names before keeping its current title since 1864. Although the Mosque of Pasha Qasim is the show-stealing landmark at the top of the square, wander around and look for the other landmarks, like the neo-Baroque city hall on the western side of the square (where the Pécs Pont is also located). Opposite on the eastern side is the County Hall, a beautiful building adorned with Zsolnay ceramics and roof tiles. Next door to the County Hall is the House of Arts and Literature, whose internal courtyard, the Hild Garden, sets the backdrop for

concerts in the warmer months. The southern side of the square is also busy with sights, the most famous being the Zsolnay Fountain, and behind it the 18th-century Fatebenefratelli Church, also known as the Hospitaller Church, that mixes historical styles. Inside you can see a Baroque altar painting depicting the martyrdom of Saint Sebastian plus frescoes dating back to 1908 by Endre Graits. Keep an eye out for the gravestones on the walls—some even have inscriptions looking like they're buried slightly below ground, although there is no known entrance to any vault under the church.

✪ ZSOLNAY FOUNTAIN

Make a special pilgrimage to the southern side of Széchenyi tér to see this remarkable structure, which also offers the best photo opportunity in Pécs. The fountain rises some 4 meters (13 feet) in height and features four pyrogranite eosin-glazed ox heads that shimmer in a dual tone of green and yellow. It's a wonderful example of Hungarian Art Nouveau, with curious Eastern elements included that give it an almost Babylonian look. Miklos Zsolnay, son of the founder of the famous ceramics emporium, donated this spectacular fountain in memory of his father. It was once seriously damaged when someone broke off one of the ox heads, but luckily the Zsolnay factory rescued and repaired it. If you stand behind the fountain, in front of the church, you have an amazing view of the Mosque of Pasha Qasim in the background.

SYNAGOGUE

Fürdő utca 1, tel. 06/72-315-881, Mon-Sat 10:30am-12:30pm Nov-Mar, Mon-Sat 10am-5pm Apr-Oct, HUF 800

Before the Turkish occupation,

The Zsolnay Fountain features four pyrogranite eosin-glazed ox.

Jews already lived in Pécs, but many couldn't settle in the city again till much later. In 1692, following the liberation from the Ottomans, the predominantly German-speaking demographic of the city swore that no non-Catholic person could reside here. Yet despite this anti-Jewish sentiment, the Jewish population grew and prospered. In the 19th century, the Jewish community commissioned architects Frigyes Feszl, Károly Gerster, and Lipót Kauser to build this synagogue. The top center of the building features the Hebrew words "For my house, be called to the house of prayer for all peoples," meaning that all people from any religious faith are welcome here. Above the inscription from the Torah are the Tablets of Moses with the ten commandments.

Inside the synagogue, not unlike the Catholic cathedral, its main feature is the organ with some 1,500 pipes. It's also worth visiting for the ornate, colorful murals in hues of deep red, indigo blue, and accents of gold, along with the geometrically carved oak galleries.

The Jewish community here dwindled to 150 people following World War II, when almost 3,000 Jews were deported.

NATIONAL THEATER

Színház tér 1, tel. 06/72-512-660, www.pnsz. hu, see website for show schedules and prices
This beautiful 19th-century theater is worth stopping by for the architecture, even if you're not planning to see a play (although there is a program available in English for subtitled shows). This neo-Renaissance structure designed by Adolf Lang was built on the site of a military hospital after the townspeople demanded a permanent stone theater. Pécs already had a vibrant theater culture, but shows and comedies were performed at inns, cafés, and dance halls—locals wanted a social place to meet friends and enjoy professional productions. The

theater occupies a pleasant Italian-looking square with black and white floor tiling and a fountain decorated by bronze work from local sculptor Sándor Rétfalvi depicting genres of acting with cafés and shops in the background. However, the theater building itself is enough to capture your attention, with its central crowning cupola and a statue of Genius posing above it. Figures from Hungary's 19th-century theatrical scene occupy the façade, along with the pyrogranite ornaments from the Zsolnay factory. Regular performances include opera, theater, and ballet. Try to see the ballet, as the Pécs company has a world-famous reputation.

✪ CSONTVÁRY MUSEUM

Janus Pannonius utca 11, tel.
06/30-313-8442, www.pecsimuzeumok.hu,
Tue-Sun 10am-6pm, HUF 1,500

This museum resides on the top floor of a neoclassical building that belongs to the Janus Pannonius Museum complex. It's dedicated to Hungarian Postimpressionist and Expressionist painter Tivadar Kosztka Csontváry, who is famed for his surreal and colorful landscapes. A year after the artist died, his family auctioned off his paintings, believing the expensive canvases would fetch a good price as tarpaulins. (Although Csontváry was not famous in his lifetime, like other artists he propelled to fame once deceased.) The museum opened in 1973 on the 120th anniversary of the artist's birth. Some of his paintings are featured in the Hungarian National Gallery in Budapest, but you won't find a better collection than this five-room museum in Pécs. You may only spend an hour at this museum, but you can easily immerse yourself in the details of his art—incredible, surreal

landscapes created in epic proportions depicting the bridge at Mostar in Bosnia and Herzegovina, Roman ruins in Sicily, and his expressive *The Lonely Cedar* painting of a tall, wind-twisted cedar tree overlooking an arid landscape.

ZSOLNAY MUSEUM

Káptalan utca 2, tel. 06/72-514-045,
www.pecsimuzeumok.hu, Tue-Sun 10am-6pm,
HUF 1,500

If you don't have time to go to the Zsolnay Cultural Quarter or you can't get enough of the beautiful ceramics, then it's worth a visit to this downtown museum just north of the famous mosque. What's especially interesting about this two-story museum, beyond its wonderful collection of Zsolnay vases and ornaments, is the building it resides in—the oldest house in Pécs. You can see Gothic niches inside dating back to the 1320s. The building also gets the bragging rights of having been the first library of Hungary, established by Zsigmond Hampó in 1440.

The museum itself covers the history of the factory's ceramic production. It takes you on a chronological journey through its vases and figurines, where you can see how tastes in ornamentation changed over the years from more traditional Hungarian motifs to those inspired by Persia, Egypt, or Japan. The collection shows how new innovations changed the Zsolnay brand, with its high-fire pyrogranite architectural ceramics and metallic eosin glaze. Curious highlights of the museum include a fountain surrounded by eosin-glazed ducks and curious vases with realistic-looking mushrooms "growing" out of them. Expect to spend an hour to two here.

VASARELY MUSEUM

Káptalan utca 3, tel. 06/30-934-6127,
www.pecsimuzeumok.hu, Tue-Sun 10am-6pm,
HUF 1,500

Pécs-born artist Victor Vasarely donated his collection of paintings, drawings, serigraphs, tapestries, and sculptures to this museum housed in an old two-story townhouse directly opposite the Zsolnay Museum. The museum resides in a quiet courtyard marked by a gate surrounded by fragrant lilacs, but inside you are transported into a world of bright colors and optical illusions. Paintings, sculptures, and drawings play with your sense of perspective and may leave you dizzy upon exiting. Vasarely's style covers an extensive collection of his surreal optical art, also known as Op-Art. He was a pioneer of the style in the 1960s, and his work went on to influence fashion and mainstream art. The museum funnels you along the ground-floor corridor with three large rooms to the side, and then up the stairs to two large rooms. It's not a very big museum, and you'll be out in an hour or less, but it's easy to spend more time playing with the optical illusions. Highlights include a large mind-bending carpet that looks three-dimensional and an acrylic chess set that seems both futuristic and retro at the same time. Descriptions are written in Hungarian, and you will be stalked by the museum staff who won't want to lose sight of you as you go into any of the rooms, but once you get over that this is a fun little museum.

MODERN HUNGARIAN GALLERY

Papnövelde utca 5, tel. 06/72-891-328,
www.pecsimuzeumok.hu, Tue-Sun 10am-6pm
Apr-Oct, Tue-Sun 10am-4pm Nov-Mar,
HUF 700

Art lovers will delight in this extensive collection of Hungarian art from the 20th century. There are over 12,000 works of modern art in this glass-clad revamped baroque townhouse, covering a range of art from different movements such as Postimpressionism, Modernism, and Postmodernism. The museum leads you through a chronological journey into 50 years of Hungarian modern art history. You enter on the second floor through the glass doors—much of the old house is covered in a glass casing that adds a new dimension to the museum—and the exhibition is laid out over three floors connected by an elevator. The glass structure allows you to see the Baroque details of the old house and blends the old and the new together, though much of the museum is set inside the original house. Highlights include paintings by József Rippl-Rónai, Károly Ferenczy, and Lajos Tihanyi. Expect to spend at least two hours in this extensive museum.

PÉCS CATHEDRAL

Szent István tér 23, tel. 06/30-373-8900,
Mon-Thu 9am-5pm, Fri-Sat 9am-5pm and
7:30pm-10pm, Sun 11:30am-5pm May-Sep,
Mon-Sat 9am-5pm, Sun 11:30-5pm Oct-Apr,
HUF 1,900

It's a subtle five-minute climb to reach Pécs Cathedral, which occupies a less prominent position in town than its formerly Muslim counterpart, but once you reach the grand white façade that faces south, it's an imposing structure with more than a thousand years of history. The building you see today is a tapestry of styles, built upon another church that fell into decay in 1064. The Cathedral has a northern Italian look to it, with its Romanesque arches and pointed bell towers, and that is no coincidence: many of the architects involved in its construction came from the Lombardy region in Italy. Over time the cathedral grew, with two more towers being added in the Middle Ages, but of course the basilica suffered under the Turkish occupation. Much of its reconstruction happened in the 19th century, and more contemporary elements slipped into the church's style, especially the façade featuring statues of the Apostles. Most of the statues here were actually made by Károly Antal in the 1960s. Inside, the highlight is the Cathedral's huge organ in the choir with over 6,000 pipes. If you can climb up the southeastern tower, you will get great views over the city.

✪ SOPIANAE EARLY CHRISTIAN MAUSOLEUM

Szent István tér, tel. 06/72-224-755, www.pecsorokseg.hu, Tue-Sun 10am-5:45pm

Apr-Oct, Tue-Sun 10am-4:45pm Nov-Mar, HUF 1,900

Underneath the Cathedral, you can descend back in time to Roman Pécs. This old complex of richly decorated burial chambers, mausoleums, and chapels is the resting place for many wealthy families who lived in the Roman town of Sopianae in the 4th century AD. This subterranean network of early Christian monuments spans two levels. The bottom layer is made up of brick tombs and a few stone sarcophagi, and the top layer houses a memorial chapel. It's easy to spend a good couple of hours here admiring the frescoes depicting Christian imagery, like Adam and Eve covering themselves with fig leaves. The entire site is also enhanced with video stories, 3D maps of the ruins, and downloadable audio material. There is even a game you

Pécs Cathedral is a mix of styles, as it was built upon another 11th century church.

can play with your smartphone using QR codes placed around. The tombs lie behind covered glass and are kept under temperature- and humidity-controlled conditions. Metal walkways and stairs allow you to explore the site independently, but there are elevators and accessible ramps for mobility-limited visitors. This historic place is a UNESCO World Heritage Site and gives you an excellent glance back into the city's ancient history.

✪ ZSOLNAY CULTURAL QUARTER

Felsővámház utca 52, tel. 06/72-500-350, www.zsolnaynegyed.hu, daily 9am-5pm Nov-Mar, 9am-6pm Apr-Oct

It's worth getting out of the city center to visit the Zsolnay Cultural Quarter. The former grounds of the famous Zsolnay porcelain factory is now a hub of museums, cafés, shops, a library (located in an old kiln), a puppet theater, a concert hall, and even a planetarium. There are some 15 protected buildings and 88 public statues scattered around the park-like complex. Even if you don't have time to visit the museums, take a stroll through the lush green grounds. Its buildings in shades of turmeric yellow, papaya pink, and turquoise are decorated with ceramic details and yellow-green tiled rooftops.

Zsolnay is famous for its glazed ceramics and architectural tiles. It saw a golden age in the 19th and early 20th centuries, but for decades many of the factory buildings lay mostly abandoned after the Zsolnay family was ejected from the property by the Communists. The factory still produced simple tableware under the nationalized name of the

Pécsi Porcelángyár (Pécs Porcelain Factory), and only in 1982 did it get its original name back and resume making its iconic ceramics. Its 5 hectares (12 acres) of land got a facelift in 2009-2011 when a huge renovation project revamped the grounds for the European City of Culture Project, and it's now a stunning cultural complex.

Highlights of the complex include the **Gyugyi Collection** (Thu-Sun 10am-5pm Nov to Mar, daily 10am-6pm Apr-Oct, HUF 1,600), which features a stunning collection of Zsolnay ceramics and vases. Highlights are the Art Nouveau vases with their iridescent shimmers thanks to their eosin glaze. The **Zsolnay Family and Factory Exhibition** (Tue-Sun 10am-5pm Nov-Mar, Tue-Sun 10am-6pm Apr and Oct, daily 10am-6pm May-Sep, HUF 1,400) chronicles the history of the factory and its family. Make sure you stroll through the **Street of Artisans' Shops** near the Felsővámház utca gate for some souvenir shopping from ceramics and jewelry to old-fashioned candies and handmade chocolates.

Entry to the cultural center grounds is free; a ticket for all the museums is HUF 5,500. You can get tickets online (www.zsolnaynegyed.hu/en/information/ticket-sales) or at the information points in the complex like the Visitor Center (signposted from any of the entrances), the Zsolnay Infopoint and Shop (at the end of the Street of Artisans' Shops), or the Zsolnay Guesthouse.

ZSOLNAY MAUSOLEUM

Zsolnay Vilmos utca 37, tel. 06/30-929-7803, www.zsolnaynegyed. hu, Tue-Sun 10am-6pm Apr-Oct, Tue-Sun 10am-5pm Nov-Mar, HUF 1,300

Just 200 meters (220 yards) away from

the Zsolnay Cultural Quarter, the Zsolnay Mausoleum resides on the top of a small slope. To reach the mausoleum, walk up the paved promenade flanked by 42 stone lions poised on the wall. Once you reach the top, the neo-Roman mausoleum lies behind the large stone and iron gate, surrounded with trees. Naturally, ceramics adorn this family tomb, where the conical rooftop is clad in marine-green roof tiles, and inside the cylindrical structure the walls and ceilings are decorated with patterned and eosin-glazed tiles and colorful frescoes. Expect to spend 20 minutes in and around the mausoleum, and definitely factor in a good 5 minutes to walk up the 130-meter-long (140-yard-long) promenade leading to the tomb. However, if you're like Vilmos Zsolnay, maybe

The Zsolnay Mauseoleum is the resting place of the family.

you'll enjoy sitting on this hillside as he did. It was a favorite spot for the founder to observe his factory from a distance. You can easily combine the Zsolnay Cultural Quarter with the mausoleum, and in fact a combined ticket for the museums includes entry to the Zsolnay Mausoleum as well.

Nightlife

Pécs is a university city, so students make up the main demographic of its nightlife scene. Although Pécs won't be as lively as Budapest, you can find quite a few fun bars and clubs clustered around Király utca.

BARS
CoolTour Café
Király utca 26, tel. 06/742-1009, Mon-Wed 9am-midnight, Thu 9am-1am, Fri-Sat 9am-2am, Sun 2pm-midnight

This three-floor ruin bar in downtown Pécs is the perfect place to have a drink in the early evening. The bar is decked out with retro mismatched sofas and armchairs, with eclectic antique rugs covering the tile floor. You need to head up to the bar to get your

drinks, but once you've relaxed on one of the sofas you may find you're too chilled out to go anywhere for a while. In the summer, make sure you grab a table in the graveled fairy-light-clad garden.

CoolTour has a ruin pub feel.

Nappali

Király utca 23-25, tel. 06/72-585-705,
Sun-Thu 9am-2am, Fri-Sat 9am-3am

This multifunctional bar in the middle of Király utca is a café and co-working space by day and transforms into a bar, concert hall, and nightclub by night. It's a large open space with maroon-colored walls and large windows; in the evening, it's easy to find by the crowds spilling out onto the street. It's a popular nighttime venue for locals, especially since you'll find a different kind of program on every night.

Művész Presszó

Kolozsvár utca 24, tel. 06/30-769-7743,
Tue-Sat 2pm-midnight, Mon 2pm-10pm

It's like a trip back in time to the 1960s and '70s, but with 100 local craft beers on the menu. The walls are clad in old-fashioned tiles depicting folk motifs of chickens and flowers, and there's vintage furniture and faded lace tablecloths. In the summer a street side terrace is open. However, the best thing about this bar is its beer selection from local microbreweries. If you're passionate about beer, you'll want to come thirsty. It's a little off the beaten track, close to the Pécs train station, but may be a good stopping point for a drink before grabbing the train.

CLUB

Pécsi Est Café

Rákóczi út 46, www.pecsiestcafe.hu,
Wed, Fri, Sat 8pm-5am

When the other bars close for the night, Pécsi Est is just getting started. This club can fit 450 people and caters to all music types: pop, rock, metal, hip-hop, punk, electronica, and even jazz concerts. Many of Hungary's top pop and rock acts feature on the events calendar, but some international ones will also make the bill. Either way, there is usually something exciting here on the weekend.

Shopping

If you're looking for a place to gather a few souvenirs in one place, then you may want to peruse the colorful Street of Artisans' Shops in the northern part of the Zsolnay Cultural Quarter. You can find more traditional souvenirs like magnets and books at the Infopoint, the information point for the quarter, but it's really worth coming here for the artisanal chocolate and interactive candy-manufacturing shops.

FOOD ITEMS

Csoko-Láda

Street of Artisans' Shops, Zsolnay
Cultural Quarter, tel. 06/20-315-7773,
www.csokolada.hu, Tue-Sun 10am-5pm

Pick up some handmade chocolate from this artisanal chocolatier on the Street of Artisans' Shops in the Zsolnay Cultural Quarter. A charming little shop with maroon walls, glass cabinets displaying freshly made bonbons, and wooden shelves packed with beautiful chocolate boxes, it is a great place to pick up a gift or two. Each chocolate is made by hand with its own casting and packed in a special, unique package.

Nostalgic Candy Factory

Street of Artisans' Shops, Zsolnay
Cultural Quarter, tel. 06/70-371-4286,
Tue-Sun 10am-5pm Oct-Mar, 10am-6pm
Apr-Sep

The Nostalgic Candy Factory is more than just a shop—it's an experience. Gyula Kovács has been making candy for more than 30 years, and you can see him and his small team make candy in this colorful shop for free between 11am and 3pm. You can also join in the fun by preparing your own lollipops for HUF 600 apiece. Otherwise, just pop in to buy some handcrafted candy to take home as a gift (or enjoy on your day in the Zsolnay Quarter).

CERAMICS

Zsolnay Brand Store

Jókai tér 2, tel. 06/72-310-220,
Mon-Fri 10am-6pm, Sat 10am-2pm

Since Zsolnay is famous for its porcelain, why not take home a souvenir? Pay a visit to the brand shop in the city and pick up an eosin vase, a porcelain plate, or perhaps something made from pyrogranite. A visit to the shop is like visiting a museum, with all the unique and valuable ceramics on display—the main difference is you can take them home at a price. (There is also a Zsolnay shop in the Cultural Quarter, close to the Street of Artisans' Shops.)

Food

Pécs lies close to the Croatian and Serbian borders, which is why the local cuisine has Balkan influences like grilled meats, *ajvar* (a paste made of peppers), and flatbreads. Another culinary influence in the region is Swabian food. The Swabs were a German-speaking group who lived west of the Danube in Hungary, and their food combines German and Hungarian dishes. Otherwise you'll find the usual Hungarian specials like goulash or chicken paprikas.

Most of the restaurants are located in the city center; however, you can get snacks inside the Zsolnay Cultural Quarter. The E78 (www.e78.hu) is a café and a bar that sells a few bites like sandwiches, scones, and chocolate bars. Just outside the Cultural Quarter, the trendy Room Bistro (www.roombistro.com) serves a daily menu with a paleo option.

HUNGARIAN

Aranykacsa

Teréz utca 4, tel. 06/72-518-860,
www.aranykacsa.hu, Tue-Thu 11:30am-10pm,
Fri-Sat 11:30am-midnight, Sun
11:30am-4:30pm, entrées HUF 1,700-2,700

This curious restaurant has three distinct rooms with different aesthetics spread over three floors. The main restaurant on the ground floor is a cozy hangout with its mahogany bar and burgundy walls. The Zsolnay room, also on the ground floor, has been decorated with eosin-glazed ceramics and is usually used for private events. The top-floor Dakk bar is more like a lounge and club room, and there is a wine cellar, the Vinarium, in the basement. Dishes are Hungarian, and some of the restaurant's more nostalgic ones are based on their menu from 1982, like goulash soup made with tripe. Try the catfish paprika stew!

Tettye Restaurant

Tettye tér 4, tel. 06/72-532-788,
www.tettye.hu, Tue-Sun 11am-11pm,
entrées HUF 1,500-4,300

Even though it's off the beaten track (from the Mosque of Pasha Qasim, it's a 30-minute walk uphill, or a 10-minute journey if you take bus number 33 from the Alagút stop, a 5-minute walk up Hunyadi János utca), this restaurant is worth a trek for the views. Residing in a large house with an impressive terrace, Tettye overlooks Pécs from the hills above, and there is even a medieval ruined Dervish monastery on its doorstep. The menu focuses on Swabian dishes, so you can try specials like trotters

cooked in Bavarian beer with stewed cabbage and spicy potato wedges. You can also get Hungarian specials like veal paprika stew or game dishes, plus a few vegetarian options. Portions are generous.

BALKAN
Balkán Bisztró

Ferencesek utcája 32, tel. 06/30-891-6809,
www.balkanbisztro.hu, Tue-Sun
11:30am-10pm, entrées HUF 1,850-2,850

Bright, airy, and modern, the Balkán Bisztró serves a selection of Balkan meat platters from *cevapcici* (spicy kebabs), to *plejskavica* (meat patties), served with *ajvar* (a spicy pepper sauce) and salads. You can also go for Balkan-themed burgers, or if you have a sweet tooth try one of their fragrant homemade baklavas or a potent Turkish coffee served on a traditional Bosnian copper set. The look of the restaurant is modern,

Balkán Bisztró serves delicious Balkan specials fused with modern Hungarian flavors.

with white walls and a mural depicting a map of the Balkans, in addition to lots of creatively arranged dangling lightbulbs.

Blöff Bisztró

Jókai tér 5, tel. 06/72-497-469, daily 11am-1am, entrées HUF 1,800-4,800

Being so close to the Croatian border, Pécs is big on Balkan food, and Blöff Bisztró is no exception. It's a simple-looking restaurant with wood flooring and wooden tables, but its minimalist look allows the food to shine. Try any of their fish dishes from the ever-changing seasonal menu. You can also get great steaks and classic Balkan dishes like *cevapcici* with *ajvar* or *pljeskavica* stuffed with ewe's cheese. Pair it all with some of the Hungarian and Croatian wines available.

INTERNATIONAL
Korhely Restaurant and Pub

Boltív köz 2, www.korhelypub.hu, daily 11:30am-11:30pm, entrées HUF 1,700-7,200

Walking into this pub, whose name means "guzzler," is like stepping back into a surreal parody of the Wild West. The décor is a mix of straw scattered on the floor, stained-glass windows on the ceiling, and old records and newspapers plastered on the walls. The menu is distinctly Tex-Mex, with an impressive selection of steaks, fajitas, and enchiladas. There are also Hungarian dishes on the menu, and if you can't wait for your food, there is a bowl of peanuts in their shells on the table you can snack on.

Pezsgőhaz Etterem

Szent István tér 12, tel. 06/72-522-599, www.pezsgohaz.hu, Thu-Fri 11:30am-3pm and 6pm-10pm, Sat 11:30am-10pm, Sun 11:30am-3pm, entrées HUF 2,600-5,900

Set in a former wine cellar, Peszgőhaz Restaurant specializes in fine dining and top wines, including a wide range of sparkling wines from the surrounding regions. Try some of their more creative dishes like duck liver with onion and quince, or black spaghetti with prawns and lemony vegetables. Dishes here are more international than Hungarian, with fusion influences from French and Italian kitchens and accents from Asia, but all dishes are made with local produce.

Accommodations

✪ Hotel Palatinus

Király utca 5, tel. 06/72-889-400, www.danubiushotels.com/hu/szallodak-pecs/hotel-palatinus, HUF 15,000-21,000 d including breakfast

It's worth staying in the Hotel Palatinus for the architecture alone. The three-star hotel resides in an Art Nouveau landmark on the vibrant Király utca, just minutes from the National Theater and Széchenyi tér. The lobby, restaurant, and staircase capture the *fin-de-siècle* grandeur of the original hotel (the hotel fell into neglect for years and underwent a 13-year-long renovation in the 1970s and 1980s), with stained glass, Zsolnay ceramics, and elaborate murals; the rooms, however, are quite simple although comfortable. Breakfast is a sumptuous spread in the restaurant with cold cuts,

CHASING AWAY WINTER IN MOHÁCS

When it's time to chase the winter away, the small town of Mohács, a half hour's drive east of Pécs, comes to life with its wild UNESCO-recognized carnival celebrations. **Busójárás** dates back to medieval times, and the festival's highlight is the men dressed up in scary demon-like costumes made out of wool with red painted masks adorned with animal horns—they make a lot of noise to chase the winter season away, while also grabbing and pursuing girls. In most settings, this kind of behavior would count as harassment, but it's part of the tradition and just for fun. That being said, if you do feel uncomfortable at costumed strangers getting touchy-feely, you may want to give this festival a miss.

Busójárás is a vibrant carnival where locals dress up in sheepskin and demonic-looking masks to scare the winter away.

Some say the celebration also commemorates the defeat of the Turks: legend has it that the men from Mohács hid in the swamps and surprised the Turks by wearing demonic masks and scared them off. The carnival lasts six days, usually in February but it depends on when Easter occurs that year. The main festivities take place on Sunday, called *Farsang vasárnap*, Carnival Sunday, but if you can make it down Tuesday for the *Farsangtemetés*, the Carnival Burial, you'll be treated to a large bonfire where the Farsang coffin is burned to mark the end of winter.

Find out more about the festival at the **Mohács Tourinform Office** (Széchenyi tér 1, Mohács, tel. 06/69-505-515, www.mohacsibusojaras.hu, free). To reach Mohács, drive 210 kilometers (130 miles) south on the M6 from Budapest. The drive takes just under 2 hours.

---

pastries, and cooked dishes like scrambled eggs and sausages. There is also a sauna and steam bath.

The Hotel Palatinus is an Art Nouveau sight that's worth stopping by even if you're not planning to stay here.

Adele Boutique Hotel

Mária utca 1, tel. 06/72-510-226, www.adelehotel.hu, HUF 20,000-30,000 d

Although Adele Boutique is one of the newer hotels in Pécs, the building it occupies dates back to the 1700s and once belonged to a baroness. This four-star hotel, set just 200 meters (220 yards) from the Mosque of Pasha Qasim, opened in 2015 and has 19 rooms, with three apartments and three suites. After a long day exploring the museums and sites, you can unwind in its sauna and relaxation area or enjoy the courtyard garden. A continental breakfast is available (around HUF 2,300).

Corso Hotel

Koller utca 8, tel. 06/72-421-900,
www.corsohotel.hu, HUF 15,000-25,000 d

If your taste in hotels is more modern, then the Corso has you covered. The building has a chic design that's colorful and playful with 81 individually decorated rooms, some sporting print wallpaper while others are more subdued in elegant shades of tan. The four-star hotel offers rooms in classic, Mediterranean, and modern styles, so you can pick the one that suits you. Make sure you check out the rooftop terrace! There is a buffet breakfast available (HUF 2,500) and also an on-site restaurant.

Hotel Arkadia

Hunyadi János utca 1,
tel. 06/72-512-550, www.hotelarkadiapecs.
hu, HUF 17,300-19,900 d

There are 32 rooms in this four-star boutique hotel in downtown Pécs. This Bauhaus-inspired hotel resides in two buildings connected by a glass corridor and is decked in designer furniture. The look is modern and sleek, with exposed brick, white walls, and functional design.

Transportation

GETTING THERE

The most comfortable and convenient way to get to Pécs is by train—especially if you take the fast train.

TRAIN

MÁV operates regular train service from Budapest Keleti to Pécs every two hours, and it takes just under three hours. Tickets cost around HUF 4,500. There are slower and cheaper trains that take around four hours from Budapest Deli and cost HUF 3,950.

It's a 20-minute walk from the station to Széchenyi tér, or 10 minutes by taxi. (Call Volán Taxi Pécs at tel. 06/72-333-333.) Numerous buses depart from outside the station to the center as well; the fare is HUF 500 if you buy from the driver. You can also get tickets (singles cost 350 HUF) at the public transport cashier at the train station (Indóház tér 6, Mon-Fri 6:45am-6pm, Sat-Sun, public holidays 8.10am-6pm).

BUS

Buses from Budapest take longer, around 3 hours 20 minutes, but are cheaper than trains at HUF 3,690. Bus services operated by Volánbusz go from the Népliget station to Pécs bus station, which is in the center of the city and a 10-minute walk from Széchenyi tér.

CAR

From Budapest, drive 210 kilometers (130 miles) south on the M6 to reach Pécs. The drive takes around 2 hours. Parking is restricted in many locations in the heart of the city, but you can park close to the center for around HUF 400 per hour. There are also underground parking garages in Kossuth tér or at the Király Ház (66 Király utca).

LEAVING PÉCS

The last direct train back to Budapest leaves around 7pm; the last bus goes much earlier, around 5:30pm.

ESSENTIALS

Getting There 252
Getting Around 255
Visas and Officialdom . . 256
Festivals and Events. . . . 257
Food and Nightlife 258
Accommodations 259
Conduct and
    Customs 260
Health and Safety 261
Practical Details 262
Traveler Advice 264
Hungarian
    Phrasebook 265

Getting There

Travelers arriving via air will fly into Budapest's Ferenc Liszt International Airport (BUD, tel. 06/1-296-7000, www.bud.hu).

FROM THE UNITED STATES

Until recently, Budapest had no direct flight connections from the US and required transfers in London, Frankfurt, Munich, or even Reykjavik.

At the time of writing, LOT Airlines (www.lot.com) just launched new routes from Budapest with direct flights to New York and Chicago, with flight times around 10-11 hours. You can also fly from Budapest to Philadelphia with American Airlines (www.aa.com) in around 10 hours, and they also have flights to New York to go to either Frankfurt or Cologne and change trains again in Vienna to reach Budapest—total journey time (with the fewest connections) of 14-16 hours. Tickets for onward journeys from Brussels could cost an extra €150-250. This is not the cheapest or fastest way to travel, but definitely the most adventurous!

FROM EUROPE

The great thing about traveling in Central Europe is choosing from an abundant selection of transport modes. You can go by bus, train, car, plane, or in some instances by ferry.

AIR

Low-cost airlines are an option if you're traveling from further afield, like the UK. Airlines like EasyJet (www.easyjet.com), WizzAir (www.wizzair.com), and Ryanair (www.ryanair.com) offer inexpensive flights to Budapest from many European destinations. It takes between 2 and 2.5 hours from London by plane.

TRAIN

Traveling by train through Europe is a pleasure. You get to see the landscape change as you go. If you're heading to Hungary from Western Europe, chances are you're in for a ride through the Alps. You can plan your train itinerary on the website Bahn.de, which shows plenty of train timetables and connections so you can prepare more efficiently.

If you're in the UK and feeling adventurous—or simply hate flying—you also have the option of traveling to Central Europe by train. The Eurostar (www.eurostar.com) goes to Brussels every two hours from London St. Pancras Station (around €100-200). However, from Brussels you will need

BUS

Buses can be the cheaper option. Although maybe not as relaxing as trains, buses like Eurolines (www.eurolines.eu) and FlixBus (www.flixbus.com) are quite comfortable, usually with toilets on board, and operate throughout Europe. Taking the bus across Europe is quite the odyssey, and I would recommend it only if you really want to save money traveling overland—and with low-cost airlines offering frequent flights, you're not really saving that much.

There are no direct buses from London to Budapest.

FERRY

If you want to move between countries in Central Europe, your best bet is to go on a multi-country river cruise across Europe—some even start from Amsterdam and sail all the way down to Budapest, connecting to the Danube via canals. AMA Waterways (www.amawaterways.com) and Viking River Cruises (www.vikingrivercruises.co.uk) run river cruises from Amsterdam to Budapest (and vice-versa), which take around 15 days.

CAR

Europe has a well-connected highway network, so depending on how far you're planning to drive, it's relatively easy to reach Hungary. Highways are smooth and well maintained through-out the region, but you may find some roads in the countryside, in Hungary especially, in poorer condition. Most roads are well lit and well maintained but do note that you must use winter tires during the winter if you're planning to drive across Central Europe as the roads—especially in the mountains in Austria—can get icy and slippery.

Border Crossings

Ever since the Schengen Agreement removed border controls between the members of the EU states, traveling by car throughout Europe has become easier. Some countries may check at the border at random, though, so always have your papers—like your passport or ID, license (International Drivers Permit, if applicable), registration, insurance papers—to hand over. Peak seasons may lead to queues at the border.

Safety

In the winter, mountain passes may be slow, or even closed off if the weather is bad. If you're driving through the Alps, it's best to keep an eye on the news and drive through smaller roads at low speeds. You must also fit your car with winter tires or all-season tires between November and April. You should also carry snow chains with you this season. Winter conditions tend to be the worst from December to February, but it's not impossible to have snow hit as late as early November, late March or even early April. Winter controls are enforced at control points, especially in Austria. And—all year round—if you're planning on driving through

Germany note that some highways won't have speed limits so expect some crazy roadrunners.

Car Rentals

If you want to head out on an epic road trip from one European country to another with a rental car, pick a company like Europcar (www.europcar.com), Sixt (www.sixt.com), or Hertz (www.hertz.com), which have offices in other countries that allow you just to drop the car off—but these will include a "drop fee," which is an extra added charge to return the car to another office. Talk to your rental company about your itinerary. You can find the best rental deal with price comparison sites like Skyscanner (www.skyscanner.com) or Kayak (www.kayak.com). The minimum age to rent a car in Budapest is 21. Some companies require you to be at least 25 years of age, so confirm with your rental car company.

Should you prefer to cross Europe by car, but don't drive yourself or prefer not to drive, you can also try the the car-sharing service Bla Bla Car (www.blablacar.com) a carpooling service that matches up drivers and passengers at reasonable prices, with intercity trips costing around HUF 2,000-3,500. However, be aware that at the time of writing the app and website will only show available rides when you browse in the Hungarian-language version (and if you download the app while traveling, your phone will set it in Hungarian with no option to change it back). Finding rides in Hungary is not available in the English-language version of the app, so you may need some help translating to use it.

FROM AUSTRALIA AND NEW ZEALAND

There are no direct flights from Australia and New Zealand to Central Europe. The quickest and most direct route is to connect through Bangkok, Doha, Dubai, or Shanghai. Emirates (www.emirates.com) and Qatar (www.qatarairways.com) serve most of the flights from Australia and New Zealand, which take around 22 hours or more, including transfers. Air China (www.airchina.com) and Thai Airways (www.thaiairways.com) also have services connecting the region to Oceania.

FROM SOUTH AFRICA

There are no direct flights from South Africa to Budapest. The easiest way is to fly with Emirates or Qatar Airways and change in Dubai or Doha. Flights take around 15 to 18 hours or more. Some routes from Johannesburg also go through Paris Charles de Gaulle with Air France or Zurich with Swiss Airlines.

Getting Around

CITY TRANSPORT

Budapest has excellent public transport, with a well-connected subway service, a vast network of tram lines, and of course buses. All the public transit systems are operated by one managing entity, so you use the same passes on multiple forms of transit, such as bus and metro. You can purchase single-ride tickets, and there are also passes that are sold in chunks of time, so you can get a pass for 24 hours, 48 hours, etc. You can buy tickets from automated machines, tobacconists, or ticket offices.

VALIDATING TRANSIT TICKETS

Budapest has a loyalty system when it comes to enforcing public transit tickets. It works like this: buy a ticket or a pass, validate it, and keep it with you. You typically validate a ticket when you enter the metro or get on the tram or bus—look for the validation boxes, and double-check that the validation mark shows. Passes, on the other hand, won't need validating as they are issued from the date you request.

Most of the time, there are no ticket inspectors, but if there are and you don't have a valid ticket, prepare for trouble. Ticket inspectors are usually in civilian dress, so until the armband comes on or the ID gets pulled out from under the shirt, you won't know, and they take no prisoners nor excuses. If your ticket is not validated or valid, you will get fined—and the experience can ruin your trip.

BIKE

Budapest has a bike-sharing system and rental companies, and it is a bike-friendly city, with designated bicycle lanes and paths all across the city.

GETTING AROUND HUNGARY

The easiest way to get between the destinations in this book is to go by train or by bus. Each town has direct connections. The main rail company in Hungary is MÁV (www.mavcsoport.hu), and the local bus company is Volánbusz (www.volanbusz.hu).

Road Rules

In Hungary the minimum driving age is 17, and there is zero tolerance for any alcohol detected in the blood. Drivers drive on the right side of the road.

You'll need a vignette for the main roads that have tolls. You can usually buy these from gas stations, at the border, or online (www.hungary-vignette.eu). These need to be displayed in the window of your car unless it's an electronic one tied to your number plate.

While traveling, you'll need your passport and driver's license. If you're from the US or Canada, it may be a good idea also to get an International Driving Permit (IDP). This is an official translation of your license from back home, and although you won't need it in all countries, it's a good idea if you're planning on driving in Austria, Hungary, Poland, Croatia, Greece, Slovenia, or Slovakia. You can get a permit from the American Automobile Association (AAA.com) or the Canadian Automobile Association Office (CCA.ca) for $20.

Visas and Officialdom

Hungary resides within the EU and the Schengen Area.

US TRAVELERS

As a US citizen, you will not need an entry permit (visa) to enter Hungary; you can come as a tourist for up to 90 days in any 180-day period. However, you do require a passport that is valid for at least three months after your departure from the European Union.

EU/SCHENGEN TRAVELERS

If you're from another EU state, you do not need a visa to enter any of the Schengen countries, including Hungary. When you travel from one Schengen country to another, chances are you won't even have your passport or ID checked, although it's a good idea to keep it on you as some borders still check IDs, such as on the train. UK travelers should check for new regulations post-Brexit.

TRAVELERS FROM AUSTRALIA AND NEW ZEALAND

Australians and New Zealanders can come to Hungary visa-free for a maximum period of 90 days in any 180-day period without taking up employment. Your passport must be valid for three months beyond the planned date of departure from the Schengen Area.

TRAVELERS FROM SOUTH AFRICA

South Africans require a visa to enter the Schengen Area. You can obtain a Schengen visa from any of the Schengen Area member countries, which will allow for free movement between the whole Schengen zone. It's best to apply for the country you're planning to visit first. Make sure it's a Uniform Schengen Visa (USV): this visa will grant entry for 90 days in a 180-day period.

If your first country is Hungary, then you can apply for your Schengen Visa from the Embassy of Hungary in Pretoria, or apply at the consulates in Durban or Cape Town.

Festivals and Events

IN BUDAPEST

JANUARY
New Year's Day Concerts are a local tradition in Budapest.

MARCH
March 15 is a huge national holiday in Hungary to remember the revolution of 1848 against the Habsburg rule.

MAY
Budapest 100 gets you a behind-the-scenes look inside private residential buildings that are normally closed to the public.

Falk Art Forum opens up the streets around 50 Budapest galleries for festivities, performances, music, theater, and food.

JULY
Formula 1 Grand Prix (Budapest) is one the most important events in motorsports, bringing thousands to Budapest each year for the races.

AUGUST
Sziget Festival is one of Europe's largest music festivals, taking place on Óbuda Island. The week-long festival pulls in thousands from around Europe.

SEPTEMBER
Budapest Wine Festival gets the best Hungarian winemakers up to Buda Castle. Sip and taste wines from the region with fantastic views over the river.

OCTOBER
Budapest Design Week takes over the city during the first half of October. Exhibits of Hungarian contemporary fashion, art, and design are scattered throughout Budapest, and most events are free.

Art Market Budapest takes place every October and is the leading art fair of Central and Eastern Europe. All manner of art is showcased here, to view and to buy, and there is a different guest country participant every year.

DECEMBER
Christmas Markets set up shop from the end of November till the end of December, and are a considerable draw to the region.

New Year is an epic party in any city, and in the center of Budapest, it becomes quite the street party.

OUTSIDE BUDAPEST
Busójárás is a carnival in Mohács, a town near Pécs, that celebrates both

the end of winter and victory against the Ottoman occupation. It's a lively carnival with sheep-skin-clad demons, lots of noise, and a bonfire.

Hollókő Easter Festival is one of the liveliest events in the country around Easter, with locals wearing folk costumes and girls being splashed with buckets of water.

Volt Festival in Sopron is the largest music festival in the country after Sziget.

Food and Nightlife

Food in Hungary is dominated by meat, particularly pork. Starchy ingredients like potatoes and dumplings also make up the base for food in this part of the world, and vegetables tend to come in pickled form.

MEALTIMES

Most people in Hungary will have breakfast between 7am and 10am, with lunch usually taking place at noon-1:30pm, and dinner around 7pm but can be as early as 6pm or late as 8:30pm.

TIPPING

Tipping is not required but is customary for good service. The general rule is to round up for small amounts (e.g., HUF 2,500 for a HUF 2,350 meal) or around 10 percent for a nice meal. You should tell your server how much you want to pay when handing them cash or your card (e.g., Server: "That's 3,600 forints." You: "4,000, please."). Don't leave cash on the table, and your credit card slip will not come with a line to add the tip. In Hungary, if you give a note and say "thank you," the waiter will assume that includes tip and you won't get change.

DIETARY RESTRICTIONS

Central Europe's vegetarian scene is slowly improving, with lots of raw and vegan restaurants opening in recent years. However, in many Hungarian restaurants, the meat-free menu is still limited to fried cheese (*rántott sajt*), and vegans may struggle to find anything suitable outside of restaurants that specifically cater to their diet. Seafood, ham, bacon, lard, and even rabbit have been known to pop up on vegetarian sections in village pubs, so double-check with your server to be 100 percent sure.

Some restaurants are better than others when it comes to dairy or gluten sensitivity. Requests to leave out certain ingredients are usually honored when possible, but substitutions or asking for ingredients on the side is not common practice and will likely be met with confusion or annoyance—especially in rural areas. Restaurants are required to list certain allergens on their menus. For severe allergies, printing a list of the specific words in Hungarian may help communicate your needs.

Accommodations

HOTELS

Hotels in Central Europe get graded on a star system running from one to five stars. Just how many stars a hotel will have depends on factors like the services and facilities available in the hotel, the infrastructure, and quality. Five-star hotels will offer luxury; there will usually be a spa and fine-dining options. Three-star hotels are generally comfortable for most travelers (and sometimes there is little difference between three or four stars in terms of standard, just the four-star hotel may have a spa). The term "boutique hotel" will pop up while traveling. This usually refers to a smaller hotel with 10 to 100 rooms, and it may even have a design twist that gives it a unique selling point for visitors. Most hotels will have en suite bathrooms—especially for hotels three stars and above—but it's best to check before booking if you're uncertain. Basic toiletries will always be provided, like soap and shampoo, for hotels over three stars.

Hotels will ask for your ID or passport upon arrival and may also want to photocopy your documents. Sometimes a city tax will be added to your bill on top of your hotel fee, and check to make sure if breakfast is included in the price of the room. Many hotels include a complimentary breakfast in the price. When it comes to tipping hotel staff, it's enough to give a bellhop or porter HUF 500 per bag. If you're happy with the cleaning service, then you can leave a similar gratuity on the bed each night for the housekeeper.

BED AND BREAKFASTS

Bed and breakfasts are usually smaller than a hotel and independently owned. Breakfast is often included in the price, often cooked by the owner. If you're looking for a place with a familial feel, then a B&B is a good choice. Rates are usually much lower than in a larger hotel, and you will get a more authentic feel in the area.

Do note though that some B&Bs occupy old residential apartments and houses, so bathrooms and toilets may not be located in the room and are down the hall. You can usually request en suite when booking the B&B.

HOSTELS

Young travelers, backpackers, and those on a budget will love hostels. Most hostels offer rooms in six- to eight-bed dorms, but some may have single or double rooms at budget prices too, however bathrooms and toilets will usually be shared and located outside the room. Some travelers also love hostels for the community spirit, as they usually come with a common room or a shared kitchen that provides an excellent opportunity for travelers to meet and mingle. Breakfast is usually extra, if offered by the hostel. However, if peace, quiet, and a good night's sleep are what you're after, steer clear of the Party Hostels, with their regular happy hours and in-house bars or clubs. However, if you want to get to see the city's nightlife or make friends with other travelers, they can be great.

APARTMENT RENTALS

If you prefer to self-cater or have the experience of living like a local in the city you're visiting, then an apartment rental may be the option for you. The most popular way of doing this is Airbnb, but this has caused significant controversy for pushing up the rents of locals, especially in Budapest. Booking.com also rents out apartments. Just note in some apartment rentals, the toilet may be shared and located out in the hall, so do your research before you book one. Also, note that with the independence an apartment will give you, you won't have the support concerning tourist information and orientation that you would have with a hotel.

Conduct and Customs

LOCAL HABITS

Don't expect service with a smile: some places have friendly staff, but as a rule, most waitstaff, especially in classic cafés, will be on the surly side. Although smiles are not mandatory, politeness is. Always say hello or good day in Hungarian if you can whenever you go into a shop or a café, stand on the right of the escalator in the metro, and give up your seat to the elderly on the bus. When it comes to tipping, say how much you'd like to pay in total when paying; don't leave change on the table.

GREETINGS

Greetings are especially important in Central Europe. It's expected you say good day when you enter a shop. In Hungary, you can say "*Jó napot kívanok*," pronounced "your nap-ot kee-van-ok," which means "I wish you a good day." It's also considered polite to say goodbye when leaving.

Greeting one another with a couple of kisses on the cheek is also common in Central Europe, but this usually happens between men-women and women-women. In some cases such as close family or older men, you may see the men do it, too. Kisses are generally exchanged at the beginning and the end of most social encounters. In business settings or between two men, a handshake is often the norm.

ALCOHOL

Alcohol rules in Hungary are more relaxed than in the United States, with the legal drinking age being 18. In Hungary, particularly in the countryside, don't be surprised to see locals doing a shot first thing in the morning.

There are restrictions on the sale of alcohol at certain times. In Budapest, certain districts put a cap on late-night shops selling alcohol after 11pm. And don't think of driving, even if you've had one beer—drinking and driving is taken very seriously and can incur punishment if any alcohol shows up in a test.

SMOKING

Smoking is legal from the age of 18 in Hungary, but you can only buy cigarettes from National Tobacco Shops (Nemzeti Dohány Bolt), which have brown signs and an 18 logo inside a red circle and the colors of the Hungarian flag—red, white, green.

A lot of Hungarians smoke, but it's not allowed inside and only in designated areas outside in restaurants and cafés.

DRUGS

The Central European region has never had a reputation as being a drug hotbed, but dealing still happens around train stations and transport hubs. Hungary has strict drug laws compared to other countries in the region (like the nearby Czech Republic, where cannabis is decriminalized); even cannabis is entirely illegal and drug possession can lead to up to two years' imprisonment in Hungary. It's best to play it safe while traveling and avoid consuming or possessing drugs—even in small quantities.

PROSTITUTION

Although prostitution has been legalized in Hungary and sex workers pay tax, there is no official red-light district in Budapest.

DRESS

Hungary has a fairly relaxed dress code. You'll see people walking around in jeans and T-shirts, and most restaurants—unless we're talking somewhere elite—won't enforce a strict dress code. In most churches, women will be expected to cover shoulders and wear skirts below the knee.

Health and Safety

EMERGENCY NUMBERS

The number to dial in an emergency is the same throughout continental Europe: 112.

CRIME AND THEFT

When it comes to violent crime, Budapest is generally safe. Pickpockets perhaps present the primary risk in crowded places like the metro or festivals, so keep an eye on your belongings when out and about. Scams are another thing to be aware of, like the classic Budapest scam when young, attractive women approach you (if you are male) on Váci utca asking for directions and then invite you to a drink—and take you to bar with no menus that will fleece you for as much money as you have. It's important not to let your guard down, but with a little common sense and avoiding areas with a bad reputation—such as the train stations—you should be fine.

MEDICAL SERVICES

Vaccines are not required in Hungary, but if you're traveling in the window between November to March, you may want to invest in a flu shot. Also, if you're planning to head out into nature, you may want to get a Tick-Borne Encephalitis vaccine as ticks are a growing risk in Central Europe. In local pharmacies you can also pick up bug spray that is good to ward of mosquitos and ticks, so if you haven't been vaccinated, it's a good idea to take precautions when in parks or wooded areas—even within the city.

In Hungary, standards will vary depending on the hospital, with some being better than others. Public health services in Hungary are understaffed and overburdened.

DRINKING WATER

The water is not only safe in Budapest, it's actually pretty good, so go ahead and feel free to bottle some tap water.

PHARMACIES

Pharmacies can help you pick up any medications, vitamins, or herbal supplements you may need while traveling. Drugs like ibuprofen and paracetamol (acetaminophen) don't require a prescription in European pharmacies, but some drugs like antibiotics or sedatives will require a local prescription from a doctor of that country. European pharmacies also sell more than just medication; you can buy skincare products and toiletries developed by dermatologists (if you've heard beauty bloggers rave about French pharmacy skincare products, the good news is you can find the same French brands like La Roche-Posay and Nuxe in larger pharmacies). You may also find pharmacies that sell alternative medicines like homeopathy as well.

You can spot a pharmacy in Hungary by the bright green cross symbol. You can find a pharmacy that's open any time of day or night, including an assigned all-night pharmacy like those in Budapest.

SECURITY

Budapest to date has not seen any terrorist attacks. Just like any city in Europe, it's best to be vigilant and consult your embassy for travel advice. Also, if offered, register your travel with your embassy before traveling so that you're entitled to consular help.

Practical Details

WHAT TO PACK

When it comes to packing, the best bet is to pack smart-casual attire and plenty of layers. The climate in the region is changeable, so keep a jacket or a cardigan in your bag for those days when the cooler evening chill sets in.

Expect to do a lot of walking, so pack a pair of comfortable shoes. The old town in Budapest has cobbles, so bear that in mind when considering footwear. Since the climate is changeable—in the summer it can go from blazing heat to flash storms—pack layers and an umbrella or a raincoat. If you're going in the winter, pack warm clothes as the temperatures can plummet below freezing.

It's a good idea to bring swimwear if you're traveling to Budapest, so you'll be prepared to visit its famous thermal baths.

If you're coming from the UK or the States, make sure you pack an adapter so you can use your electronics. Plugs in Central Europe use two round prongs with a voltage of 220V. You will definitely want a camera or at least a good quality phone to snap pics, but bring extra memory cards, because you will need them!

Finally, earbuds or headphones can be useful for accessing museum audio guides that you can download onto your phone.

MONEY

Hungary uses the Hungarian Forint (HUF).

You'll find that **ATMs** will take foreign cards and most shops will take Visa, Mastercard, or Maestro. Some won't take American Express, so best to check before ordering. If you prefer, you can also change money at official money changers, either in banks or official changers (they usually have a Western Union sign outside, too).

Some restaurants and shops will only take cash; most markets are cash only. It's a good idea to carry some smaller bills with you if you're planning on paying in cash. Most large supermarkets and restaurants will break larger notes, but you might get a few irritated servers or sellers if you try to pay with a HUF 20,000 note in a smaller venue. Keep some small change on you at all times, especially for public toilets.

OPENING HOURS

Shops usually open around 9am or 10am and close around 6pm, perhaps later in large shopping malls, Mondays to Saturdays. In Budapest shops in the city center will open for shorter hours on Sunday. Sometimes, smaller stores will close for lunch hours.

Museums, in general, tend to close on Mondays, but check the opening times of any place you're interested in visiting—some popular attractions open every day of the week, others may have a rest day on Tuesday or Sunday. Jewish sites usually close on Saturdays.

PUBLIC HOLIDAYS

During high holidays, like Christmas and New Year's Day, most shops and attractions will be closed. Businesses also tend to close for religious holidays, but also national holidays like October 23, March 15, and August 20 in Hungary.

COMMUNICATIONS
PHONES AND CELL PHONES

The country code for Hungary is 36. If you're calling from the US, dial the international access code 011 from a US or Canadian landline, or use the plus sign and add the country code, then dial the number (drop the 0 before calling). From the UK, just dial 00 and then the country code.

Within Hungary, just dial the number without dropping the 0, if there is one, and for long-distance call, dial 06. Don't get nervous if phone numbers seem irregular in number. Standards are a little harder to predict. Mobile phone numbers can come with their own prefixes, and landline number length may also vary.

To call out of the country, dial 00 or the plus sign and the country code. For US and Canada this is 1, and then add in the phone number with the area code.

Most smartphones will work in Central Europe with a US, UK, or Canadian SIM card, but talk to your provider to make sure you don't rack up any unwanted roaming charges when you go abroad.

INTERNET ACCESS

It is easy to get online in Budapest. You should find Wi-Fi access in your hotel, but most cafés, malls, and even hotspots in the city center should get you connected online for free. Some free Wi-Fi services may ask you to register with an email and click on their terms and conditions.

SHIPPING AND POSTAL

If you're looking only to post a card, then you may want to skip the queues at the post office and buy a stamp at a newsagent. Should you go to a post office, some require you press a button and take a number for the queue.

Traveler Advice

ACCESS FOR TRAVELERS WITH DISABILITIES

With its cobbled streets, stairways leading up from one lane to another, and old metro stations, Central Europe can be a challenge for disabled travelers. In Budapest, historic buildings may not have an elevator, and some of the older metro stations may be stairs only. It's best to do some additional research; contact the Hungarian Federation of Disabled Persons' Associations (www.meosz.hu/en).

TRAVELING WITH CHILDREN

Hungary offers something for the whole family. Kids get discounts on public transport and museums, and some restaurants even offer a children's menu. There's plenty to keep the little ones busy when traveling here. Some tourist offices will provide brochures with family-friendly ideas. It's worth researching museums to see if any have play areas for children.

WOMEN TRAVELING ALONE

Budapest is relatively safe cities for solo female travelers, but exercise the same caution as you would in any other European city. Most downtown areas are okay to explore your own, even at night. However, if you feel anxious walking down quiet streets after dark, then try to pick accommodations on a main road, since there are side streets that may unnerve you after dark. Taxis can be a great option to get back if you don't like taking public transport late at night, or there are no services to where you're staying, but make sure you take a licensed operator. And should you go to a bar, take care never to leave your drink unattended.

SENIOR TRAVELERS

Senior travelers may struggle with the cobbled streets and the less accessible sites in Hungary, but on the whole, it's great for older travelers. The thermal baths in Budapest attract people of all ages, including older ones. Most museums have elevators and benches, and of course discounts for senior citizens. Public transport in Budapest is free for EU citizens aged 65 and over. Just take care not to book a hotel in Budapest's Jewish Quarter if you're looking for a peaceful night's sleep.

GAY AND LESBIAN

Hungary has conservative views, but attitudes are changing, especially in Budapest, as the numbers grow in Pride each year with more and more allies joining the march. There have been some violent demonstrations from the far-right in the city, but beyond the noise, there is an increasing amount of gay-friendly spaces in the city center.

When traveling outside Budapest, members of the LGBTQ community may feel a little uncomfortable in rural areas. In rural Hungary—and even in Budapest—members of the LGBTQ community tend to remain invisible, and public displays of affection are not seen. The Spartacus International Gay Guide (http://spartacus.gayguide.

travel/gayguide) offers a lot of useful information for LGBTQ travelers.

TRAVELERS OF COLOR

Travelers from some ethnic or religious backgrounds, particularly those with darker skin, may experience xenophobic attitudes and unwanted attention in Budapest.

You'll notice most of the population is quite homogeneous in Hungary, so travelers of color may get stared at. The country doesn't have the best reputation when it comes to racism and discrimination, especially given the anti-migrant campaigns following the recent refugee crisis. The capital city tends to be more liberal and open-minded, and you should not experience anything more than a few curious stares in the city center.

However, anti-immigrant or anti-Muslim marches are usually met with an equal or larger march in support of diverse societies, but this is a divisive political issue.

Outside of the cities, travelers of color may be met with stares from locals—especially in rural regions—but there is no need to be concerned about safety when visiting the day trips recommended in this book. These are all popular with visitors from across the world and welcome travelers of color.

Hungarian Phrasebook

Hungarian is a language that has nothing in common with its Slavic, Germanic, and Latin neighbors around. The good thing is Hungarian is in Latin script, so you should be able to read signs and the basics, but the bad news is apart from borrowed words from English there won't be much you'll understand. Hungarian is quite tricky for English speakers to pronounce, but here are a few basics to help:

s   is pronounced sh

sz is what we think is an s

ny is easiest explained as sounding like the Spanish ñ, but if you don't speak Spanish think of it like the ny in the singer's name Enya.

gy is more like d'ya, the g is very soft

ő   is like a long o and an e put together

ű   resembles a long e and u together

dzs is like our j

j   is like a y

ó   sounds like or, as in Eeyore

é   is a long e

í   is a long i

á   is like a sigh of relief, aah

ú   sounds like oo

ö   is a short and rounded o

ü   is a short and rounded u

ESSENTIAL PHRASES

Hello *Szervusz/Szia* (informal)
Good morning *Jó reggelt*
Good afternoon *Jó napot*
Good evening *Jó estét*
Good night *Jó éjszakát*
Good bye *Viszontlátásra*
Nice to meet you *Örvendek*
Thank you *Köszönöm*
You're welcome *Szívesen*
Please *Kérem*
Do you speak English? *Beszél angolul?*
I don't understand. *Nem értem.*
Yes *Igen*
No *Nem*

TRANSPORTATION

Where is...? *Hol van...?*
How far is...? *Milyen messze van...?*
Is there a bus to...? *Van egy busz...?*
Does this bus go to...? *Ez a busz megy...?*
Where do I get off? *Hol kell leszállni?*
What time does the bus/train leave? *Mikor indul a busz/vonat?*
Where is the nearest subway station? *Hol van a legközelebbi metró?*
Where can I buy a ticket? *Hol tudok jegyet venni?*
A round-trip ticket/single ticket to... *Egy menettérti jegyet/jegy...*

FOOD

A table for one/two... *Egy ember/két ember számára kérek asztalt*
Do you have a menu in English? *Van angol menü?*
What is the dish of the day? *Mi a napi étel?*
We're ready to order. *Szeretnénk rendelni.*
I'm vegetarian. *Vegetáriánus vagyok.*
I would like to order a... *Szeretnék rendelni egy...*
The check, please. *A számlát, kérem.*
beer *sör*
breakfast *reggeli*
cash *készpénz*
check *számla*
coffee *kávé*
dinner *vacsora*
glass *pohár*
hors d'oeuvre *előétel*
ice *jég*
ice cream *jégkrém*
lunch *ebéd*
restaurant *étterem*
sandwich *szendvics*
snack *falatozás*

waiter *pincér*
water *víz*
wine *bor*

SHOPPING

money *pénz*
shop *bolt/üzlet*
What time do the shops close? *Mikor zárnak a boltok?*
How much is it? *Mennyibe kerül*
I'm just looking. *Csak nézelődök.*
Is there a local specialty? *Van egy helyi specialitás?*

HEALTH

drugstore *gyógyszertár*
pain *fájdalom*
fever *láz*
headache *fejfájás*
stomach ache *hasfájás*
toothache *fogfájás*
burn *égés*
cramp *görcs*
nausea *hányinger*
vomiting *hányás*
medicine *gyógyszer*
antibiotic *antibiotikum*
pill/tablet *tabletta*
aspirin *aszpirin*
I need a doctor. *Szükségem van egy orvosra.*
I need to go to the hospital. *Kórházba kell mennem.*
I have a pain here... *Fájdalom van itt ...*
She/he has been stung/ bitten. *Elcsípett/megharapott.*
I am diabetic/pregnant. *Cukorbeteg/ Terhes vagyok*
I am allergic to penicillin/ cortisone. *Allergiás vagyok a penicillinre /kortizonra.*
My blood group is... positive/ negative. *A vércsoportom... pozitív/ negatív.*

NUMBERS

0 *nulla*
1 *egy*
2 *kettő*
3 *három*
4 *négy*
5 *öt*
6 *hat*
7 *hét*
8 *nyolc*
9 *kilenc*
10 *tíz*
11 *tizenegy*
12 *tizenkettő*
13 *tizenhárom*
14 *tizennégy*
15 *tizenöt*
16 *tizenhat*
17 *tizenhét*
18 *tizennyolc*
19 *tizenkilenc*
20 *húsz*
21 *huszonegy*
30 *harminc*
40 *negyven*
50 *ötven*
60 *hatvan*
70 *hetven*
80 *nyolcvan*
90 *kilencven*
100 *száz*
101 *száz és egy*
200 *kétszáz*
500 *ötszáz*
1,000 *ezer*
10,000 *tizezer*
100,000 *százezer*
1,000,000 *millió*

TIME

What time is it? *Mennyi az idő?*
It's one/three o'clock *Egy/Három óra van*
midday *dél*
midnight *éjfél*
morning *reggel*
afternoon *délután*
evening *este*
night *éjszaka*
yesterday *tegnap*
today *ma*
tomorrow *holnap*

DAYS AND MONTHS

week *hét*
month *hónap*
Monday *Hétfő*
Tuesday *Kedd*
Wednesday *Szerda*
Thursday *Csütörtök*
Friday *Péntek*
Saturday *Szombat*
Sunday *Vasárnap*
January *Január*
February *Február*
March *Március*
April *Április*
May *Május*
June *Június*
July *Július*
August *Augusztus*
September *Szeptember*
October *Oktober*
November *November*
December *December*

Index

A

accommodations: 123–129, 259–260. *See also specific place*
air transportation: 131, 252–253, 255
alcohol: 260. *See also* bars and nightlife; wine
Andrássy Avenue: accommodations 126; bars and nightlife 90–92; food 118–119; orientation 38; performing arts and concert halls 95–96; sights 60–61
apartment rentals: 260. *See also* accommodations
Aquincum: 79
architecture: The Bálna 76; Budapest 100 97; Dohány Street Synagogue 58–59; Geological Institute of Hungary 66; Gresham Palace 55–56; Hungarian House of Art Nouveau (Bedő House) 55; Hungarian State Opera 60; National Theatre (Budapest) 79; National Theatre (Pécs) 240–241; Ödön Lechner 57; Palace of Arts 78–79; Pécs 19; Sopron 5; Vajdahunyad Castle 61–63
Art Market Budapest: 97, 257
Art Mill: 143, 147
Art Nouveau: 55–56, 57, 234
arts and artwork: Art Market Budapest 97, 257; Budapest Design Week 97, 257; Hollókő 212–213; Palace of Arts 78–79; Róth 65; as souvenirs 106; Szentendre 18, 149–150; Tihany 184. *See also* museums; performing arts
ATMs: 263

B

Badacsony: 13, 185–186; accommodations 187–188; food 187; itinerary 22; transportation 188; wineries and wine tasting 18, 186–187
Bakery House: 225–226
Balatonfüred: 178; accommodations 180–181; food 180; itinerary ideas 22, 176; map 179; sights 178–180; transportation 181
Balaton Pantheon: 179
Bálna, The: 76
bars and nightlife: 88; bars and pubs 90–91; clubs 93–94; craft beer 92–93; general information 258; live music 93; Pécs 245–246; ruin bars 32, 33, 88–90; Siófok 189, 191; Sopron 226–227; wine bars 91–92, 230
Bartók Béla Avenue: 122
baths: 7, 16, 32, 80, 81–87
beaches: 10, 19, 99–100, 173, 183–184, 190–191
bed and breakfasts: 259. *See also* accommodations
Bedő House (Hungarian House of Art Nouveau): 55
Benedictine Abbey of Tihany: 173, 182
biking: 101–102, 152–153, 255
Bla Bla Car: 254
Blagoveštenska Orthodox Church: 143, 144, 147
boating: 103, 156, 169. *See also* Danube River cruises
boat travel: 133, 153, 166, 169, 170–171
Bogdányi Street: 143, 148–149
border crossings: 169, 254. *See also* entry requirements
bridges: Chain Bridge 52–53; Margaret Bridge 68–69; Mária Valéria bridge 169
Buda: 5, 33. *See also* South Buda
Buda Castle: 32, 44–46; labyrinth 48–49; Wine Festival 97
Buda Hills: 44, 80–83; orientation 39
Budapest: history 33–36; map 34–35; orientation 37–39
Budapest 100: 97, 257
Budapest Card: 30
Budapest Design Week: 97, 257
Budapest History Museum: 47
Budapest Operetta Theater: 96
Budapest Pinball Museum: 68
Budapest Wine Festival: 257
budgeting: 29
business hours: 129
Busójárás: 250, 257–258
bus travel: around Budapest 133; to Budapest 131, 253; Eger 204; Esztergom 171; Gödöllő 141; Hollókő 215; Lake Balaton 185; Pécs 251; Szentendre 152–153; Tihany 185; Visegrád 166

C

car rentals: 20, 254
car travel: around Hungary 256; to Budapest 131–132, 253–254. *See also specific place*
Castle District: accommodations 124; food 110–113; map 45; orientation 37; shopping 107–108; sights 44–49; thermal baths 83–84
Castle Garden Bazaar: 49
castles and palaces: Buda Castle 32, 44–46, 48–49; Eger Castle 194, 195, 196–198; Gödöllő Royal Palace 12, 17, 18, 137–139; Hollókő Castle 206, 207, 208–209; Lower Castle (Salamon Torony) 164; Royal Palace 165; Taródi Castle 226; Vajdahunyad Castle 61–63; Visegrád Citadel 163–164
cathedrals. *See* churches and cathedrals; Mosque of Pasha Qasim; synagogues
Cave Church: 71–72
cave tours: 102–103
cell phones: 263
cemeteries, mausoleums, and tombs: Gül Baba's Tomb 69–70; Kerepesi Cemetery 77–78; Sopianae Early Christian Mausoleum 234, 235, 243–244; Zsolnay Mausoleum 238, 244–245
Central Market Hall: 73
ceramics: 247. *See also* porcelain
Chain Bridge: 52–53
children, traveling with: 264
Children's Railway: 80–81
Christmas markets: 98
churches and cathedrals: Benedictine Abbey of Tihany 173; Blagoveštenska Orthodox Church 143, 144, 147; Cave Church 71–72; Eger Basilica 196, 199–200; Esztergom Basilica 156, 167; Goat Church 219, 224; Matthias Church 48; Pécs Cathedral 242–243; St. John the Baptist Catholic Church 144; St. Mary Magdalene's Tower 47; St. Stephen's Basilica 56–58; Szent Márton Church 207, 209–210; Vác Cathedral 161. *See also* Mosque of Pasha Qasim; synagogues
Church of Our Lady of Buda Castle (Matthias Church): 48
Citadel, The: 70–71; map: 71
City Park: accommodations 126–127; food 119–120; map 62; orientation 38; recreation and activities 99, 103; sights 61–66; thermal baths 84–85
classes: 105

clothing: 26, 95, 109–110, 261
color, travelers of: 265
communications: 263
conduct and customs: 258, 260–261
consulates, foreign: 130
crime and theft: 130, 261
Csontváry Museum: 234, 235, 241
cuisine. *See* food and drinks
culture / customs: 258, 260–261
currency: 28, 29, 262–263
cycling: 101–102, 152–153, 255

D

Dandár: 87
Danube Bend: 14, 155–156; accommodations 162, 165–166, 170; Esztergom Basilica 156; food 161–162, 165, 168–169; getting to 162, 166; highlights 156; itinerary ideas 18–19, 157–160; map 157; orientation 156; planning your time 156–157; Rám Canyon 162; sights 18, 160–161, 163–164, 167; Tragor Ignác Museum 156, 160–161; Visegrád Citadel 156. *See also* Esztergom; Vác; Visegrád
Danube River cruises: 54–55, 169
day trips: 14. *See also specific place*
dietary restrictions: 258
dining. *See* food and drinks
disabilities, travelers with: 264
discrimination: 265
dobostorta: 117
Dohány Street Synagogue: 32, 58–59
Dominican Convent Ruins: 68
dress: 26, 95, 261
drinking water: 262
drugs: 261. *See also* pharmacies
Dumtsa Jenő Road: 143, 148–149

E

Eat&Meet: 119
Eger: 5, 193–194; accommodations 203–204; food 201–202; highlights 194; itinerary ideas 23–24, 195–196; map 197; orientation 194; planning your time 194; sights 196–200; transportation 28, 194, 204; wine cellars and tasting 18, 194, 200–201, 202, 203
Eger Basilica: 196, 199–200
Eger Castle: 194, 195, 196–198
Eger Minaret: 194, 195, 199
electrical system: 28, 29
Elizabeth Lookout: 81, 101

embassies: 130
emergency numbers: 130, 261
entry requirements: 28, 256–257. *See also* border crossings
escape rooms: 104
Esztergom: 12; accommodations 170; food 168–169; itinerary 20, 159; map 168; sights 167; transportation 28, 170–171
Esztergom Basilica: 156, 167
events. *See* festivals and events

F

Fabricius House: 219, 223–224
Falk Art Forum: 98, 257
Ferenczy Museum: 146
Ferris wheel: 173, 190
ferry travel: 166, 253
festivals and events: 96–98, 257–258; Art Market Budapest 97, 257; Budapest 100 97, 257; Budapest Design Week 97, 257; Budapest Wine Festival 257; Busójárás 250, 257–258; Christmas markets 98, 257; Falk Art Forum 98, 257; Formula 1 Grand Prix 257; Hollókő Easter Festival 214, 258; Sziget Festival 96–97, 257; Volt Festival 231, 258
Fire Tower: 219, 222–223
Fisherman's Bastion: 32, 47–48
food and drinks: bakeries 117; dietary restrictions 258; Eat&Meet 119; general information 258; Hungarian specialties 111; mealtimes 258; shopping and souvenirs 106, 108–109, 213, 246–247. *See also specific place*; wine
foreign consulates: 130
Formula 1 Grand Prix: 257

G

gardens. *See* parks, gardens, and squares
gay and lesbian travelers: 264–265
Gellért Hill: 32, 70–71
Gellért Thermal Baths: 86–87
Geological Institute of Hungary: 66
Ghetto Memorial Wall: 60
Goat Church: 219, 224
Gödöllő: 134–135; Baroque Theater 135, 136, 139; day trip 14, 17; food 140; highlights 135; itinerary ideas 136–137; map 137; orientation 135; planning your time 135; sights 12, 17, 135, 136, 137–140; tourist information 135; transportation 29, 141

Gödöllő Royal Palace: 12, 17, 135, 136, 137–139
greetings: 260
Gresham Palace: 55–56
Gül Baba's Tomb: 69–70
Gyugyi Collection: 237, 244

H

Handicraft Printer's Museum: 207, 210–211
health and safety: crime and theft 130, 261; drinking water 262; emergency numbers 130, 261; medical services 130, 261, 262; women traveling alone 264
Heroes' Square: 64–65
hiking: 100–101, 182–183
holidays: 263
Hollókő: 13, 205–206; accommodations 214; Easter Festival 214, 258; food 211–212; highlights 206; itinerary ideas 25, 207; map 208; orientation 206; planning your time 206; shopping 206, 212–213; sights 206, 207, 208–211; transportation 28–29, 215; village life 19
Hollókő Castle: 206, 207, 208–209
Holocaust. *See* memorials
Holocaust Memorial Center: 77
Horthy's Bunker: 135, 136, 139–140
Hospital in the Rock: 48
hospitals and pharmacies: 130
hostels: 259. *See also* accommodations
hotels: 259. *See also* accommodations
House of Terror: 60–61
Hungarian House of Art Nouveau (Bedő House): 55
Hungarian Jewish Museum and Archives: 59
Hungarian National Gallery: 46–47
Hungarian National Museum: 32, 76–77
Hungarian Open Air Museum: 143, 144, 147–148
Hungarian Parliament Building: 30, 32, 49–52
Hungarian phrases: 265–267
Hungarian Secession. *See* Art Nouveau
Hungarian State Opera: 32, 60, 95–96

IJK

ice skating: 103–104
information and services: accommodations 259–260; business hours 129; car rentals 20; crime and

theft 130, 261; drinking water 262; emergency numbers 130, 261; entry requirements 28, 256–257; festivals and events 257–258; food and nightlife 258; foreign consulates 130; Hungarian phrases 265–267; luggage storage 20, 194, 218, 235; medical services 130, 261, 262; packing 29–30, 262; practical details 28, 262–263; tourist information 129, 135, 183, 194, 206, 218, 235; traveler advice 264–265

Inner City: accommodations 128–129; bars and nightlife 92–93; food 121; orientation 38–39; performing arts and concert halls 96; shopping 107, 108, 109–110; sights 73–79

internet access: 263

Irány Pécs card: 235

itineraries: 15–26, 40–44. *See also specific place*

Jewish Quarter: accommodations 125–126; bars and nightlife 88–90, 91, 92, 93; food 115–118; orientation 37; shopping 105–107, 108, 110; sights 58–60

Kazinczy Street Synagogue: 59

Kecske Hegy: 100–101

Kerepesi Cemetery: 77–78

Király Bath: 83–84

Kiscelli Museum: 79–80

Kopászi Dam: 100

Kossuth Lajos Spring: 173

Kunsthalle: 64

L

Lake Balaton: 5, 10, 172–173; accommodations 180–181, 184–185, 187–188, 192; bars and nightlife 189, 191; beaches 10, 19, 173, 183–184, 190–191; food 180, 184–185, 187, 192; highlights 173; hiking 182–183; itinerary ideas 22, 176–178; map 174, 175; orientation 173–174; planning your time 174–175; shopping 184; sights 18, 178–180, 182, 189–190; transportation 28, 181, 185, 188, 192; wineries 186–187. *See also* Badacsony; Balatonfüred; Siófok; Tihany

Lechner, Ödön: 57, 66

LGBTQ travelers: 264–265

Liberty Monument: 71

Liberty Square: 53–54

Lipótváros: accommodations 124–125; food 113–115; nightlife 93; orientation 37; performing arts and concert halls 94; shopping 108, 109; sights 49–58

Liszt Ferenc Music Academy: 96

local, traveling like: 26, 44

Lower Castle (Salamon Torony): 164

Ludwig Museum: 79

luggage storage: 20, 194, 218, 235

Lukács Thermal Bath: 85

Lupa Tó: 100

Lyceum: 196, 198–199

M

March 15 holiday: 257

Margaret Bridge: 68–69

Margaret Island: accommodations 127; food 120; map 67; orientation 38; recreation and activities 99; sights 66–70; thermal baths 85–86, 87

Mária Valéria bridge: 169

markets: 39, 73, 98, 105–107, 257

Matthias Church: 48

Mátyáshegy Caves: 103

mealtimes: 258

medical services: 130, 261

Memento Park: 32, 72–73

memorials: Ghetto Memorial Wall 60; Heroes' Square 64–65; Holocaust Memorial Center 77; Liberty Monument 71; Raoul Wallenberg Holocaust Memorial Park 58–59; Shoes on the Danube memorial 53; Soviet War Memorial 53; Victims of German Occupation memorial 53–54

metro: 133

Miksa Róth Memorial House: 66

Millennium Quarter: 78–79

Modern Hungarian Gallery: 242

Mohács: 250, 257–258

MOL BuBi: 101–102

Molnár János Cave: 103

money: 28, 29, 262–263

Mosque of Pasha Qasim: 234, 235, 238–239

Museum of Agriculture: 62

Museum of Fine Arts (Szépművészeti Múzeum): 63–64

museums: Art Mill 143, 147; Budapest History Museum 47; Budapest Pinball Museum 68; Csontváry Museum 234, 235, 241; Ferenczy Museum 146; Handicraft Printer's Museum 207, 210–211; hours 30, 39, 263; House of Terror 60–61; Hungarian Jewish Museum and Archives 59; Hungarian National

Gallery 46–47; Hungarian National Museum 32, 76–77; Hungarian Open Air Museum 143, 144, 147–148; Irány Pécs card 235; Kiscelli Museum 79–80; Kunsthalle 64; Ludwig Museum 79; Miksa Róth Memorial House 66; Modern Hungarian Gallery 242; Museum of Agriculture 62; Museum of Fine Arts (Szépművészeti Múzeum) 63–64; Palóc Doll Museum 207, 210; Pharmacy House 224–225; Post Museum 211; Serbian Ecclesiastical Art Museum 147; Tragor Ignác Museum 156, 160–161; Vasarely Museum 242; Vaszary Villa 179; Village Museum of Hollókő 206, 207, 210; Zsolnay Museum 241; Zwack Unicum Museum 77, 78
music, live: 93. See also performing arts

NO

Nagymező utca: 95
National Széchényi Library: 47
National Theatre (Budapest): 79
National Theatre (Pécs): 238, 240–241
nightlife. See bars and nightlife
North Pest, map: 50–51
Óbuda: 5; accommodations 129; food 123; orientation 39; sights 79–80
Old Synagogue: 217, 219, 223
Ottoman relics: 69; Eger Minaret 194, 195, 199; Mosque of Pasha Qasim 234, 235, 238–239

P

packing: 29–30, 262
Palace of Arts: 78–79
palaces. See castles and palaces
Palatinus: 87
pálinka: 106, 111
Palóc Doll Museum: 207, 210
Pálvölgyi Caves: 102
paprika: 69, 106, 111
parks, gardens, and squares: Heroes' Square 64–65; Liberty Square 53–54; Margaret Island 99; Memento Park 32, 72–73; Philosopher's Garden 70; Raoul Wallenberg Holocaust Memorial Park 58–59; Széchenyi Tér 239. See also City Park
Paskál Thermal and Open-Air Bath: 87
Pécs: 5, 233–234; accommodations 249–251; food 247–249; highlights 234; itinerary ideas 235–238; map 236–237; nightlife 245–246; orientation 234–235; planning your time 235; shopping 246–247; sights 13, 19, 238–245; transportation 28, 251; Visit Pécs! Card 30
Pécs Cathedral: 242–243
performing arts: concert halls 32, 60, 94–96; concert venues 94; live music 93; Nagymező utca 95; Sopron 227; Sziget Festival 96–97
Pest: 5. See also North Pest, map; South Pest
Petőfi Promenade: 189–190
pharmacies: 130, 262
Pharmacy House: 224–225
Philosopher's Garden: 70
phones: 263
pinball machines: 68
porcelain: 13, 106. See also ceramics
postage: 263
Postal Savings Bank: 54
Post Museum: 211
prostitution: 261

R

racism: 265
Rám Canyon: 162
Raoul Wallenberg Holocaust Memorial Park: 58–59
recreation and activities: baths 7, 16, 32, 80, 81–87; beaches 10, 19, 99–100, 173, 183–184, 190–191; boating 103, 156, 169; cave tours and spelunking 102–103; classes 105; cycling 101–102, 152–153; escape rooms 104; hiking 100–101, 182–183; ice skating 103–104; parks 99; Rám Canyon 162; tours 104–105
reservations: 30, 39–40
restaurants. See food and drinks
river cruises: 54–55, 169
Római Open-Air Baths: 87
Római Part: 99–100
Roman baths: 80. See also thermal baths
Roman relics: 79, 80, 224
Róth, Miksa: 65; Miksa Róth Memorial House 66
Royal Palace: 165
Rudas Thermal Baths: 86
ruin bars: 32, 33, 88–90
Rumbach Street Synagogue: 60

S

Sajkodi Beach: 183–184
Sas Hegy: 101
Scarbantia Forum: 224
seasons: 27–28, 254
senior travelers: 264
Serbian Ecclesiastical Art Museum: 147
services. See information and services
shipping: 263
Shoes on the Danube memorial: 53
shopping: clothing and accessories
109–110; design shops 107–108;
Hollókő 206, 212–213; Lake Balaton
184; markets 39, 73, 98, 105–107, 257;
opening hours 263; Pécs 246–247;
shopping districts 105; Szentendre
143, 148–150; Tihany 184
sightseeing: on number 2 tram 56; passes
30. See also specific place
Siófok: 188–189; accommodations 192;
bars and nightlife 189, 191; beaches
190–191; food 192; itinerary 22–23,
176–177; map 189; sights 189–190;
transportation 192
Siófok Water Tower: 190
Slovakia: 169
smoking: 260–261
Sopianae Early Christian Mausoleum:
234, 235, 243–244
Sopron: 5, 216–217; accommodations
230–231; food 228–230; highlights
217; itinerary idea 219; map 220–221;
nightlife 226–227; orientation 217–
218; performing arts 227; planning
your time 218; sights 217, 222–226;
transportation 28, 232; village life 19;
Volt Festival 231
Sopron Old Town: 217, 222
South Buda: accommodations 127–128;
bars and nightlife 93; food 120–121;
orientation 38; sights 70–73; thermal
baths 86–87
South Pest: bars and nightlife 92–93;
food 121–123; map 74–75; markets
107; orientation 38–39; performing
arts and concert halls 96; shopping
108, 109–110; sights 73–79; thermal
baths 87
souvenirs: 106
Soviet War Memorial: 53
Sparties: 30, 32, 39, 83, 90
spelunking: 102–103
squares. See parks, gardens, and squares
State Hospital of Cardiology and the
Kossuth Lajos Spring: 179–180

St. John the Baptist Catholic Church: 144
St. Mary Magdalene's Tower: 47
Storno House: 225
St. Stephen's Basilica: 32, 56–58
souvenirs: 106
synagogues: Dohány Street Synagogue
32, 58–59; hours 30, 39; Kazinczy
Street Synagogue 59; Old Synagogue
217, 219, 223; Pécs 239–240; Rumbach
Street Synagogue 60. See also
churches and cathedrals; Mosque of
Pasha Qasim
Széchenyi Baths: 16, 32, 84–85
Széchenyi Tér: 239
Szemlőhegyi Caves: 102
Szentendre: 10, 142–143;
accommodations 151; day trip 14;
food 150–151; highlights 143; itinerary
ideas 18–19, 144–145; orientation 143;
planning your time 143; shopping
143, 148–150; sights 143, 144, 146–149;
transportation 29, 151–153, 154
Szent Márton Church: 207, 209–210
Sziget Festival: 96–97, 257

TU

Tagore Promenade: 178–179
Taródi Castle: 226
taxis: 133, 167, 171, 188, 204, 232
thermal baths: 7, 16, 32, 81–87. See also
Roman baths
Tihany: 181; accommodations 184–185;
beaches 183–184; food 184–185;
hiking 182–183; itinerary ideas 176;
map 181; shopping 184; sights 182;
transportation 185
tipping: 258
tours: 104–105
Tragor Ignác Museum: 156, 160–161
train travel: 131, 255–256. See also specific
place
tram and trolleybus travel: 56, 133
transportation: around Budapest 28,
132–133, 255; around Hungary 255–
256; bike sharing and rentals 101–102;
to Budapest 28, 131–132, 252–255;
car rentals 20, 254; outside Budapest
28–29; public transport 26, 28,
132–133, 255; sightseeing on number
2 tram 56; taxis 133, 167, 171, 188, 204,
232; tram, bus, and trolleybus 56, 133;
transit passes 132–133; transit ticket
validations 132, 255. See also specific
place
unicum: 77, 78, 106

V

Vác: 10, 160; accommodations 162; food 161–162; itinerary 20, 157–158; map 160; sights 160–161; transportation 28, 162

Vác Cathedral: 161

vaccines: 261

Vajdahunyad Castle: 61

Valley of Beautiful Women: 13, 24–25, 194, 196, 202

Vasarely Museum: 242

Vaszary Villa: 179

Veli Bej Bath: 85–86

Victims of German Occupation memorial: 53–54

Village Museum of Hollókő: 206, 207, 210

Visegrád: 163; accommodations 165–166; food and drinks 165; itinerary 19–20, 157–158; map 163; sights 163–164; transportation 29, 166–167

Visegrád Citadel: 156, 163–164

Visit Pécs! Card: 30

Volt Festival: 231, 258

Vörösmarty tér Cristmas market: 98

WZ

water, drinking: 262

Water Tower, Siófok: 190

Water Tower on Margaret Island: 66–68

wine: Badacsony 186–187; bars 91–92, 230; Buda Castle Wine Festival 97; Budapest Wine Festival 257; in Hungarian diet 111; shopping and souvenirs 106, 108–109, 213; tasting 18, 194, 200–201, 202, 203

women, traveling alone: 264

zoo: 63

Zsolnay Cultural Quarter: 13, 234, 237–238, 244

Zsolnay Family and Factory Exhibition: 238, 244

Zsolnay Fountain: 234, 237, 239

Zsolnay Mausoleum: 238, 244–245

Zsolnay Museum: 241

Zwack Unicum Museum: 77, 78

List of Maps

Budapest
Budapest: 34–35
Itinerary Ideas: 42–43
Castle District: 45
Liptóváros, Jewish Quarter, and
    Around Andrassy Avenue: 50–51
City Park: 62
Margaret Island: 67
South Buda: 71
Inner City and South Pest: 74–75

Gödöllő
Gödöllő: 137

Szentendre
Szentendre: 145

Danube Bend
Danube Bend: 157
Itinerary Ideas: 158
Vác: 160

Visegrád: 163
Esztergom: 168

Lake Balaton
Lake Balaton: 174–175
Itinerary Ideas: 177
Balatonfüred: 179
Tihany: 182
Siófok: 189

Eger
Eger: 197

Hollókő
Hollókő: 208

Sopron
Sopron: 220–221

Pécs
Pécs: 236–237

Photo Credits

More Guides for Urban Adventure

ASHEVILLE & THE GREAT SMOKY MOUNTAINS

BOSTON

BUENOS AIRES

CHICAGO

CHARLESTON

CLEVELAND

LOS ANGELES

MEXICO CITY

MONTRÉAL

NASHVILLE

NEW ORLEANS

NEW YORK CITY

OSLO

PORTLAND

QUÉBEC CITY

REYKJAVÍK

SAN DIEGO

SEATTLE

VANCOUVER

WASHINGTON DC

MAP SYMBOLS

═══	Expressway	○	City/Town	ⓘ	Information Center	♠	Park
═══	Primary Road	◉	State Capital	Ⓟ	Parking Area	⚸	Golf Course
═══	Secondary Road	◉	National Capital	♠	Church	✛	Unique Feature
⋯⋯	Unpaved Road	◎	Highlight	♥	Winery	⋇	Waterfall
⋯⋯	Trail	★	Point of Interest	Ⓣ	Trailhead	Δ	Camping
⋯⋯	Ferry	•	Accommodation	Ⓡ	Train Station	▲	Mountain
⊷⊷	Railroad	▼	Restaurant/Bar	✕	Airport	⛷	Ski Area
═══	Pedestrian Walkway	■	Other Location	✕	Airfield	⬭	Glacier
⊐⊐⊐	Stairs						

CONVERSION TABLES

°C = (°F - 32) / 1.8
°F = (°C x 1.8) + 32
1 inch = 2.54 centimeters (cm)
1 foot = 0.304 meters (m)
1 yard = 0.914 meters
1 mile = 1.6093 kilometers (km)
1 km = 0.6214 miles
1 fathom = 1.8288 m
1 chain = 20.1168 m
1 furlong = 201.168 m
1 acre = 0.4047 hectares
1 sq km = 100 hectares
1 sq mile = 2.59 square km
1 ounce = 28.35 grams
1 pound = 0.4536 kilograms
1 short ton = 0.90718 metric ton
1 short ton = 2,000 pounds
1 long ton = 1.016 metric tons
1 long ton = 2,240 pounds
1 metric ton = 1,000 kilograms
1 quart = 0.94635 liters
1 US gallon = 3.7854 liters
1 Imperial gallon = 4.5459 liters
1 nautical mile = 1.852 km

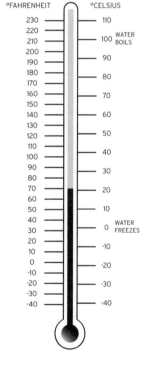

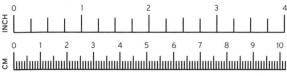

MOON BUDAPEST & BEYOND
Avalon Travel
Hachette Book Group
1700 Fourth Street
Berkeley, CA 94710, USA
www.moon.com

Editor: Nikki Ioakimedes
Managing Editor: Hannah Brezack
Copy Editor: Matt Hoover
Graphics and Production Coordinator: Lucie Ericksen
Cover Design: Faceout Studio, Charles
Interior Design: Megan Jones Design
Moon Logo: Tim McGrath
Map Editor: Kat Bennett
Cartographers: Karin Dahl and Brian Shotwell
Proofreader: Lori Hobkirk
Indexer: Rachel Lyon

ISBN-13: 978-1-64049-809-9

Printing History
1st Edition — March 2020
5 4 3 2 1

Front cover photo: Chain Bridge in the evening © Zsolt Hlinka/Getty Images
Back cover photo: Szentendre © Adonis Villanueva/Dreamstime.com
Inside cover photo: view of Budapest over river Danube © Spectral-design/Dreamstime.com

Printed in China by RR Donnelley